Jefferson Davis's Generals

Gettysburg Civil War Institute Books

Published by Oxford University Press
Edited by Gabor S. Boritt

Why the Confederacy Lost

Lincoln, the War President: The Gettysburg Lectures

Lincoln's Generals

*War Comes Again: Comparative Vistas
on the Civil War and World War II*

Why the Civil War Came

The Gettysburg Nobody Knows

Jefferson Davis's Generals

Other books by Gabor S. Boritt

Lincoln and the Economics of the American Dream

The Lincoln Image
(with Harold Holzer and Mark E. Neely, Jr.)

The Confederate Image
(with Mark E. Neely, Jr., and Harold Holzer)

The Historian's Lincoln
(with Norman O. Forness)

*The Historian's Lincoln, Rebuttals:
What the University Press Would Not Print*

*Of the People, By the People, For the People
and Other Quotations from Abraham Lincoln*
(with Jakob B. Boritt, Deborah R. Huso and Peter C. Vermilyea)

Jefferson Davis's Generals

EDITED BY

GABOR S. BORITT

New York   Oxford
OXFORD UNIVERSITY PRESS
1999

Oxford University Press

Oxford   New York
Athens   Auckland   Bangkok   Bogota   Buenos Aires   Calcutta
Cape Town   Chennai   Dar es Salaam   Delhi   Florence   Hong Kong   Istanbul
Karachi   Kuala Lumpur   Madrid   Melbourne   Mexico City   Mumbai
Nairobi   Paris   Singapore   Taipei   Tokyo   Toronto   Warsaw

and associated companies in
Berlin   Ibadan

Published by Oxford University Press, Inc.,
198 Madison Avenue, New York, New York 10016

Oxford is a registered trademark of Oxford University Press

Library of Congress Cataloging-in-Publication Data
Jefferson Davis's generals / edited by Gabor S. Boritt.
p.   cm.   "Gettysburg Civil War Institute books."
Includes bibliographical references.
ISBN 0-19-512062-0
1. United States—History—Civil War, 1861–1865—Campaigns.
2. Davis, Jefferson, 1808–1889—Military leadership.
3. Confederate States of America. Army—History.
4. Generals—Confederate States of America—History.
I. Boritt, G. S., 1940–   .
E470.D38 1999
973.7′3—dc21 98–49045

1 3 5 7 9 8 6 4 2

Printed in the United States of America
on acid-free paper

By late June it is usually warm,
even hot in Gettysburg.
In the night at our farm,
the fireflies glow in the dark,
fleeting specks illuminating the woods and
turning Marsh Creek into a pageant.
In the daytime along the side of the road,
orange tiger lilies proclaim their eternal message.
My heart overflows;
it is time to see old friends again,
time to make new ones.
It is the time for the Gettysburg Civil War Institute.

GABOR S. BORITT

President Jefferson Davis Arriving in the Field of Battle at Bull's Run.
Lithograph probably by Hoyer & Ludwig, Richmond, ca. 1861. (Fort
Wayne, Indiana, Lincoln Library and Museum)

Contents

Introduction

ROBERT E. LEE moved toward Pennsylvania and Ulysses Grant besieged Vicksburg. Much hung in the balance, and for Confederate president Jefferson Davis the waiting seemed almost unbearable. By July 2, 1863, as the Army of Northern Virginia assaulted Little Round Top, the Peach Orchard, the Wheatfield, Cemetery Ridge, and Culp's Hill, Davis took to bed. He did not know what was happening on the fields of battle. July 3, 4, and 5, still in bed. He was so ill that he could not meet even close associates. People in Richmond wondered if he would die.

Then news came that Lee had lost at Gettysburg. "Gen. Barksdale is killed, Gen. Garnett and Armistead are missing . . . Gen. Pender and Trimble are wounded in the leg, Gen. Hood in the arm." Davis was up by then. The message from Vicksburg came, surrender and unprecedented losses: "1 lieutenant general, 4 major-generals, 8 brigadier-generals, and 1 State brigadier, with their staffs; the regimental and other officers, and rank and file and men amount to some 29,000." Meanings unmistakable. This was the "hour" of our "sorest need," Davis wrote.[1]

The president's strategic notions were in disarray, but he dealt firmly with the disasters. He supported some generals unstintingly; embittered others. How he dealt with his major commanders, and how they with him—most of the historians of this volume maintain—played a central part in the outcome of the war. Through it all Jefferson Davis remained in charge. He endured.

Joseph E. Johnston was his first important general, with the first important command in the East. Craig Symonds explains in Chapter 1 that at one time the president's and the general's wives were best of friends, but tension developed quickly between the men. Johnston is often quoted as saying—apropos of the Peninsula campaign of 1862, when the Army of the Potomac reached within five miles of Richmond and Lee replaced the wounded Johnston—that "the shot that struck me down was the best ever fired" for the Confederacy. But Chapter 1 puts the focus on the less quoted concluding part of the statement that provides its context: the above was so because Lee had Davis's "confidence"; Johnston did not. Indeed, as the war went on, trust continued to wither between the two as they warred for a cause—and with each other. Why they did so is the burden of Chapter 1. As for who was at fault, Symonds assigns the greater blame to the general, but wherever fault may be found, the dysfunctional relationship came to be "a major factor in Confederate defeat."

Lee, who succeeded to head the Army of Northern Virginia, has long been depicted as forming a "powerful team" with his commander in chief, two men who deeply respected each other. Lee courted Davis, and vice versa, and the two agreed that an offensive-defensive strategy had the best chance of success. But harmony was more apparent than real, according to Emory Thomas in Chapter 2. Lee believed, (though he did not make it plain to his chief) that the Confederacy would grow weaker the longer the war lasted and only a decisive battle or campaign would save it. On the other hand Davis had strong faith that his country could outlast the United States in a long contest of wills and, if all else failed, guerrilla war would clinch the victory. Both Antietam and Gettysburg illustrated where unresolved differences led. Indeed, Thomas concludes, in the end those differences served as one source of Confederate defeat.

Braxton Bragg, who held independent command in the West, is generally seen as much less than competent, but a general stubbornly supported by his president. Not quite so, according to Steven E. Woodworth in Chapter 3. Bragg had substantial talents that Davis "squandered." Not permitted to assemble his own officer corps, as Lee did in the East, Bragg was also saddled with Leonidas Polk, an inept, disruptive bishop turned soldier who was the president's crony. Nor did the commander in chief understand, until too late, the need for a clear, unified, workable command system in the West. By the time Davis realized his mistake, a potentially serviceable general, in an army that badly needed such generals, had been harmed beyond help. His reputation destroyed, Bragg was effectively lost to the Confederates. This, Woodworth argues, was "one of Davis's greatest failures in the West."

P. G. T. Beauregard commanded an army in the West, too, as well as in the East and in the South, thanks to the president of the Confederate States of America. The flamboyant, much adored hero's relationship with Davis also reeked of mutual loathing. From the hostilities that erupted between president and general in the aftermath of the Confederacy's first victory at Manasses, to Appomattox and long beyond, the war between the two men never ended. And yet, according to the provocative argument of Michael Parrish in Chapter 4, in contrast to the Johnston case, deep antagonism did not cripple their successful work together. They had misunderstandings aplenty, but the Confederacy did not suffer significantly from their mutual hatred because both made substantial and successful efforts to separate professional judgment from personal feelings. Ultimately, the democratic constitutional traditions of America dictated that the general submit to civilian authority. Beauregard did.

If Davis's dislike of "the Creole" did not affect in measurable ways the Confederate performance on the battlefield, his liking of John Bell Hood may have. In Chapter 5 Herman Hattaway (showing a deep indebtedness to historian Richard McMurry) traces Hood's rise, from graduating eighth from the bottom of the West Point class of 1853, to becoming a full general in command of an army in 1864. He came to the Confederate president's attention early in the war; they met for the first time in the spring of 1862, and grew close. The grievous wounds that Hood received at Gettysburg and Chickamauga did not slow the general's trajectory, until at last he destroyed his Army of Tennessee in 1864. By then Hood had risen well beyond his level of competence, although his chief may not have easily found a better commander. In any case, Davis remained the fighting soldier's defender to the death.

And what of the private side of war—of wives of the president and the generals? They rarely receive attention, yet Lesley Gordon argues in Chapter 6 that women could play a vital role in their men's lives, affecting their outlook as well as their career and performance. The women ranged from the traditional wives and mothers to trusted military advisors. Some generals benefited from strong marriages of equals; others found themselves in strained, even estranged circumstances. Yet no direct relationship has appeared between success in marriage and success on the battlefield. As for the president's wife, Varina Davis proved during the war to be a devoted helpmate possessing useful social skills, a woman ready to share triumph and humiliation.

Both of these fates got conjured up in the graphic images artists created of Jefferson Davis. In Chapter 7 Harold Holzer shows that when Davis and his generals came to be depicted together in prints, the president almost always received the dominant role. To this extent the civilian supremacy of American traditions that Chapter 4 emphasizes ruled the popular arts, too. The military bearing Davis cultivated, and artists granted him, contrasted sharply with Abraham Lincoln's image as the quintessential civilian. The martial Davis filled the Southern white public's nationalistic needs—and Northern coffers, since much of the postwar popular art was Yankee creation. Davis in uniform, at times with his generals, received honored places in many a Southern parlor. That military image got shaken after his capture at the end of the war, when myriad cartoon versions of an emasculated and hoop-skirted ex-president appeared in countless Northern taverns and the like. But the humiliated chief, clapped into Fort Monroe, even into shackles for a moment, grew into a martyr—and then the military image returned not to be dethroned again. Davis and his generals: heroes for eternity.

In the final chapter James McPherson surveys the terrain of this book, places it into a broad context, and advances his own interpretation. He starts by noting that the troubled personal relationships between commander in chief and generals often weakened the Confederate war effort. The partnership of Davis and Lee, however, worked well and the dissonance between the two—with Lee emphasizing the first half of the offensive-defensive strategy, Davis the second—grows quite small when actual campaigns are examined. How important were the personalities, how important strategic concepts? McPherson emphasizes the latter; readers will make up their own minds. But therein lie, perhaps, the seeds of another Civil War Institute session.

And so to an expression of thanks to the many who helped bring this book alive. Peter Ginna, my new editor at Oxford, is a pleasure to work with. I am also grateful to Rosemary Wellner for copy editing and to Helen Mules for seeing the book through production.

At the Civil War Institute the staff, Tina M. Grim, Linda Marshall, and Marti Shaw, make our hardworking life happy. Without their creative work there would be no CWI sessions. Without Marti's excellent help this book would have taken much longer to complete. I must also add Dan De Palma, who volunteers so much time that he qualifies to be known as a staff member.

The student assistants at the CWI make the place lively and their work efficient: Rebecca Clay, Charles Dittrich, Benjamin Knuth, Paul Lapato, Jill MacArthur, Lavinia Rogers, Jon Roscoe, Chris Schumacher, Sarah Sherman, and Jay Spiese. Charley, Paul, and Sarah, together with Ron Schorpp, worked specifically on research tasks. In addition to these fine young people, at the 1997 session Nicki Bangert, Daniel Boritt, Paul Hutchinson, and Mike Karpyn served as assistants. Peter Vermilyea made the CWI session specially memorable for our contingent of scholarship students. William Hanna, with the help of Dennis Smyth, performed a similar task for the group of teachers who also came with scholarships, generously donated by CWI students.

In mentioning Dan Boritt among the above names, I already came, as always, to my family. As my youngest son he showed up as an extra at our first session at age three in 1983, grew up with the CWI, became an assistant at a very young age, and could put in a full eight hour day when ten years old (no child labor laws in the Boritt family). He has never missed a session. The acceptance of my scholarly world by Daniel, my wife, Liz, and our other sons, Jake and Norse, is precious. Norse once more created the Pennsylvania Dutch design of the dedication page.

I wish to express my appreciation to the historians for

making the the CWI session devoted to Davis and his generals lively and thought-provoking; to those who read and commented critically on each other's papers; and to three anonymous readers.

My final thanks go to George D. Kornitzer, M.D., surgeon, my close friend since we were six years old in the first grade. On a peaceful visit to his Buzzard's Bay home on the New England shore, I completed work on this book. Thanks for that visit, and for the friendship of a lifetime.

Summer 1998   G. S. B.
Farm by the Ford
Gettysburg
and
Wind Rose
Marion, Massachussetts

Jefferson Davis's Generals

1

A Fatal Relationship: Davis and Johnston at War

CRAIG L. SYMONDS

Synergy. I recall clearly the moment in the late 1960s when I first heard the word. I was listening to a lecture by one of the mass-market philosophers of that era, Buckminster Fuller, who explained that things were synergistic if a particular combination of elements made possible achievements that might otherwise be impossible. In more mundane language, the term implied that it was entirely possible for the whole to be greater than the sum of its parts. Heady stuff for the 1960s. I was thinking about that concept in considering the relationship between Jefferson Davis and Joseph E. Johnston, and it led me to wonder if there were an antonym for the word synergy—for, if so, it would be singularly appropriate to describe their partnership. Here, surely, was a relationship where the whole was considerably *less* than the sum of its parts. Davis was not as bad a president as his many critics have claimed; nor for all his faults was Johnston as poor a general as his critics have claimed. But there was no synergy here. Indeed, if forced to choose one word from the dictionary of popular psychology to describe their professional relationship, the one that springs to mind is dysfunctional.

There were more than 420 Confederate officers who bore the title of general during the Civil War—and probably twice that number who claimed it afterward. But of all the "generals in gray" whose thin skins and large egos caused Jefferson Davis anxiety and frustration as commander in chief, none was more troublesome than Joseph E. Johnston. In one respect it is ironic that this should be so, for in many ways the two men were very much alike. They were roughly the same age—Davis had graduated just one year ahead of Johnston (and Robert E. Lee) at West Point. They were both proud men who suffered, almost physically, when their efforts went unappreciated by others. They were also sensitive men who reacted feelingly to perceived slights and indulged in occasional bouts of self-pity. Each felt that he martyred himself to the cause he served.

It is not too much to assert that the mutual antagonism between Davis and Johnston was a major factor in Confederate defeat. If the Confederacy had any hope at all of overcoming the North's tangible advantages of manpower and industrial resources, it had to have two things: commonality of purpose and unity of direction, and the feud between Davis and Johnston helped ensure that it had neither. The failure of Confederate leadership in the 1864 Atlanta campaign was particularly critical. Many students of the war place responsibility for that failure squarely on Johnston for his inability or unwillingness to make any serious effort to stop Sherman's advance from Dalton in north Georgia to the Chattahoochee River on the very outskirts of Atlanta. Others blame Davis for failing to support Johnston, and even more for replacing him in July with the brash, even reckless, John Bell Hood. Although a good case can be made by either side, a more fundamental problem was that the working relationship between Davis and Johnston had been poisoned long before the campaign in north Georgia even began. By the spring of 1864, neither president nor general was willing or able to cooperate effectively with the other.

What brought these two men to such a pass? Participants in the feud, and historians ever since, have spent a great deal of time and expended a lot of ink trying to allocate responsibility. Davis's advocates point the finger at Johnston, citing his personal touchiness, his willingness to cooperate with Davis's political foes, and his timidity in the field, all of which were certainly salient characteristics of Joe Johnston. Johnston's advocates, unsurprisingly, blame Davis, citing the president's own touchiness, his proclivity for micromanagement, and his tendency to judge field commanders by their personal loyalty to him rather than their performance in the field. And, again, all of these were very real characteristics of Jefferson Davis. In addition, there were active third-party participants in the feud, men who pursued their own political agendas by encouraging an antagonistic relationship between the president and his western general. This is not to say that there would have been no friction between Davis and Johnston without the encouragement of others. Their common characteristics, and a prewar history of disagreement, ensured that their relationship would be a rocky one. But without the political element provided by anti-Davis politicians in Richmond who used Johnston as a cat's-paw to assail the president, it is at least conceivable that the two men might have managed some minimal level of cooperation. Instead their feud became a primary factor in Confederate defeat.[1]

There are many stories about the origin of the feud. One is that it began while Davis and Johnston were cadets at West Point. According to this tale, they quarrelled over a girl. There is no contemporary evidence of any such quarrel and almost certainly it is a myth invented years later by one side or the other. Although first given currency by an early Davis biographer who claimed that Johnston bested the older and taller Davis in the fight, the story may have originated with Johnston's friends. It may even have given Johnston some secret satisfaction to think that others might believe him capable of defeating Davis in a romantic rivalry. After all, Davis was not only older and taller, he was also at that time a happy-go-lucky, risk-taking, demerit-earning, hard-drinking denizen of Benny Havens's Tavern—in short, just the kind of bold and dashing, even slightly dangerous, cadet who might be simultaneously threatening and interesting to a young lady. Johnston, by contrast, was an upright—and uptight—do-gooder who earned almost no demerits in his four years and whose nickname was "the colonel," a title that in those days probably suggested an ancient and doddering individual who was fussy and conservative in his personal habits. It is hard to imagine that a young lady who was attracted to one of these men would find the other the least bit interesting.[2]

Note that at this age the two men were very different. But while Johnston's personality remained largely unchanged through the years, Davis underwent a transforming experience in 1835, seven years after his graduation from West Point. He met, wooed, and married Sarah Knox Taylor, the daughter of his commanding officer (and future president) Zachary Taylor. On their honeymoon, both Davis and his pretty young bride contracted malaria and, while Jeff Davis survived, Sarah did not. She died in September and her widowed husband was never again quite the same. The devil-may-care young man filled with *joie de vivre* was gone, replaced by the dour and largely humorless statesman whom we remember today. Davis all but gave up on being happy—he nearly gave up on life. For another seven years he basically dropped out, spending most of that time managing a plantation given him by his brother Joseph at Davis Bend south of Vicksburg. It was Joseph who arranged the meeting, at Christmastime in 1843, with the seventeen-year-old Varina Howell. Two years later, the forty-one-year-old widower married the nineteen-year-old Varina. That, plus the outbreak of the Mexican War that same year, reenergized him and brought him into national prominence.[3]

Joe Johnston, meanwhile, had been laboring away in the army seeking opportunity for advancement and promotion. Eagerness for promotion may seem a bit indecorous, but it was nearly universal in the officer corps of the Old Army where promotions came very slowly. For Johnston as well as Davis, the war with Mexico brought new opportunity and both men took advantage of it. Davis had long since left the army, but as a volunteer colonel he won plaudits for the performance of his regiment—the Mississippi Rifles—at Buena Vista. Johnston won plaudits of his own, mainly for leading the battalion of voltigeurs that successfully stormed the Mexican citadel of Chapultepec. They both emerged from the war as heroes.

Davis parlayed his newfound notoriety into a political career; Johnston found the promotion he had long sought within the army. Indeed, Johnston won two brevets during the war. These were temporary promotions granted during wartime in recognition of unusual heroism, and generally officers reverted to their substantive rank once the war ended. After the victories of the Mexican War, however, Congress was in an expansive mood and declared that army officers could keep all brevets they had won during the war. For Johnston this was wonderful news. He had entered the war as a captain in the regular army. Early in the campaign he had been raised to the rank of major, then he won a brevet to lieutenant colonel, and another brevet—for his heroism at Chapultepec—that raised him to colonel. Or so he thought. In the 1850s, he was hugely disappointed when the secretary of war, Charles Conrad of Louisiana, ruled that since Johnston had begun the war as a captain and had won two brevets, he was a *lieutenant* colonel, not a colonel. Undeterred, Johnston renewed his claim to a colonelcy after Jefferson Davis became secretary of war in 1853. Like Conrad before him, Davis denied Johnston's petition, although he did give Johnston a plum assignment as second in command of the United States First Cavalry regiment. Nevertheless, Johnston remained convinced that he had been unfairly denied a promotion he had earned; in the 1850s he argued that his initial promotion to lieutenant colonel (in 1847) entitled him to seniority over his new commander, Colonel Edwin Vose Sumner, whose commission as lieutenant colonel dated from 1848. Davis rejected this argument too. In hindsight, this episode may seem to have been the first straw in the wind of the coming storm. But despite Johnston's unseemly persistence on the issue, there is no evidence that it marked the beginning of any long-term hostility between the two men. At this point, their relationship was still salvageable.[4]

When the Civil War broke out in the spring of 1861, Joseph E. Johnston was a brigadier general in the United States Army. He had finally gotten his promotion to colonel—due largely to the influence of James Buchanan's secretary of war John B. Floyd, who was a distant cousin of Johnston's by marriage—and soon afterward was promoted again by virtue of his appointment as quartermaster general of the United States Army, a job that carried with it a brigadier's star. For his part, Davis had long since left the war office and taken a seat in the Senate.

Both Davis and Johnston plighted themselves to the Confederacy: Davis in an emotional and challenging speech in the

Senate, Johnston in a tearful resignation in the War Department. As it turned out, Johnston was the only general officer in the United States Army to resign his commission and go south. Lee, his friend and West Point classmate, was still a colonel.

As Confederate president, an assignment he accepted with many misgivings, Davis was eager to secure Johnston's services for the army then forming. He made Johnston a brigadier general in the army (the highest rank then possible by law) and placed him in command of the force gathering at Harpers Ferry, Virginia. It was from there that Johnston brought his small army of some 9,000 men east by rail to join Beauregard at Manassas Junction, arriving almost literally in the nick of time to swing the balance of forces in favor of the South. By then the Confederate Congress had created the rank of full general, and Davis had elevated Johnston to that status. As a result, Johnston was the senior Confederate officer at the Battle of Bull Run on July 21, 1861. It was Johnston who recognized that the Federal attack on Henry House Hill was the enemy's main effort and who directed his reinforcements into position. Once there, however, it was Beauregard who assumed tactical command at the fighting front while Johnston returned to the rear to forward reinforcements. As a result, the ensuing victory brought more public fame to Beauregard than to Johnston, a fact that rankled a bit at the time and even more later. Still, Manassas enhanced Johnston's stature as well, and despite some post-battle squabbling over the failure to pursue the fleeing Yankees, his relationship with Davis seemed to be settled on firm ground.[5]

The rest of the summer passed quietly. Johnston mounted a tentative advance northward to Fairfax, then fell back again to Centreville. He declined to undertake a general offensive that summer on the grounds that his forces were inadequate to the task. Davis did not press him, and their correspondence retained a cordial, even friendly, tone. Then in the fall of 1861, Davis announced the names—in order of rank—of the five men who were to be confirmed as full generals in the Confederate Army. Johnston was among them to be sure, but he was listed fourth: behind Samuel Cooper (who was, in effect, chief of staff and who never held field command), Albert Sidney Johnston, and Robert E. Lee. Davis had ranked his generals by their seniority within the arm of service in which they currently served. Though Johnston had held the rank of brigadier general in the U.S. Army while serving as the Army's quartermaster, he had never held a general's rank as an infantry officer. In that capacity, he was junior to Cooper, A. S. Johnston, and Lee. But Johnston believed that he had been ill-treated. He was aware that an act of the Confederate Congress had declared that the seniority of officers holding the same rank would be determined by their relative seniority in the "Old Army"—the United States Army. Since Johnston had been senior to Cooper, Lee, and Sidney Johnston in that army, he believed he should have been ranked above them now. He wrote a long, rambling, and self-justifying letter to Davis to complain about it.[6]

Surprised and angered by Johnston's impertinence, even insubordination, Davis took Johnston's letter to a cabinet meeting and read it aloud. His own reply was brief, cool, and very official.[7] Johnston's ill-considered letter of complaint marked the beginning of a deterioration of their working relationship. There was never again the kind of cordial and confident exchange of views that is the ideal relationship between a head of state and his commander in the field. Even now, however, the breach was probably not irrevocable; Johnston did not resign and Davis did not seek to replace him.

In addition to this quarrel over seniority, Davis and Johnston had very real differences of opinion about Confederate strategy. Davis generally believed in defending the Confederacy everywhere it was physically possible to do so. This view was dictated by both military and political circumstances. A strategy of an extended defense gave nothing away to the Yankees and compelled them to occupy only what they could take by force. Moreover, Davis saw that it was impolitic for the leader of a confederated government willingly to give up part of one state in order to defend another. Could he, for example, tell the governor of North Carolina that he must send North Carolina troops to Virginia to defend Richmond while Union Navy and Army forces occupied Hatteras Inlet, Roanoke Island, and threatened New Bern? Davis, therefore, sought to defend as much Confederate territory as it was practical to defend, spreading out the Confederacy's manpower resources as necessary.[8]

Johnston saw it differently. He felt that as a soldier, he was under no obligation to take political factors into consideration. He therefore dismissed out of hand Davis's sensitivity to the concerns of nervous governors. The military circumstances, he believed, were self-evident, and it was up to the executive to explain to the governors the realities of the moment. His own strategic views were based on those realities. Because the North had a four-to-one manpower and materiel advantage over the South, the Confederacy simply could not spread out its defenses and leave it to the superior enemy to choose the time and place for its attack. Instead, he argued, the South must concentrate its forces into one or two large field armies and seek decisive battle at a place of its own choosing. If that meant the temporary abandonment of one or another part of the Confederacy, so be it. In the long run, military victory in the field would restore what had been temporarily surrendered to achieve it.[9]

It is a bit surprising, perhaps, to hear such high-risk and offensive-minded stuff coming from the likes of Joe Johnston. After all, there are few cases on record of his actually undertaking an offensive. But these were the views he urged on Jefferson Davis in their February and March meetings in 1862 when McClellan was preparing his Peninsular campaign. It is worth noting that Johnston's views on this particular issue were also those of Robert E. Lee. But lacking Lee's sensitivity and tact, Johnston failed to sell this vision effectively to Davis. Instead, he tended to assert his views and assume that their evident correctness would carry the day.

The divergent views between Davis and Johnston became more than theoretical in the spring of 1862 when George B. McClellan, a close friend of Johnston's from the Old Army, brought his Federal army to the Virginia peninsula. Davis wanted to leave Johnston's army where it was on the south bank of the Rappahannock and rely on other forces under John B. Magruder to watch McClellan's growing army at Fort Monroe. But as McClellan's strength grew, the president ordered Johnston to send reinforcements to Magruder a bit at a time. Johnston perforce obeyed these orders, but he did so with misgivings. His army on the Rappahannock slowly waned from 40,000 to 23,000 as Magruder's force on the peninsula grew from 10,000 to over 30,000. Johnston believed that such dispositions threw away the advantage of interior lines. Instead of using that advantage to concentrate Confederate forces against first one and then the other of the Federal armies in the field, Davis apparently intended to contest the issue at both places simultaneously. As Johnston saw it, the result would be that neither Confederate army would be strong enough to ensure success. He argued that all the Confederate forces should be committed either to the peninsula or concentrated on the Rappahannock.[10]

Johnston's first choice was to concentrate the army outside

Richmond—not only his own forces from northern Virginia, but those from Georgia and the Carolinas as well. If northern Virginia and the Carolina coast had to be surrendered temporarily, he believed that all would be regained by a decisive victory outside Richmond. If Richmond fell, holding the Rappahannock and New Bern would hardly matter.

In the first week of April, McClellan's army sallied from Fort Monroe and began a cautious advance up the peninsula. Davis wired Johnston to come personally to Richmond to discuss the crisis. In his first inspection of the defensive lines that Magruder had erected on the peninsula, Johnston was unimpressed. The works were too lengthy to be effectively manned, he insisted, but, more important, they could be turned on either flank by the Union Navy operating on the York or the James Rivers. He urged that Magruder be withdrawn, that reinforcements be brought at once from Georgia and the Carolinas, and that a massive Confederate army be assembled outside Richmond. It would strike, Johnston said, once McClellan had advanced beyond the range of the protective gunboats.[11]

Here was a high-risk strategy, indeed. In the name of the concentration of force, Johnston was willing to give up not only the line of the Rappanhannock and the coasts of Georgia and the Carolinas, but also Norfolk and its Navy yard. Davis was skeptical, and he was supported by both the war secretary (at that time George Randolph) and by Lee who was acting as the president's military advisor. Lee argued that the peninsula was a fine place to offer a defense of Richmond—it presented a narrow front that minimized the Union superiority in numbers.

Johnston accepted this decision, albeit reluctantly, and personally went to command at Yorktown. He had no intention whatsoever of fighting it out with McClellan's army on the Yorktown line; he would stay only as long as circumstances allowed, then would fall back on Richmond. But if the defensive lines at Yorktown had not impressed Johnston, they certainly impressed McClellan, who decided they were so formidable that he had no option but to embark on a regular siege using the same tactics that Vauban had developed in the seventeenth century to capture castles and fortified cities. Johnston harassed these efforts, but the Union advance was inexorable and the result, he believed, inevitable.[12]

Even those historians who tend to be skeptical of Johnston as a fighting general have acknowledged the timeliness of his withdrawal from the Yorktown line on May 3. Had he stayed even another day, it is likely that McClellan would have had his heavy guns in position to pin the Rebel army within those lines. Instead, Johnston made a successful evacuation after having delayed McClellan at Yorktown for a month. Of course, holding that line had not been his idea in the first place, and what was even worse for the Davis–Johnston relationship was that Davis found out about Johnston's withdrawal only the day before it took place. He immediately wired Johnston to tell him that "Your announcement . . . that you will withdraw tomorrow takes us by surprise." Johnston wired back a defensive response: "I determined to retire because we can do nothing here. . . . We MUST lose. By delay we may insure the loss of Richmond too." Davis was skeptical of the urgency to fall back, but, short of accusing his army commander of at the very least bad judgment, he would have to live with it.[13]

This episode highlights the single greatest failing in the Davis–Johnston relationship: the lack of full and free communication. This is primarily Johnston's fault, of course. As the junior partner in the relationship, it was his responsibility to keep Davis informed, particularly since he was aware of Davis's obsession for information. But he made little serious effort to cultivate the president's support, and his failure to do so was deliberate. It was not that Johnston wanted a confrontational relationship with his commander in chief, but he believed that sending daily informational letters and repeated invitations for Davis to offer suggestions was entirely inappropriate for a commander in the field. "I did not consult the president," he wrote later, "because it seemed to me that to do so would be to transfer my responsibilities to his shoulders. I could not consult him without adopting the course he might advise, so that to ask his advice would have been, in my opinion, to ask him to command for me." This was probably more than simple justification. Johnston really believed that it was a field officer's duty to accept responsibility, not to ask questions—or to seek advice. But if that explains why Johnston did not ask Davis's advice, it does not explain why he did not at least keep the president better *informed* than he did. He apparently conceived it to be the job of a field general to plan, fight, and win battles—then to notify the head of state afterward.[14]

Johnston did not want to send a message to Davis until he could report a success. Although he maintained the public posture that his retrograde movement up the peninsula was a thoughtful and considered strategic maneuver, he also knew how it would look to the government and the public. In a passage loaded with unconscious irony considering subsequent events, Johnston wrote his wife a week after evacuating Yorktown: "I am still going back. I flatter myself that if practice makes perfect, I shall soon learn to conduct a retreat." Rather than report these retreats to Davis on a daily basis, he would wait until he could announce a victory.[15]

Alas, Johnston did not win many victories either. When he finally did attack McClellan's slowly advancing horde—at the Battle of Seven Pines—he achieved only modest results, pushing the Federals back, but failing to inflict the kind of defeat that would compel McCellan to give up the campaign. Worse yet, he again failed to keep Davis informed; the president did not even know that a battle was being planned until he heard the sound of the guns. Seven Pines was a personal nightmare for Johnston, although he claimed afterward and for the rest of his life that the battle was an unappreciated Confederate victory. It was his first experience in commanding so large an army. The records are in dispute, but it appears likely that he had upward of 70,000 men available to hurl at McClellan. Moreover, McClellan had provided him with a golden opportunity by dividing his own forces into two unequal halves with the rain-swollen Chickahominy River between them. Johnston's plan was to hit the smaller element of McClellan's army with the larger part of his own. Alas, his own inexperience, the unwieldy size and organization of the army, and perhaps most of all the cupidity of James Longstreet, made a mockery of his plans. Johnston hoped to use the road network outside Richmond to bring no fewer than twenty-one brigades against a lone Federal corps. Such a plan required him to bring together the commands of Huger, D. H. Hill, and Longstreet in converging columns, on different roads, and have them all arrive more or less simultaneously.

It began to come apart almost at once. Huger was delayed; Longstreet, for reasons never explained convincingly, took the wrong road. Their columns converged prematurely and clogged the roads even more. At Gilles Creek, instead of splashing through the waist-deep water, the lead brigade constructed a makeshift bridge and the whole force tiptoed across it single file. In the afternoon, Johnston rode personally to the front and threw himself into the fight in an attempt to recoup the situation. In doing so he exposed himself to both rifle and artillery fire. Even as his army was turned back, he fell to the ground badly wounded. While being carried to the rear, his stretcher bearers encountered Davis, who was riding to the front. All their differences temporarily forgotten in this moment, Davis was quickly off his horse and kneeling by Johnston's side. Was he badly hurt? Was there anything he could do? Johnston shook his head and was carried to the rear.[16]

Now Davis faced an even more serious problem than an uncooperative army commander—no army commander. Officially the job fell on Johnston's second in command, Major General Gustavus Woodson Smith, an indifferent officer who had joined the Confederacy late and whose loyalty was suspected by some. In the long run, Smith would not do. Davis therefore turned to his military advisor riding alongside and asked Robert E. Lee if he would take over the command duties. Johnston would never get back his starting assignment.

As the army's new commander, Lee initiated the series of battles known as the Seven Days that drove McClellan from Richmond and ensured Lee permanent command of the army. Historians have often quoted the line attributed to Johnston after the war by his friend Dabney Maury that "the shot that struck me down was the best ever fired for the Southern Confederacy" because it brought Lee to command. This might be construed to suggest that Johnston was being magnanimous and self-effacing, acknowledging the brilliance of his West Point classmate. But the rest of the passage is revealing. Johnston went on to say that Lee's command was likely to be successful because he had "the confidence of this Government." In other words, what Johnston meant was that Lee's ascension to command was valuable to the Confederacy mainly because he could manipulate Davis and

Johnston couldn't. If, indeed, Johnston ever made this state-ment (we have only Dabney Maury's word for it), it was a rare moment of insight.[17]

Ironically, the six months that Johnston spent convalescing from his wounds proved to be the most decisive period of the war in terms of its impact on his relationship with Davis, for what finally doomed that relationship was not so much strategy as politics. Only days after the Battle of Seven Pines, Johnston received a visit from Texas Senator Louis T. Wigfall and his wife Charlotte. Johnston had known Wigfall briefly from the short time that the Texan had commanded a brigade in Johnston's army at Centreville. Now Wigfall offered the hospitality of his home as a place where Johnston could con-valesce in comfort and Johnston gratefully accepted. It was a fateful decision, for Wigfall emerged soon thereafter as one of Davis's most persistent critics, and over the next several months Johnston's presence in the Wigfall home identified him publicly with Davis's political foes.

As the relationship between Johnston and Wigfall strengthened, that of Johnston and Davis deteriorated. Oth-ers took sides in the quarrel and egged on both principals. Johnston accepted solace and promises of support from Wig-fall and from other Davis foes in the Confederate Congress; they in turn used Johnston's name and reputation—still very high among the general public—to assail Davis. Johnston himself never became an active player in these political maneuvers. If someone had suggested to him that he was playing politics or that he was being disloyal, he would have professed astonishment. All he did, after all, was accept the support of high-ranking members of the government who told him he was being ill-treated. Johnston was unquestion-ably politically naive in this role, but he was also more than a little self-deceptive. He could not have been unaware that

Wigfall and his allies were using him for their own purposes. Even without his active participation, his toleration of the use of his name and reputation by Davis's political enemies so undermined his credibility with the president that a genuine working partnership between the two men became impossible.[18]

By the time Johnston had recovered from his wounds, Lee's record of successes in the field was such that even Johnston appreciated that he had no hope of reclaiming command of the army in Virginia. But despite Johnston's new political prominence, Davis did give him another assignment. The president sent him west. There Johnston held a rather curious command as the coordinator of two field armies—Braxton Bragg's Army of Tennessee and John C. Pemberton's Army of Mississippi. Although he commanded neither army directly, he was (in Davis's view of things) supposed to shuttle forces back and forth between these two armies as needed. It never worked the way Davis imagined—indeed, it never really worked at all, in part because the theater was simply too big (and Confederate transport too unreliable) to make timely transfers possible, and in part because Johnston never enthusiastically embraced the idea. The fall of Vicksburg in July 1863 put the final unhappy punctuation mark on the end of this command experiment, and, so far as Davis was concerned, on Johnston as well. Johnston had never managed to assemble a force strong enough to lift Grant's siege of Vicksburg and, after that, Davis all but gave up on him. When Josiah Gorgas remarked to Davis that Pemberton's starving garrison in Vicksburg had been forced to surrender for want of provisions, Davis retorted, "Yes, from want of provisions inside, and a general outside who wouldn't fight."[19]

Davis was determined never to give Johnston an important command again. Of course, Johnston's friends in Richmond—who were also, and not coincidentally, Davis's political foes—complained about this constantly. But to Davis this was all the more reason for keeping Johnston at arm's length. In the end, however, Davis could not resist the pressure to reinstate Johnston. After the debacle of Missionary Ridge in November 1863, Davis was compelled to dismiss Bragg and, against his own better judgment, named Johnston to replace him. When the spring campaign began in May 1864, the only two effective field armies left in the Confederacy were those commanded by the West Point classmates Robert E. Lee and Joseph E. Johnston.

While Grant and Lee slugged it out in Virginia—in the Wilderness, at Spotsylvania, and Cold Harbor—Davis watched with more alarm than surprise as Johnston fell back before Sherman's advance in Georgia, giving up mile after mile to the invader and making what seemed to Davis no serious effort to stop him. Already skeptical of Johnston's prowess as a general, and suspicious of his political associations, Davis was further distressed by Johnston's apparent timidity in declining to attack Sherman and by the infrequency of his reports. Davis wanted to be made a full partner in the campaign via reports from the field. But Johnston made only minimal efforts to keep Davis informed, and never wrote to ask Davis's advice. Johnston's loyal wife Lydia urged her husband to write more frequent reports to Davis, but Johnston doubted that it would do any good. "I do report in a general way," he wrote her, "but the people of Richmond take no interest."[20]

As for his retrograde movements, Johnston claimed after the war, in his *Narrative of Military Operations* (1874), that this was a deliberate policy on his part. "I thought it our policy to stand on the defensive, to spare the blood of our soldiers by fighting under cover habitually, and to attack only when bad position or division of the enemy's forces might give us advantages." This is certainly what Johnston *did* during the campaign, but it is less clear that it is what he *planned*. Instead, he seized on this strategy only after Sherman had successfully flanked him out of several strong positions. Still, the notion was a viable one. The further Sherman penetrated into Georgia, the longer his supply lines became. A credible threat to those supply lines might have slowed him even more. If Sherman had been kept out of Atlanta past the fall elections in the North, the course of the war might have been changed. But when Johnston asked Richmond for cavalry support from other theaters to strike at Sherman's supply lines, he met skepticism and refusal. To Davis this sounded all too familiar: more excuses to avoid fighting.[21]

Whether or not a strategy of striking Sherman's supply lines would have worked remains a subject for latter-day armchair strategists, but the point to be made is that it was never tried because Johnston had already squandered his credibility with Davis not only by his timidity in the field and the infrequency of his reports, but also by his unprofessional association with Louis T. Wigfall and Davis's political foes in Richmond. These factors, plus Braxton Bragg's poisonous innuendos, and John Bell Hood's secret and self-promotional letters from the front, created a climate of intrigue in the Army of Tennessee that would have made members of the Roman Senate blush.

By July, Davis had seen and heard enough. He dismissed Johnston and replaced him with Hood, who subsequently led the army into a series of fierce and unsuccessful battles around Atlanta and then a quixotic invasion of Tennessee that resulted in the army's virtual destruction. Johnston went into retirement.

But there was an epilogue. All through the winter of 1864–65, as Hood led the Army of Tennessee to its destruction outside Nashville and Lee survived a bitter and wasting siege in Richmond, Johnston lived in relative comfort in Columbia, South Carolina. Staring defeat in the face, the Confederacy looked for a miracle, and in January 1865 the Congress tried to conjure one by naming Robert E. Lee as commander in chief of Confederate armies, thus effectively stripping that power from Davis. At the same time, Congress recommended, but did not require, "the assignment of General Joseph E. Johnston to the command of the Army of Tennessee."[22]

Davis was both humiliated and defiant. He sat down and compiled a fifteen-page indictment of Johnston for the purpose of explaining to Congress why he could not, under any circumstances, again give Johnston the command of a Confederate army. "At different times during the war," Davis wrote, "I have given to General Johnston three very important commands, and in each case, experience has revealed . . . defects which unfit him for the conduct of a campaign." Davis asserted that Johnston had failed to hold Harpers Ferry in Virginia during his first command; he had given up Centreville without a fight; he had retreated from Yorktown; and for more than two months he had given way before Sherman's army in Georgia without once making a serious effort to halt Sherman's destructive campaign. Item by item, in his precise and detailed way, Davis painted a portrait of a man so hopelessly incompetent that he should never again be entrusted with important military responsibility. "My opinion of General Johnston's unfitness for command has ripened slowly . . . into a conviction so settled that it would be impossible for me again to feel confidence in him as the commander of an army in the field."[23]

Davis never sent this lengthy memorandum to Congress. It was Lee who convinced him that, if nothing else, Johnston's restoration to command would improve morale in the ranks in that dark and bitter winter and would encourage veterans to return to the colors. Against every instinct, Davis acceded.

The news of his reinstatement brought Johnston no joy. Given the history of his relationship with Davis, he was convinced that the president had returned him to command only to ensure that he would be the one to bear the opprobrium of the final surrender. When he got Lee's order "to concentrate all your forces and drive back Sherman," he replied tersely: "These troops form an army too weak to cope with Sherman." The next day, he chanced to run into Mary Chesnut, who was living nearby. That night she wrote in her diary that Johnston professed to be "very angry to be ordered to take command again." And apparently his anger was genuine, for his wife Lydia wrote confidentially to a close friend that her husband was "in the very devil of a bad humor" because of his conviction that "he was only put back to be the one to surrender."[24]

On three days in mid-March 1865, Joseph E. Johnston fought his last battle. The Battle of Bentonville was also the last major battle of the Civil War. It is easy to see how for Joe Johnston, this was an opportunity for redemption. A victory here would redeem his own reputation as a general who would not fight; it would redeem the honor of the Army of Tennessee, slandered by Hood as timorous in a self-serving explanation for his own failures in Tennessee. It is easy to imagine that Johnston saw the fight as a chance to show "them."

If Bentonville was not a Confederate victory, it was at least a serious check to Sherman's hitherto unopposed advance through the Carolinas. Johnston was pleased. Sherman had been punished, and he would have to be more careful. Then, too, Johnston believed that his soldiers had disproved Hood's criticism. Pointedly, he wired Lee in Richmond: "Troops of Tennessee army have fully disproved slanders that have been published against them."[25]

But the moment did not last. Only days afterward news arrived at Johnston's headquarters that Lee had been forced from Richmond and that the government had been compelled to flee the city. Davis ordered Johnston to report to him at Greensboro on April 12. When Johnston dutifully arrived, he heard the news that Lee had surrendered. As far as he was concerned, that meant the war was over. There was nothing but a longer casualty list that could be gained by prolonging the war even another day. When he reported to Davis, however, the president wanted to talk only about how to continue the war. Johnston was appalled. Evidently Davis sensed it, for he stopped abruptly and asked Johnston for his views. There was a moment of awkward silence as the two men regarded each other. Then Johnston spoke: "My views, sir," he began, "are that our people are tired of the war, feel themselves whipped, and will not fight."

Davis looked down, and worried a small piece of paper in his hands, folding it over and over.

Johnston continued: "Our country is overrun, its military resources greatly diminished, while the enemy's military power and resources were never greater and may be increased to any extent desired. . . . My men are daily deserting in large numbers and are stealing my artillery teams to aid in their escape. . . . Since Lee's surrender they regard the war as at an end."

Still Davis did not look up. He asked Beauregard his thoughts. That officer replied: "I concur in everything that General Johnston has said." There was another long period of silence. Finally Davis asked Johnston what he proposed. Johnston suggested that he send a note through the lines to Sherman to request a general armistice, not only for his own army but for all Confederate armies. Davis didn't believe anything good could come of it, but he gave his permission.[26] Given that opening, Johnston met Sherman at the Bennett House near Durham Station, and the two men patched together a surrender document that called not only for the end of hostilities, but also for the restoration of state governments. By the time that document arrived in Washington, however, the death of President Lincoln had dramatically changed the mood in the capital. Sherman was instructed that the arrangement he had made with Johnston was unsatisfactory and was ordered to renew hostilities at once. Notified of these events by Sherman, Johnston agreed to meet a second time at the Bennett House; this time he surrendered what was left of his army without any discussion of political solutions. Davis never forgave him. Lee had surrendered because he had had no other choice, Davis asserted. Johnston had merely quit.

Even the end of the war did not end the feud. It extended into the postwar years as each man wrote his memoirs, and in this battle Davis emerged the clear victor. Neither man produced a particularly readable or enlightening memoir. But Davis's account was at least relatively restrained whereas Johnston's was confrontational and combative. The bitter and unyielding tone of his postwar writings probably did more to undermine his historical reputation than all of his actions—or inaction—on the battlefield.

In the end, however, the relationship between Davis and Johnston is suggestive of the fact that—Buckminster Fuller notwithstanding—there are some partnerships where the whole is *less* than the sum of the parts. Their dysfunctional partnership was an unalloyed disaster for the cause they served. As the junior member of that partnership, it was Johnston's duty to make the greater effort to adjust. Instead he allowed himself to be seduced by his own hurt feelings and the calculated solace of Davis's political enemies. As a result, by the time of the critical Atlanta Campaign of 1864, he had lost all credibility with the administration. Whatever merit there may have been to the strategic vision he communicated to his friends in Richmond, it was unlikely to attract the enthusiastic support of a president who had come to view him as the enemy. For that, Johnston himself must bear a major responsibility—and with it a major responsibility for the failure of the Confederate war effort.

2

Ambivalent Visions of Victory: Davis, Lee, and Confederate Grand Strategy

EMORY M. THOMAS

Rᴏʙᴇʀᴛ ᴇ. ʟᴇᴇ had every right to be frustrated. At Mechanicsville, Virginia, on June 26, 1862, after thirty-three years' experience in the military, Lee commanded an army in combat for the first time in his life. His only previous experience with command in combat had occurred on October 16, 1859, at Harpers Ferry when he led a couple dozen marines in a successful assault on the fire-engine house in which John Brown and a handful of his followers held thirteen hostages. Now Lee commanded 92,000 Confederates against Union General George B. McClellan and his army of more than 100,000 men. And Lee's initial battle, the second of the Seven Days, was going badly.[1]

Jefferson Davis, president and therefore commander in chief of the Confederate States, was on the scene at Lee's headquarters. Davis, with his staff and numerous other civilians, had ridden the short distance from Richmond to see

Lee's battle. For a long time, they all stood around on Chickahominy Bluffs and waited for something to happen. Then when something did happen, Davis and his entourage followed Lee down the bluff, across the Chickahominy River, through the village of Mechanicsville, to a small rise before Beaverdam Creek where Southern attacks were meeting bloody repulse. Stonewall Jackson and his Army of the Valley were supposed to be on the flank and in the rear of the Federal troops, who were holding the stubborn defensive line on the opposite bank of Beaverdam Creek. But Jackson and his men had yet to make an appearance. Lee could only watch his soldiers fail and fall in vain attempts to break the enemy line of battle. Davis and company also watched the futile action while artillery rounds landed nearby, potentially threatening not only Lee, but also Davis and his crew.

Finally, Lee rode over to Davis and inquired, "Who is all this army and what is it doing here?"

"It is not my army, General," Davis responded.

Lee then stated, "It is certainly not my army, Mr. President, and this is no place for it."

After an awkward pause, Davis agreed to leave the field and did so, while Lee observed to ensure that he did. No doubt Lee was concerned for the safety of the president and his entourage. That his careful plans had gone awry also exasperated him, and he did not appreciate having civilian spectators watch the abortive battle. But Lee also did not want Davis looking over his shoulder during a campaign in progress.[2]

At issue was more than the natural reticence of a subordinate to persistent observation by a superior or the usual discomfort of a general with interference, implied or otherwise, from a civilian. Lee knew Davis well enough to know that the president had a different strategic vision from his own. And

Lee was not at all eager for Davis to realize that Lee proposed to fight one kind of war and Davis another. The difference in strategic outlook between Lee and Davis was subtle, but significant. This difference was not apparent during the war because Lee was too shrewd to express ideas at cross purposes to Davis's assumptions. And because the general never wrote or spoke his heresy, historians have believed, as the Confederate president believed, that Lee and Davis were in strategic accord when, in fact, they were not. To understand the separate strategic visions of Lee and Davis it is necessary to examine each one in turn.

In the spring of 1861, Robert E. Lee possessed an abundance of reputation and a dearth of experience as credentials for command in combat. Lee was the son of Light-Horse Harry Lee who had won fame but not much else in the Revolutionary War; young Lee, however, had spent most of his career in the United States Army as an engineer. His reputation rested principally on his service on the staff of Winfield Scott during the Mexican War and on the praise Scott lavished on Lee thereafter. Lee had commanded cavalry in Texas from 1855 until he resigned his commission in April 1861, but had spent much of this period sitting on courts martial and more than two years on leave in a vain attempt to settle the estate of his father-in-law G. W. P. Custis. Lee had led expeditions against Comanche warriors and Mexican marauders, but had himself seen no action in either case. So beyond some genetic advantage inherited from his father and the good opinion of a fellow Virginian who commanded the army of the enemy, Lee seemed to have little to commend him as a Confederate general.

During the first year of the war, Lee did little to enhance this standing. Initially, he commanded the armed forces of Virginia and performed worthy service raising, training, and equipping volunteers. But when Lee's regiments mustered into Confederate service, Lee became a general without an army. He served as unofficial aide/advisor to the president during the summer of 1861 and in that capacity went in the fall to Western (now West) Virginia to oversee Confederate efforts in the Kanawha Valley. This campaign, however, became a disaster, and Lee returned to Richmond. Next, Davis assigned Lee to command the Department of South Carolina, Georgia, and Florida. In this capacity, Lee made the wise but unpopular decision to withdraw troops and guns from the coast and barrier islands in favor of deploying Confederate defenses up the rivers where Southern armies had some chance of blocking Northern penetration. Lee returned to Richmond during the spring of 1862, and resumed his duties as advisor to Davis—at most, an unofficial chief of staff. During the early phase of McClellan's Peninsula Campaign, Lee had the uncomfortable chore of mediating between Joseph E. Johnston and the president, neither of whom had much confidence in the other. When Johnston suffered battle wounds at Seven Pines on May 31, Davis appointed Lee to command Johnston's army.[3]

Thus far, Lee's experience as a Confederate had been nothing if not frustrating. From this experience, however, Lee learned lessons that informed his strategic thinking when he assumed command. He learned that many Southerners seemed to lack any sense of urgency about this war. "Our people have not been earnest enough," Lee wrote to one of his daughters on March 2, 1862, "have thought too much of themselves and their ease, and instead of turning out to a man, have been content to nurse themselves and their dimes, and leave the protection of themselves and families to others." He remembered lessons learned with Scott in Mexico that volunteer troops were essentially civilians, that political generals were politicians, and that bold, decisive action was likely the only way to retain the attention and energy of these civilians masquerading as soldiers.[4]

Lee appropriated the Napoleonic concept of the offensive defense and once observed, "It is [as] impossible for him [the enemy] to have a large operating army at every assailable point in our territory as it is for us to keep one up to defend it. We must move our troops from point to point as required. . . . Partial encroachments of the enemy we must expect, but they can always be recovered, and any defeat of their large army will reinstate everything." While adhering to the offensive defense, Lee definitely emphasized offense.[5]

He came to believe that the best chance for Confederate victory lay in a battle or campaign of annihilation. Lee also thought that the best chance for a climactic battle or campaign was sooner rather than later. "We should not . . . conceal from ourselves that our resources in men are constantly diminishing, and the disproportion in this respect between us and our enemies . . . is steadily augmenting," Lee wrote at the very time that Confederate armies reached their peak of numerical strength. So Lee pursued a showdown as soon as possible and risked boldly to achieve a moment of truth.[6]

Jefferson Davis adopted a larger view than Lee regarding Confederate victory. Like Lee, Davis was a graduate of West Point (1828). He served for seven years in the United States Army, then resigned to become a planter in Mississippi. Davis commanded a volunteer regiment in the Mexican War and obtained fame along with a battle wound at the Battle of Buena Vista. He served as Secretary of War in the cabinet of Franklin Pierce and then as U.S. Senator from Mississippi. Davis hoped that he would serve the Confederacy as a general and took seriously his presidential role as commander in chief.[7]

"All we want is to be left alone," Davis insisted when he addressed the Congress in the wake of firing on Fort Sumter.

The president was aware that the Confederacy could win simply by not losing. Like those other American rebels between 1775 and 1781, Confederates merely had to keep the faith and maintain armies in the field to wear down their enemies and achieve independence.[8]

Initially, Davis succumbed to political pressure and attempted to defend the entire frontier of his new nation against Federal invasion. By the spring of 1862, however, Davis had greatly modified his strategic thinking and policy. "I acknowledge the error of my attempt to defend all of the frontier," he wrote to a friend in March 1862. Then Davis protested that he did not plan "to carry on the war upon a 'purely defensive system.'" On the contrary, he insisted, "The advantage of selecting the time and place of attack was too apparent to have been overlooked, but the means might have been wanting." Davis, too, had begun to think in terms of the offensive defense.[9]

But Davis's emphasis was on defense. He still fell back on his belief that Confederate Southerners could outlast their enemies in a war of wills. Thus, Davis emphasized husbanding Confederate resources and discouraged taking risks that might lead to destruction of one or more of his armies. If all else failed, Davis believed, the Confederacy would survive in guerrilla warfare as long as any significant number of Southerners remained faithful to the cause.

So when conventional means seemed about to fail, Davis wrote what became his final proclamation to the Confederate people. On April 4, 1865, as his government on wheels paused at Danville, Virginia, the president said:

> We have now entered upon a new phase. . . . Relieved from the necessity of guarding cities and particular points, important but not vital to our defense, with an army free to move from point to point and strike in detail detachments and garrisons of the enemy, operating on the interior of our own country, where the

supplies are more accessible, and where the foe will be far removed from his own base and cut off from all succor in case of reverse, nothing is now needed to render our triumph certain but the exhibition of our own unquenchable resolve. Let us but will it and we are free.[10]

From hindsight, Davis's words sound almost farcical. And Jefferson Davis's version of "the long march" culminated near Irwinville, Georgia, with his capture in ignominious circumstances.

Irony attends the fact that only a few days after Davis dispatched his call to partisan arms, Lee confronted the possibility of becoming a guerrilla himself. Edward Porter Alexander proposed to Lee at Appomattox on April 9, 1865, that the Army of Northern Virginia should "scatter like rabbits and partridges in the woods." Lee responded to Alexander's suggestion and said among other things:

> The men would have no rations and they would be under no discipline. They are already demoralized by four years of war. They would have to plunder and rob to procure subsistence. The country would be full of lawless bands in every part, a state of society would ensue from which it would take the country years to recover. Then the enemy's cavalry would pursue in the hopes of catching the principal officers, and wherever they went there would be fresh rapine and destruction.[11]

Clearly, Lee was more afraid of anarchy than he was afraid of Yankees. But more to this point, Lee's strategic thinking was diametrically opposed to that of the president. Aware of Davis's commitment to a guerrilla alternative to defeat in a conventional war, Lee addressed the issue when he rendered his final report to Davis on April 20, 1865. "A partisan war may be continued," Lee stated, "and hostilities protracted, causing individual suffering and the devastation of the country, but I see no prospect by that means of achieving a separate independence." Then Lee urged the president to take steps toward the "suspension of hostilities and the restoration of peace."[12]

Beyond this explanation of his surrender and his plea for peace, Lee did not address the issue of his difference with Davis. Much later Davis said of Lee, "Laborious and exact in details, as he was vigilant and comprehensive in grand strategy, [he had] a power . . . [that] soon became manifest in all that makes an army a rapid, accurate, compact machine, with responsive motion in all its parts."[13]

And much later than that, Frank E. Vandiver voiced the verdict of most historians when he asserted of Lee and Davis: "They made a powerful team."[14] William C. Davis echoes Vandiver's conclusion: "In the understanding and rapport they achieved, and in the way they cooperated, Davis and Lee formed a civil-military team surpassing any other of the war, even Lincoln and Grant."[15] Clement Eaton states of Davis, "He seldom interfered with Lee."[16] Archer Jones claims that after the Seven Days' battles, a chastened Lee "followed the conservative strategy which he and Davis had agreed upon."[17] Richard M. McMurry observes, "Lee knew that the Richmond authorities were naturally concerned about the progress of his campaigns, and he went to great lengths to keep them informed about the details of his army's movements, the enemy's activities, and his plans."[18] Douglas Southall Freeman proclaims, "Lee understood the President thoroughly, and from the day he assumed command he employed his knowledge to remove misunderstandings and to assure co-operation."[19] And in his study of relationships between leaders in the Civil War, Joseph T. Glatthaar repeats the familiar theme; about Davis and Lee, Glatthaar concludes, "Together they formed a solid, professional working relationship."[20]

The essential historiographic exception to the legend of a

Lee–Davis love feast, other than my own, is Steven E. Woodworth's *Davis and Lee at War*. In his preface Woodworth writes:

Although Lee did pursue a largely offensive grand strategy, his policy was in fact one of two possible ways in which the South could conceivably have obtained its independence. The other, the thoroughly defensive, survival-oriented grand strategy, so much praised by many modern scholars, was the strategy of Jefferson Davis, and the tension between Davis's ideas and Lee's offensive quest for early victory is the central feature of the climactic stages of Davis's war for Virginia and the Confederacy.[21]

Because Woodworth's book and my biography of Lee appeared within a year of each other, I can only conclude that here we have an idea whose time has indeed come. Until 1993, Lee himself was probably the only person who realized the depth of his division with Davis.[22]

Lee had better sense than to confront the president over grand strategy, and Davis was unaware of the difference between them. And because Davis feuded with most of his other generals, his relations with Lee have seemed all the more harmonious—just as Lee wanted them to seem.

Ideas, however, have consequences. The difference in the strategic visions of Lee and Davis may not have provoked discord between general and president. But because their difference remained unaddressed, so all the more unresolved, Lee and Davis pursued their separate strategies. And beyond some point, these strategies were mutually exclusive. In his quest for a climactic battle, Lee bled his army to exhaustion eventually, far beyond the capacity to rally Confederate Southerners to the full-scale guerrilla war Davis envisioned. In his quest to husband Southern resources for the protracted conflict he projected, Davis at critical moments withheld the support in men and material that Lee requested to achieve his battle of annihilation. And because Lee knew that he and Davis possessed varied strategic visions, Lee on occasion made plans based more on circumstances in Richmond than on the situation in Washington.

Lee had learned from his time spent serving Davis as advisor/chief of staff/consultant. From his often-awkward position as intermediary between the president and Joseph E. Johnston, Lee knew from experience that Davis wanted to know what his commanders were doing. Accordingly, when Lee left the immediate proximity of Richmond for the first time after acceding to command of the Army of Northern Virginia, he informed Davis:

> Unless I hear from you to the contrary I shall leave for G[ordonsville] at 4 A.M. tomorrow. The troops are accumulating there & I must see that arrangements are made for the field. I received a letter from Longstreet today requesting my presence. I will keep you informed of everything of importance that transpires. When you do not hear from me, you may feel sure that I do not think it necessary to trouble you. I shall feel obliged to you for any directions you may think proper to give.[23]

Between this letter of August 14 and August 30, 1862, Lee wrote fifteen letters and telegrams to Davis in seventeen days.[24]

For his part, Davis wrote often to Lee (six letters during the same seventeen-day period), and the President sent his old friend William N. Pendleton to Lee and explained:

> I conversed fully with Genl Pendleton before he left here and aske[d] him to proceed directly to your Head Qr[s] to confer with you and give you suc[h] information as would enable you t[o] show me with the necessary precision how I could best promote the success of your operations and generally secure that cointelligence between us which is desirable to both.

Pendleton remained with Lee throughout the war, usually as "nominal" chief of artillery. He did write "occasional confidential memoranda of the position, doings etc, of the army" to Davis as instructed; but his memoranda usually praised Lee and reported the army in fighting trim.[25]

Lee's last two communications with Davis during this period (August 14–30) are interesting. Lee wrote both of them on August 30. Sometime that morning he wrote a letter to Davis and said, among other things, "The movement [of Lee's forces] has, as far as I am able to judge, drawn the enemy from the Rappahannock frontier and caused him to concentrate his troops between Manassas and Centreville. My desire has been to avoid a general engagement, being the weaker force, & by manoeuvring to relieve the portion of the country referred to." Later the same day, Lee dispatched a telegram to Davis that revealed rather more ambitious goals for this campaign. "This army," Lee wrote, "achieved today on the plains of Manassas a signal victory over combined forces of Genls McClellan and Pope." This, of course, was Second Manassas/Bull Run in which Lee did not exactly "avoid a general engagement."[26]

The exchange of letters between Lee and Davis associated with Lee's first foray to the field in command of the Army of Northern Virginia reveals some lack of candor on Lee's part. He certainly did not send Stonewall Jackson's wing into the rear of Pope's army and then hurl James Longstreet's wing at Pope's exposed flank "to avoid a general engagement." But Davis could hardly complain when the result was one of Lee's greatest battles.[27]

Lee's expressed desire "to avoid a general engagement" at Second Manassas was a prelude to one of two case studies presented here of Lee and Davis operating in less than concert. The first of these examples of dissonance was the Mary-

land campaign in September 1862, culminating in the Battle
of Antietam/Sharpsburg.

On September 3, 1862, from Dranesville in northern Virginia, Lee wrote to Davis, "The present seems to me to be the
most propitious time since the commencement of the war for
the Confederate Army to enter Maryland." He admitted to
the president, "The army is not properly equipped for an
invasion of an enemy's territory. It lacks much of the material of war, is feeble in transportation, the animals being much
reduced, and the men are poorly provided with clothes and
in thousands of instances are destitute of shoes." But Lee
added, "We cannot afford to be idle, and though weaker than
our opponents in men and military equipments, must endeav-
or to harass, if we cannot destroy them. I am aware that the
movement is attended with much risk, yet I do not consider
success impossible."[28]

Next day, September 4, Lee again spoke of his plan to
invade Maryland in a letter to Davis. "I am more fully persuaded of the benefits that will result from an expedition into
Maryland, and I shall proceed to make the movement at
once, unless you should signify your disapprobation." And in
the same letter Lee proposed to enter Pennsylvania "unless
you should deem it unadvisable upon political or other
grounds."[29]

When Lee wrote his intention "to make the movement at
once," he was serious. On September 5, Lee proclaimed,
"This army is about entering Maryland," and the next day
Lee announced by telegram, "Two divisions of the army have
crossed the Potomac, I hope all will cross today." And the
day after that (September 7), Lee wrote to Davis that "all the
divisions of the army have crossed the Potomac."[30]

Had Davis opposed sending an army into Maryland, he
would have had precious little opportunity to restrain Lee
before Lee crossed the Potomac. Lee first mentioned his plan

by letter on September 3 and confirmed his intention on September 4. On September 6, Lee informed Davis by telegram that two divisions were already in Maryland and the next day wrote Davis that the entire army was in enemy country. When and how was Davis to object?

As it happened, Davis was delighted with Lee's invasion and determined to take part himself. In a letter sent to Lee on September 7, Davis expressed his desire to join Lee at Leesburg (Virginia) and discuss plans. That same day the president left Richmond with former Maryland governor Enoch Louis Lowe and traveled north as far as Warrenton. James Longstreet later claimed that Davis planned to ride at the head of his army, make a spectacle of the liberation of Maryland, and call for recognition of Confederate independence.[31]

Lee was much less than delighted with the president's plan and wrote Davis to discourage him from any attempt to join the army. Lee protested that the journey would be "very disagreeable" and that since he had abandoned his lines of supply and communication east of the Blue Ridge Mountains, Davis risked capture if he tried to reach Leesburg. To make sure that Davis understood all this, Lee sent his aide Walter Taylor to intercept the president and "explain . . . the difficulties and dangers of the journey, which I cannot recommend you to undertake."[32]

The same day he wrote these discouraging words to the president (September 9, 1862), Lee also dispatched Special Orders No. 191 to his subordinates. This was the bold division of his army designed to extend the invasion of Maryland and recapture Harpers Ferry at the same time. He sent a copy of the order to Davis on September 12, and the following day a copy fell into the hands of Union General George B. McClellan. This mischance, of course, drove the Maryland campaign thereafter, as McClellan attempted to take advantage of good fortune by assailing the fragments of Lee's army and Lee tried to reconcentrate the Army of Northern Virginia.[33]

Initially, Lee planned to withdraw across the Potomac at Shepherdstown; but on September 15 he learned that Jackson would soon receive the surrender of the Federal garrison at Harpers Ferry. Consequently, Lee decided to concentrate at Sharpsburg and give battle to McClellan along Antietam Creek.[34]

Then and since then, many have asked why. Lee had already informed Davis that his army was "not properly equipped for an invasion." On September 13, Lee wrote Davis about "the reduction of our ranks by straggling" and estimated that "from a third to a half" of the army had slipped or fallen away. So why did Lee choose to stand and fight with an ill-equipped, anemic army? "We will make our stand on those hills," he said to some of his soldiers two days before the battle. One of the best students of this and Lee's other battles has concluded, "His decision to make that stand was a bad one, probably his worst of the war."[35]

From hindsight, this judgment may indeed be valid. At the time, however, Lee's decision to "make our stand on those hills" had several factors in its favor. The army was, after all, already there or en route to Sharpsburg; Lee would not lose any more troops to straggling. The enemy was once more McClellan, and Lee knew him well enough to know that he would be cautious to the point of timidity. Lee planned to array his army on the defensive, and he of all commanders should have known the cost of offensive action. This time he intended to let the enemy pay that price. Perhaps he envisioned another Malvern Hill—with the roles reversed—or maybe he anticipated Fredericksburg in which his enemies battered themselves against an impregnable defensive position. However reduced his army was, Lee could reasonably anticipate the concentration of the strength he had against an enemy expecting to assail only fragments of Lee's forces.[36]

In light of what happened at Antietam/Sharpsburg on September 17, 1862, these speculations may sound lame. But two certainties stand out from Lee's decision to make a stand. Lee desired a major battle; Lee believed he had a chance to win this battle. And Jefferson Davis was nowhere near to mitigate Lee's moment of truth. The Maryland campaign in 1862 revealed Lee intent on fighting a climactic battle, perhaps so intent that he accepted battle under adverse circumstances in order to have his fight without interference.

The campaign that produced the Battle of Gettysburg is another example of Lee and Davis working at cross purposes. On May 30, 1863, Lee, ignoring the flush of Chancellorsville's victory, complained to Davis that his army was "diminished." He concluded, "I fear the time has passed when I could have taken the offensive with advantage. From indications that reach me, the enemy is contemplating another movement, I have not discovered what it is. There may be nothing left for me to do but fall back." When he did set the army in motion, Lee explained to Davis, "I think if I can create an apprehension for the safety of their right flank & the Potomac, more troops will be brought from their line of operations in the South. But to gain any material advantage, I should if possible have a large force, as their army by all accounts is represented as very large." To Secretary of War James A. Seddon, Lee wrote more plainly:

> As far as I can judge there is nothing to be gained by this army remaining quietly on the defensive, which it must do unless it can be reinforced. I am aware that there is difficulty & hazard in taking the aggressive with so large an army in its front, entrenched behind a river where it cannot be advantageously attacked. Unless it can be drawn out in a position to be assailed, it will take its own time to prepare and strengthen itself to renew its advance upon Richmond, and force this army back within the entrenchments of that city. This may be the result in any event, still I think it is worth a trial to prevent such a catastrophe. Still,

if the Department thinks it better to remain on the defensive, and guard as far as possible all the avenues of approach and await the time of the enemy, I am ready to adopt this course.

Lee was losing patience with the defensive posture the administration seemed intent on pursuing.[37]

By mid-June, elements of Lee's army were about to leave Virginia and advance once more into enemy country. On June 18, Lee reported to Davis, "The enemy has been thrown back from the line of the Rappahannock, & is concentrating, as far as I can learn, in the vicinity of Centreville [near Washington]." Still Lee understated his goals in this campaign. "I think I can throw Genl Hooker's army across the Potomac and draw troops from the South, embarrassing their plan of campaign in a measure, if I can do nothing more and have to return."[38]

More revealing was Lee's plea for strategic concentration to complement his invasion. He began stating his case on June 23:

At this distance, I can see no benefit to be derived from maintaining a large force on the southern coast during the unhealthy months of the summer and autumn, and I think that a part at least, of the troops in North Carolina, and of those under Genl Beauregard, can be employed at this time with great advantage in Virginia. If an army could be organized under the command of Genl Beauregard, and pushed forward to Culpeper Court House, threatening Washington from that direction, it would not only effect a diversion most favorable for this army, but would I think, relieve us of any apprehension of an attack upon Richmond during our absence.

Lee returned to this topic in a letter of June 25.

If the plan that I suggested the other day, of organizing an army, even in effigy, under Genl Beauregard at Culpeper Court House, can be carried into effect, much relief will be afforded.

One more time on June 25, Lee tried to move Davis to action:

> So strong is my conviction of the necessity of activity on our part in military affairs, that you will excuse my adverting to the subject again, notwithstanding what I have said in my previous letter of today.
>
> It seems to me that we cannot afford to keep our troops awaiting possible movements of the enemy, but that our true policy is, as far as we can, so to employ our own forces, as to give occupation to his at points of our selection. . . . I feel sure therefore that the best use that can be made of the troops in Carolina, and those in Virginia now guarding Richmond, would be the prompt assembling of the main body of them, leaving sufficient to prevent raids, together with as many as can be drawn from the army of Genl Beauregard at Culpeper Court House under the command of that officer.[39]

The president responded to these pleas in a letter Lee never received; the courier who carried it fell into enemy hands on July 2, 1862, and by then Lee needed more than Beauregard at Culpeper Court House. For the record, Davis carefully explained why Lee could have no reinforcements and why Beauregard could not come to Culpeper Court House.[40]

To Davis, Lee used modest phrases like "embarrassing their plan of campaign" to describe his intentions in Pennsylvania. But according to Isaac Ridgeway Trimble, one of Lee's subordinates, the commanding general had much more ambitious plans. On June 25, the same day he wrote to the president about "embarrassing their plan of campaign," Lee reportedly said to Trimble:

> We have outmaneuvered the enemy and are in the heart of Pennsylvania, and as far as I can learn from the papers, the Northern Army [does not] know that we have crossed the Potomac. When they hear where we are, they will throw themselves by forced marches between us and Washington, Baltimore or Philadelphia,

but strung out on a long line, fatigued, hungry and somewhat demoralized by surprise and apprehension of danger. Our forces have marched at leisure, are well rested and in fine spirits, and can be concentrated on any point east of the South Mountain in forty-eight hours or less. My plan is to throw an overwhelming force against the enemy's advance, as soon as I learn the road they take, crush them, and following up the sweep, beat them in detail, and in a few hours throw the whole Army into disorder and probably create a panic. . . .

According to Trimble, "General Lee then laid his spread fingers upon the map between Gettysburg and Emmitsburg and said, 'Somewhere hereabout, we shall fight a great battle, and if successful, will secure our independence and end the war.' "[41]

Very likely, Trimble's memory was dependent on hindsight. But Trimble's account does describe what Lee attempted to do at Gettysburg. And it is clear that Lee wanted the stakes in his grand gamble raised even higher. His pleas for reinforcement and his plan to threaten Washington with Beauregard and troops drawn from the deep South only indicate that Lee wanted the Gettysburg campaign to be decisive. Lee proposed to win or lose the war during the summer of 1863. As it was, Gettysburg may have been Lee's last chance to win. And to the degree to which Davis played the trimmer as commander in chief, the president reduced Lee's chances for the grand showdown he sought.

The Maryland campaign in September 1862 and the Gettysburg campaign are only two examples of Davis and Lee, that "powerful team," operating in less than perfect harmony. At Antietam/Sharpsburg Lee surely fought a more momentous battle than Davis, had he known the circumstances, would have approved. At Gettysburg, Davis prevented Lee from fighting an even more cataclysmic battle than he did.

Lee was more right than he realized when he asked Davis

at Mechanicsville, "Who is all this army and what is it doing here?" Thereafter, Lee certainly proved himself a clever diplomat in his relations with Davis. But in the larger cause, both men failed. Lee never won a victory so complete as to achieve annihilation. Davis gravely miscalculated the winner in the war of wills. And one source of Confederate defeat was the unresolved conflict of strategic visions at its highest command.

3

Jeff Davis Rules: General Beauregard and the Sanctity of Civilian Authority in the Confederacy

T. MICHAEL PARRISH

Iɴ ᴇᴀʀʟʏ ᴏᴄᴛᴏʙᴇʀ 1864, a month after the calamitous fall of Atlanta, President Jefferson Davis sought to benefit from General P. G. T. Beauregard's enduring popularity and thereby boost Southern morale. Meeting face-to-face in Augusta, Georgia, Davis and Beauregard put aside the personal venom that had festered and often boiled up between them during the past three years and quietly conversed for several hours, exchanging information and making decisions. According to Beauregard's own recollection, Davis "praised highly the new Commander of the Army of Tennessee, [General John Bell Hood,] predicting that he would carry out a different policy from that of General Joseph E. Johnston, who would have retreated ere long—said Mr. Davis—to the very Gulf of Mexico should [General William T.] Sherman have followed him that far south." Widely considered as the likely candidate to take command of the western army prior to Davis's choosing Hood instead, Beauregard gave his willing approval to Hood's planned attempt to lure Sherman northward, away from Atlanta. At the same time, Davis gave Beauregard command of the new Military Division of the West, an area covering five states, more than a third of the Confederacy. Fully realizing his lack of real authority as an advisor to Hood, who would report directly to Davis, Beauregard accepted his rather strange role and vowed to carry out his assignment.[1]

After his meeting with Beauregard, Davis delivered a speech to the nervous citizens of Augusta. The president affirmed his optimism for the South's beleaguered cause and predicted great results from the supremely aggressive General Hood. Toward the end of the speech Davis noted, "Beauregard goes to share the toils, the fortunes, the misfortunes, if it be so, of the army in Georgia. He goes with a single purpose: to serve wherever I direct, asking no particular place, desiring no special command, but in the spirit that made a general of a corporal, go where I say, and so going I trust he goes not to bleed but to conquer." After Davis's speech, Beauregard uttered only a few words to the crowd, saying that "he had fired the first gun at Sumter" and that he "hoped to live to fire the last of the war."[2]

Always brutally honest, Davis told the crowd in Augusta exactly what he believed and intended—not that he had staked great authority and confidence in Beauregard's abilities, but that as commander in chief he had issued orders and now expected Beauregard to help Hood avoid disaster. Mindful of Beauregard's spotty record as a field commander, Davis's forthright actions and statements at Augusta typified his dealings with Beauregard throughout the war. As Confederate president, Davis put Beauregard in various positions, transferring him, removing him, denying him reassignment, and assigning him elsewhere, convinced that he recognized Beauregard's weaknesses and always searching to use the general's talents to best advantage. For his part, Beauregard always did Davis's bidding, if often grudgingly.

During most of the Civil War, and long afterward, Davis and Beauregard mistrusted and despised one another. Yet how severely did their antagonism and hatred affect the relationship between commander in chief and high-ranking subordinate officer? Did their personal animosity truly hamper and damage the Confederate war effort? Was one more guilty than the other for contributing to the shortcomings in leadership that seem to stand so starkly as reasons for the South's defeat? If, by some miracle, they had developed personal affection for one another, how might they have cooperated significantly better than they did?

Jefferson Davis has few defenders among historians who have closely analyzed his policies and decisions as Confederate commander in chief. Even in recognizing his deliberate reliance on Robert E. Lee, historians have given far more credit to Lee than to Davis for the success they enjoyed as a team. Blind rigidity, petty prejudices, and perverse pride seem to have plagued Davis, causing failure upon failure in his political dealings, his handling of financial policy, his efforts at public relations, and most of all in his relationships with his senior general officers. The president's dismal reputation today springs primarily from his arrogant and persistent support of too many poor commanders—because he apparently liked and respected them personally. At the same time, historians have increasingly ridiculed Davis for his alleged refusal or gross inability to get along with and thereby better utilize commanders who clearly possessed considerable military talent, most notably Joseph E. Johnston and P. G. T. Beauregard.[3]

Thus, historians have often laid at Davis's feet the principal blame for the Confederacy's ultimate demise. "From the war's outset," insisted one scholar, "Davis tended to personalize disagreements and to reduce the standards by which he evaluated military competence to a moral question—whether or not he deemed an individual to have character. . . . The President concluded that [Johnston and Beauregard in particular] were too contentious, too jealous of their prerogatives and reputations, and ultimately he decided that they were petty and dishonest men devoid of character and consequently untrustworthy." Similarly, another historian avowed that "Davis's tendencies to support his friends in the military and to sidetrack heroes of the hour (Beauregard being a good example) were crippling to the Southern cause." One of the greatest of all Civil War scholars, Allan Nevins, argued pointedly, "Davis lacked the sense of proportion that statesmen ought to have. Highly sensitive to criticism, he gave way to fits of temper. . . . He had an intense dislike for P. G. T. Beauregard and Joseph Johnston, which did these generals wrong."[4]

In evaluating Johnston and Beauregard, historians have often applied a brand of judgment equally severe as that heaped on Davis. Ironically enough, as if to spread the blame around in full measure, some scholars who have blasted Davis most harshly for his disgust toward Beauregard have also argued that Davis should not be faulted too badly after all. The Confederate president could always rely on the talented and gentlemanly Robert E. Lee, the argument goes, but Davis needed other exemplary commanders to win the war and no others even came close to matching Lee. In pointing the finger at Beauregard, the Creole's biographer, T. Harry Williams, repeated a wartime journalist's assertion that "Beauregard was not a first-class military man but a first-rate second-class man" and that "maybe the tragedy of the Confederacy was that it did not have enough first-class generals to go around." The peerless Lee, it seems, remains the only member of the Confederate high command who largely escapes censure.[5] Williams and others have reached their conclusions about Beauregard by emphasizing his rigidity, selfish pride, and wild strategic notions, traits that damaged his effectiveness as a commander, ruined his relations with Davis, and permanently tarnished his historical reputation. One distinguished scholar recently called Beauregard "prickly" and "immature," a grandiose strategist "for whom nothing seemed impossible." The prominent British military historian John Keegan concluded, "Military in appearance rather than talent, [Beauregard] was, like so many of the generals of both armies of the Civil War, overpromoted." Such statements appear to imply rather starkly that if Beauregard, Johnston, and their ilk had only cooperated with Davis as well as Lee did, the Confederacy might have triumphed.[6]

Animus between Davis and Beauregard erupted in the aftermath of the first Battle of Manassas (Bull Run) during the autumn of 1861, a period of mounting public disappointment about the failure to follow up the Confederacy's first major victory, a battle Beauregard took credit for winning. Grateful for Beauregard's heroics at Fort Sumter and his timely triumph at Manassas, Davis had promoted him on the field from the rank of brigadier to full general. In an effort to deflect the widespread blame for his army's remaining idle and on the defensive in Virginia, however, Beauregard unwisely used his official report of the battle to belittle the president's lack of appreciation for Beauregard's grand strategic plan to launch an offensive against the North. The general claimed to have sent an aide to Richmond prior to Manassas to submit the plan in detail to the president. Unfortunately for Beauregard, his post-battle report criticizing Davis was printed in its earliest form in a Richmond newspaper. An exchange of tense letters between Davis and Beauregard reached a climax in late October when Davis rejected his claim as utterly false. "[I]f we did differ in opinion as to the measures and purposes of contemplated campaigns," Davis concluded, "such fact could have no appropriate place in the report of a battle . . . and especially because no such plan as that described was submitted to me." Even worse, Davis upbraided the colorful, publicity-minded general by stating tersely that his battle report "seemed to be an attempt to exalt yourself at my expense."[7]

With this single retort, Davis had firmly asserted his authority as commander in chief, demonstrating most notably the principle of civilian control over the military. Beauregard well understood that principle, having served for two decades as a United States Army officer during a pivotal era that saw the emergence of a thoroughly professional body of West Point-trained officers. Davis himself, first as a U.S. senator and then as secretary of war, had acted as one of the main architects of the West Point standard for military training. Yet his rebuke caught the proud and successful Beauregard by surprise. "I did not for one instant think how far [my report] was to affect him," the general admitted to his friend and confidant, Congressman Roger Pryor.[8]

With subordination to civilian authority ingrained in the antebellum army as an inviolable ideal, Beauregard should have expected Davis's reaction. Only a few years earlier, during Davis's tenure as secretary of war, the army's crusty old commanding general, Winfield Scott, had repeatedly challenged Davis's power over him with regard to minor matters of policy. A long series of written accusations, denials, counterattacks, and insults from both men finally resulted in a congressionally mandated publication of more than 350 pages detailing the Davis–Scott correspondence. In one of several climactic barrages of invective, Davis growled, "Your petulance, characteristic egotism, and recklessness of accusation have imposed on me the task of unveiling some of your deformities. . . . It is sincerely to be hoped that those who follow you in the honorable profession in which you have been eminent, notwithstanding your fame has been clouded by groveling vices, will select for their imitation some other model than one whose military career has been marked by querulousness, insubordination, greed of lucre and want of truth." Scott had begun his magnificent military career prior to the entrenchment of the principle of civilian control. Secretary Davis never relented in extracting from Scott a proper deference to civilian authority, and Scott could hardly bear it.[9]

Beauregard was fully aware of the history of the Scott–Davis imbroglio, but only after his collision with the president in late 1861 did the general suddenly realize that he dare not cross his commander in chief again. Davis had cut Beauregard down to size—calmly, confidently, completely. Afterward the general's adjutant Thomas Jordan noticed a pointed difference in Beauregard's demeanor. His usual confidence and bluster turned into silent brooding. "You never saw such a change," Jordan wrote to one of the general's friends. Never again during the course of the war did Beauregard criticize the Confederate president in print or in any other public forum. Just as he had done with the pompous Scott, Davis had taught one of his highest-ranking and most popular military subordinates a painful lesson.[10]

Although Davis and Beauregard had thus begun to loathe one another personally, Davis still maintained confidence in Beauregard's abilities as a commander. In early 1862, Davis consulted privately with Beauregard's friends in Congress to persuade him to accept a transfer to the western theater to serve as second in command to General Albert Sidney Johnston. Beauregard was to help Johnston formulate strategy and organize his forces for a concentration and counteroffensive against a Union invasion. When Johnston fell mortally wounded at Shiloh in southwestern Tennessee in early April, Beauregard took command of the Army of the Mississippi (the forerunner of the Army of Tennessee) and managed an orderly withdrawal from the battlefield following two days of bloody fighting. However, he could not convince Davis, or many others in Richmond, of a victory at Shiloh. After two months of stagnation behind fortifications at Corinth, Mississippi, Beauregard's lack of initiative began to grate on Davis as he despaired for other points in need of protection. "If Mississippi troops lying in camp, when not retreating under Beauregard, were at home," he commented impatiently to his wife, "they would probably keep a section of the [Mississippi] river free for our use and closed against Yankee transports."[11]

When in late May 1862 Beauregard finally abandoned Corinth—a vital strategic position—and so avoided giving battle to a Federal army commanded by the compulsively cautious General Henry W. Halleck, Davis told his wife disgustedly: "Beauregard claims by telegram to have made a 'brilliant and successful retreat.' . . . There are those who can only walk a log when it is near the ground, and I fear he has been placed too high for his mental strength, as he does not exhibit the ability manifested on smaller fields." Davis's confidence in Beauregard's abilities was evaporating rapidly.[12]

Then, suddenly, Beauregard decided to seek relief from his chronic, debilitating throat ailment by taking a medical leave from the army without first securing permission from the Confederate War Department or even informing Davis in advance. Davis quickly relieved Beauregard from command and replaced him with General Braxton Bragg. "Beauregard left his command to seek rest, and restore his health," Davis informed his wife. "The sedentary life at Corinth must have been hard to bear as he reports himself exhausted."[13]

All Beauregard could do in response was to express his personal outrage to his friends. "If the country be satisfied to have me laid on the shelf by a man who is either demented or a traitor to his trust, well, be it so!" he exclaimed to his adjutant Thomas Jordan. "I require rest and will endeavor to fit myself better for the darkest hours of our trial. . . . As to my reputation, if it can suffer by anything that living specimen of gall and hatred, can do . . . it is not then worth preserving. . . . My consolation is, that the difference between 'that Individual' and myself is—that, if he were to die to-day, the whole country would rejoice at it, whereas, if the same thing were to happen to me, they would regret it."[14]

For Davis, the issue was clear. Whatever personal contempt he held for Beauregard, it had no bearing on his decision. In a letter to General Edmund Kirby Smith several months later, the president explained resolutely, "Beauregard was tried as commander of the Army of the West and left it without leave when the troops were demoralized and the country he was sent to protect was threatened with conquest." Concerned more about the Confederacy's protection than any political damage he might suffer, Davis saw no choice but to use his authority to remove Beauregard from command.[15]

In their efforts to understand more fully what happened in the American Civil War, perhaps historians should consider more seriously what did not happen. The Civil War was not dominated by ardent extremists, politically or militarily, in either the North or the South. As a result, the war did *not* explode into a revolutionary conflict in which personal vendettas, violent coups, high-level assassinations, conspiracies, or terrorism played any significant part. The Civil War was indeed a bloody struggle, but it was a struggle that was nearly always restrained and guided by fundamental democratic principles, one of the most prominent being the supremacy of civilian control over commanders of extremely powerful military forces.

Historians should therefore distinguish carefully between the Davis–Beauregard display of personal animosity and their official conduct. Despite their loathing for one another, both Davis and Beauregard were so devoted to the Confederate cause, and so attuned to a democratically inspired sense of constitutional duty to the principle of civilian control, that they actually operated relatively well together throughout the war. Perhaps Davis was slightly jealous of Beauregard's gigantic popularity—during the fall of 1861 the general was even being touted as a possible candidate for the presidency—but Davis did not fear Beauregard as a rival for power. Exercising his authority as commander in chief at every turn, Davis put Beauregard just where he wanted him and then kept him there. Davis made these decisions calmly, soberly, as matters of military policy, because he meant to utilize Beauregard effectively. He never acted because he hated Beauregard and could not stand the notion of picking him over the hapless Braxton Bragg, the timid Joseph Johnston, or the reckless John Bell Hood to serve as commander of the ill-fated Army of Tennessee.

Indeed, in giving Beauregard his longest-running assignment, Davis put him in the one position where he truly belonged—as commander of Charleston—allowing him to do what he did best: building up and defending the fixed fortifications of a vibrant city that was essential to the morale and economic strength of the Confederacy. Although he often expressed a desire to return to a more prominent position at the head of the western army, Beauregard also sent mixed signals, writing, for example, in early 1863 to Congressman William Porcher Miles: "Should the Government desire to send me back to the West, before I have gotten through here with the abolitionists [then attacking Charleston,] I hope my friends in Congress will oppose it MOST DETERMINEDLY. . . . If I were ordered now to retrieve affairs in Tennessee, I would probably get there too late to do much good, and my health, I fear, would not stand the cold weather." To a fellow officer Beauregard admitted that he was disappointed about not being reinstated to field command, but "[Charleston] being a post of danger is acceptable to me." Alluding to his triumphal firing on Fort Sumter at the war's outset, he added, "One 'always returns to one's first love.'"[16]

Not only did Beauregard accept his important role at Charleston—hardly the "backwater" that many historians have called it—but he also excelled as a consummate military engineer, a leading expert in heavy artillery, and the creator and coordinator of coastal fortifications that successfully resisted some of the most massive and relentless combined operations of naval and land forces of the entire war. Instead of focusing solely on Beauregard's shortcomings as a field commander and his personal discord with Davis, historians should recognize once and for all that Beauregard's performance during the protracted siege of Charleston was superb, an accomplishment comparable, if not equal, to Robert E. Lee's brilliant defense of Richmond and Petersburg. According to a leading modern authority on the Confederate Navy, "General Beauregard . . . better than anyone else in the army, understood the blend between sea and land war."[17]

Indeed, he organized and commanded the war's most successful defense of a land target against an attack from the ocean. The Yankees spared no expense and effort in a long series of attempts to capture the vaunted "Cradle of Secession." During the two-year period of Beauregard's tenure there, the soldiers and civilians of the Confederacy concerned themselves primarily with the successes and failures of three entities: the Army of Northern Virginia, the Army of Tennessee, and the defenders of Charleston. Had Charleston fallen, the effect on Southern morale would have proved just as horrific as the fall of New Orleans and nearly as disastrous as the losses of Vicksburg and Atlanta.[18]

To repeat: when Davis removed Beauregard from command of the western army after the abandonment of Corinth, he had in mind purely military reasons. Davis got his excuse to do so when Beauregard took sudden, unannounced sick leave from the army. Only a few months earlier, Beauregard himself had confirmed Corinth's strategic importance: "If we are defeated here," he told authorities in Richmond, "we lose the whole Mississippi Valley and probably our cause." A victory, he exclaimed, "would not only insure us the valley of the Mississippi but also our independence. . . . Thus it becomes essential to hold Corinth to the last extremity, even at the risk of a defeat."[19]

On the very day that Beauregard abandoned Corinth, he received a letter from Robert E. Lee, Davis's primary military advisor, reinforcing the sheer need to hold the position and specifying the manner in which Beauregard might best succeed. "[Even] if the superior numbers of the enemy force you back," wrote Lee, "it is hoped you will be able to strike a successful blow at the enemy if he follows, which will enable you to gain the ascendancy and drive him back to the Ohio [River]." Lee himself would be faced with the same kind of challenge only a few weeks later during the Seven Days' Battles, when he struck a blow at George B. McClellan's huge army and drove it from the gates of Richmond. For Lee, his own emergence as an effective army commander came during the Seven Days. In contrast, feeling his reputation tarnished by Shiloh, Beauregard received his best chance for redemption and glory at Corinth and failed the test. So Davis relieved him and soon afterward assigned him to Charleston.[20]

Once that city was clearly secure in Beauregard's hands,

Davis made a rational decision by refusing to put the general back at the head of an army for the remainder of the war. In some situations perhaps Davis allowed his personal feelings to affect his judgment about military policy. With Beauregard, however, that was not the case.

At the same time, Beauregard had no choice but to submit to the president's executive authority. Always mindful of the firestorm created by his post-Manassas statements, Beauregard never cast any public doubt on Davis's ability or legitimacy as his superior. Only after the war was long concluded did Beauregard launch into a publishing frenzy of articles and books branding Davis as the most stupid, most egotistical, most dishonorable, and most destructive leader the Confederacy could have had as its president. Of course, from the moment Davis removed him from command of the western army in mid-1862 Beauregard moaned and railed viciously, but always privately, against Davis. Writing to Congressman William Porcher Miles, a friend, he expressed his contempt and outright enmity toward Davis in late 1862. "Every day I thank my creator that I am not the essence of egotism, vanity, jealousy, obstinacy, perversity, and vindictiveness!" Beauregard insisted. "If there is a sadder picture of human depravity, more pernicious in times like these [than Davis] . . . I hope never to behold it!"[21]

Despite continually blasting Davis in conversations and letters, Beauregard always followed Davis's orders, sometimes grudgingly and slowly—as he clearly did in bringing troops to Bermuda Hundred, Virginia, near Petersburg, in the spring of 1864. But there his tardiness actually matched the old pattern of reticence and ineffectiveness that only confirmed Davis's long-standing certainty of Beauregard's limitations as a field commander. "The most striking thing about Beauregard's behavior during the Bermuda Hundred campaign," observes historian Steven Woodworth, "is the remarkable continuity with his performances throughout the war. . . . As had been the case in the Western Theater in 1862, the Creole had plenty of courage but not quite enough nerve. . . . Davis had . . . suggested years earlier that Beauregard was unable to use his great mental gifts to advantage when placed in a position of extreme responsibility. In this way also, Beauregard in the Bermuda Hundred Campaign had proved true to his earlier form."[22]

Most significantly, in his personal communications with friends in the Confederate Congress—men who nearly always proved receptive to his carping about Davis as a pathetic administrator and obtuse strategist—Beauregard never advocated or even suggested that Davis ought to be impeached or otherwise forced from office. Writing in strongest terms about Davis to Congressman Charles Villere, Beauregard complained in early 1863: "I am the last fault-finding man . . . in the service, when my personal interests alone are at stake; but when the comfort of my troops or the public good is in question, I only regret that I am not a Robespierre." Yet Beauregard and Villere knew very well that it would have been utterly foolhardy and futile for them or anyone else—even with the benefit of Beauregard's great popularity—to push politics to radical extremes and attempt to seize the revolutionary power of a Robespierre. Despite a growing chorus of anti-Davis critics throughout the South, no one challenged his capacity and legitimacy in performing the duties of his office.[23]

In early 1864, erstwhile Confederate General and Congressman Robert Toombs, one of President Davis's most abusive enemies, informed his close friend Henry W. Cleveland, editor of the Atlanta *Constitutionalist*, that the anti-Davis members of the Confederate Congress were preparing to unleash "a counter-revolution with which . . . Vice President Alexander H. Stephens, the governors of several states, the secretary of war, and Generals [John C.] Breckinridge, William H. Walker, Gustavus W. Smith, Joseph Johnston, Beauregard, and even General Lee were in more or less sympathy." Not even a slender hint of Toombs's so-called "counter-revolution" ever materialized in Congress, in the army's high command, or in any other part of the Confederacy. After the war, when Cleveland asked the former Confederate vice president about the alleged conspiracy, Stephens replied, "It was all pure bluster on the part of Mr. Toombs. . . . I have never heard of any governor or general then, or since, who contemplated a revolution to depose Mr. Davis and his supporters in Congress."[24]

By the same token, in all his relationships with his generals—and especially in his actions toward Beauregard—Jefferson Davis was never so foolish as to exert his executive authority in a dictatorial fashion. Fully aware of Beauregard's unceasing favor with an admiring public, as well as his influence with key Confederate leaders, Davis quietly and deftly cooperated with Beauregard's friends in Congress to persuade the general to accept transfer to the western theater in early 1862. Several months later, after the defeat at Shiloh and Beauregard's abandonment of Corinth, Davis again handled the situation carefully by sending his personal aide William Preston Johnston to ask Beauregard to explain his decisions and describe his plans for the army's future operations, and the general complied dutifully, if grudgingly.[25]

Again, after Beauregard left the army to take extended sick leave in mid-1862, Davis welcomed a delegation of irate congressmen, patiently listened to their protests against his decision to remove Beauregard from command, and then firmly rejected their pleas to have Beauregard reinstated. With total self-assurance, Davis announced to the congressmen that he had based his decision "exclusively on the public interests" and that he would not restore Beauregard "if the whole world united in the petition." Besides, Davis rightly asserted, Charleston was "of vast consequence to the Confederacy," and "General Beauregard's qualifications peculiarly fitted him for its defense," thus making him "the best man in the army for the South Carolina and Georgia department." Finally, in sending Beauregard to Charleston, Davis eased the transition for him, skillfully encouraging authorities in South Carolina to appeal directly to the general for his skill and leadership in defending the city.[26]

Although he carped privately against Davis, Beauregard and his congressional allies not only recognized the president's authority to act as he did in each situation, but the general also sometimes admitted to his friends his own errors. A few months after Davis upbraided him for his Manassas battle report that belittled the president in the newspaper, Beauregard confessed to Congressman Roger Pryor, "I do not pretend that I never commit mistakes; for every day of my life I find that I have a great deal still to learn, especially with regards to the pretensions of others; nor do I lay claims to being a great general; but I yield to no one in devotion to my country." Shortly after the war, in a letter to his trusted adjutant general Thomas Jordan, Beauregard reminisced about Davis's decisive act in removing him from command of the army in 1862: "I do not pretend not to have committed great errors in my military career, but I was then only beginning to learn how to command troops in the field. The President determined, however, that I should never finish my education." This represented the most honest judgment Beauregard ever stated about his feud with Davis.[27]

As the leader of a fledgling nation desperate for military victories, Jefferson Davis could not afford to wait for one of his two major army commanders to finish educating himself. He could not afford to risk Beauregard's losing more major battles, his withdrawing rather than striking the enemy, his abandoning more strategic points, and his suffering from a chronic illness that rendered him weak or incapacitated under the continual stress of field command. Hatred between Davis and Beauregard was irrelevant in Davis's decisions. Davis simply believed and continued to believe that Beauregard could not function competently and capably as an army commander. Davis had given him a splendid opportunity to prove himself after Shiloh and in time Beauregard realized that he had faltered.

More important, the ongoing rancor between Davis and Beauregard was inconsequential when compared to the fact that these two strong-willed, energetic, proud men managed to adhere to the sanctity of a democratic constitutional standard vesting ultimate authority in the civilian commander in chief. Neither of them—passionate leaders in a popular cause—was ever tempted to set out deliberately and publicly to humiliate, much less ruin or harm, the other. Neither Davis nor Beauregard stooped to deceit, betrayal, confrontation, or any other method so often used by powerful leaders to crush political and military rivals in other revolutions and civil wars throughout history.

In describing the principle of civilian control over military power in U.S. history, historian Russell Weigley pointed to the bitter Civil War relationship between President Abraham Lincoln and General George B. McClellan, a pair of Yankee antagonists similar in many ways to Davis and Beauregard. "While McClellan's political allegiance was to the Democratic Party rather than to Lincoln and the Republicans, he did not challenge civilian supremacy either in word or in deed," Weigley observed. "[McClellan] sometimes treated Lincoln with less than complete personal courtesy . . . [but Lincoln] dismissed McClellan [from army command] primarily because the general had demonstrated himself to be a military failure. . . . He was simply not a competent director of operations and tactics." Thus did Lincoln's actions toward McClellan mirror Davis's toward Beauregard. Had either general gone so far as to criticize and defy their presidents openly to stir up the public, we may assume that neither Lincoln nor Davis would have hesitated to act, just as President Harry Truman did in removing General Douglas MacArthur nearly a century later.[28]

In the spring of 1865, instead of facing a military coup or an outraged army threatening to hang him as the chief scapegoat for the Confederacy's miseries, President Davis fled to Greensboro, North Carolina, where he met with two of the men he probably disliked most: P. G. T. Beauregard and Joseph Johnston. They discussed quietly and sadly the need to surrender the remnants of the Army of Tennessee and petition for terms from General William T. Sherman. Beauregard himself later recalled that the president "extended a cordial greeting . . . and taking [me] aside, questioned [me] closely and anxiously about current military events. . . . The President lent an attentive ear to the account thus given of the hopeless condition of the Confederacy, but appeared, nevertheless, undismayed."[29]

Both Johnston and Beauregard recognized that the grave choice between continuing the struggle or surrendering belonged to Davis alone. Refusing to cast blame on one another, they set aside their animosities and resentments and, with the dream of Confederate independence crashing down around them, discussed the crisis at hand. Davis asked Johnston and Beauregard for their blunt opinions. Both officers knew that the situation was hopeless. Davis agonized briefly and then assented to their advice to surrender the army to Sherman.[30]

The American Civil War was decided on the battlefield by soldiers who adhered to a clear chain of military command that finally resided in civilian authority. As a direct result, the

North experienced a clear victory and the South experienced a clear defeat, with extremely lenient terms granted by the victors to the vanquished. The Civil War was not decided by violent revolutionary upheaval inspired by extremist ideologies or by politicians and generals bent on usurping power for their own ends. Contentious leaders in high command—especially men like Jefferson Davis and P. G. T. Beauregard, and Abraham Lincoln and George McClellan—operated in the firm conviction that all power must answer ultimately to the popular will, a democratic standard sanctioned by law and embodied most patently and responsibly in the president as commander in chief. Although they mistrusted one another, Davis and Beauregard never misunderstood one another with regard to the crux of executive authority and military duty. Despite all their personal vindictiveness and professional shortcomings, Jefferson Davis ruled and Beauregard obeyed as best he could.

4

Davis, Bragg, and Confederate Command in the West

STEVEN E. WOODWORTH

THE CONFEDERACY lost the Civil War in the West. There Jefferson Davis's strategy of outlasting the Union by fending off each successive Federal onslaught failed, and blue-clad troops cleared the banks of the Mississippi, penetrated deep into the Southern heartland, and finally spilled over into the eastern theater and bore down in the rear of Robert E. Lee's cornered army in Virginia. That it was so says much about the quality of such western Union generals as Ulysses S. Grant, William T. Sherman, Philip H. Sheridan, William S. Rosecrans, and George H. Thomas. It says perhaps more about the quality of the soldiers they led, resourceful Midwestern farmboys who had come out to see the job finished. Yet it also reflects on the quality of the Confederate defensive effort, for despite the impressiveness of Northern skill and courage west of the Appalachians, the task that men like Grant and Sherman and their soldiers accomplished should have been impossible. The Confederacy could boast soldiers no less brave; if they were fewer, they also fought on their own turf, in known, largely friendly, country, and with all the advantages of defenders in a vast and rugged land. The history of the western campaigns reveals almost unbelievable courage and endurance on the part of the common soldier of the Confederacy and an almost equally amazing record of blundering and bickering on the part of his leaders. Clearly, something was seriously wrong with Confederate high command in the West.

The fundamental problem behind the Confederacy's western woes was Davis's failure to find, use, and support a general who could work successfully both with him and with his subordinates—and who would win battles. His chances for doing so suffered a serious blow early in the war when his trusted prewar friend Albert Sidney Johnston fell at the Battle of Shiloh, April 6, 1862. After his death, Pierre G. T. Beauregard proved physically unequal to the stress of command and unsatisfactory to Davis. On June 20, 1862, the Confederate president called on Braxton Bragg to assume overall command of the chief Southern army west of the Appalachians.[1]

Bragg would lead that army for seventeen months, far longer than any of its other commanders. By the end of his tenure he would come under intense criticism and Davis would be mercilessly scored as well by press and politicians for maintaining him. Bragg, the critics claimed and historians have echoed, was an old friend of the president, incompetent but supported for reasons of personal favoritism. Yet Bragg and Davis were, if anything, old enemies, and Bragg represented, in fact, Davis's best chance to find successful leadership for the Confederacy's chief western army. Although flawed in some ways as a man and a commander, Bragg possessed genuine talent and a commitment to Southern independence that gave him the potential to be a successful general at the head of an army that might successfully stave off Union advances into Tennessee. With Bragg now in command of that army, what remained was for Davis to support his efforts in such a way as to make him a success.[2] The first campaign was extremely important. If a general could establish a reputation as a winner, subsequent setbacks might be endured with confidence, personal idiosyncrasies written off as endearing eccentricities, and a prickly exterior overlooked as the personality quirk of a genius. Stonewall Jackson is a good example. The key was to win early in one's command. Beauregard, Bragg's predecessor, had won more or less fortuitous victories at Fort Sumter and Bull Run, but such easy triumphs were not Bragg's lot. He spent the early months of the war in a quiet sector, Pensacola, Florida, and then had performed with credit, in the judgment of his contemporaries, in a subordinate role at the Battle of Shiloh. Although he came into army command with a fairly good reputation, and newfound respect in the eyes of Jefferson Davis, his first active campaign would show his generals, his soldiers, and the public how to estimate him as a general.[3]

That first campaign was a dramatic one. By midsummer 1862 Union forces had overrun all of Kentucky and the western two-thirds of Tennessee and had proceeded down the Mississippi River—and up from its mouth. Bragg's army, in Tupelo, Mississippi, faced a powerful Northern opponent in northern Mississippi and West Tennessee, while another strong Union army marched across northern Alabama to threaten a vital Confederate rail junction at Chattanooga, Tennessee. If Chattanooga fell, the Federals would then control all of Tennessee and have an open gateway for the invasion of Georgia as well as a backdoor into Virginia. To prevent such ominous consequences, the Confederacy had in East Tennessee only a small force under Major General Edmund Kirby Smith.

Bragg seized on the one aspect of the Union advance that

presented an opportunity for the South—the very slowness of the movement of the ponderous Federal armies. Bragg also took advantage of a roundabout connection to Chattanooga. Sending his artillery and wagons cross country, Bragg shipped his infantry down the Mobile & Ohio to Mobile, next by boat across Mobile Bay, and then back into railroad cars for the ride up to Atlanta and finally into Chattanooga from the southeast, well ahead of the slow-moving Union host under Maj. Gen. Don Carlos Buell. That not only saved Chattanooga but also opened the way for Bragg to march around Buell into middle Tennessee, turning the Federals and forcing them to fight at a disadvantage, theoretically against the combined forces of both Bragg and Kirby Smith.[4]

Unfortunately, Davis failed in two significant ways to give Bragg the support he needed to succeed in this campaign, or, indeed, in his subsequent operations. As late as the summer of 1862, Davis still failed to grasp the importance of unified command or clearly defined authority. Having done much to set up Confederate defensive arrangements in Mississippi by directly ordering the assignment of Maj. Gen. Earl Van Dorn with a force to defend Vicksburg, Davis failed to make clear to Bragg whether Van Dorn was to be under his command. As a result, Bragg left behind him in Mississippi a confused command arrangement in which two separate Confederate forces, one under Van Dorn and the other under Maj. Gen. Sterling Price, were independent of each other but were somehow expected to cooperate in keeping up the pressure on the Federals in northern Mississippi and East Tennessee. Not surprisingly, in view of this muddle of independent commands, they failed in that mission and Bragg eventually had to face, in Kentucky, Union troops that had been drawn off from this sector.

In like manner Davis provided a muddled command arrangement in the sector to which Bragg went that paralleled the confusion behind him. Although Bragg outranked Kirby Smith and would command their combined forces any time the two were in contact, Smith would be under no obligation to take any orders from Bragg until their forces actually joined. Remarkably, Davis not only declined to remedy this situation, but even expressed his confidence that it would present no problem because Bragg and Kirby Smith were both good and patriotic officers.

The divided command presented serious problems. Despite having offered to place himself voluntarily under Bragg's command, Smith quickly showed a disregard for Bragg's strategic plans. Not waiting for Bragg to catch up and take command, Smith ignored Bragg's urgings and marched his force, including a couple of divisions on loan from Bragg, right out of Tennessee and into Kentucky, forcing Bragg to conform to his movements. The swing into Kentucky, leaving Buell's army intact in Tennessee, reduced the odds of beating Buell under every contingency but one, and that was the one on which Kirby Smith was betting—namely, that the people of Kentucky would rise en masse to support the Confederate cause. The reports of flamboyant Confederate cavalryman John Hunt Morgan from his recent raid into the Bluegrass State gave basis to such hopes; with Smith forcing the pace of Confederate advance, Bragg had no choice but to rely on that prospect as well.

The army that Bragg marched north from Chattanooga, skillfully keeping between Smith and Buell's larger Union force, was flawed by the second of Davis's fundamental failures to support the campaign. Not long before his departure from Mississippi, Bragg had written Davis requesting that a number of the army's higher-ranking generals be set aside in favor of abler, younger men. He was right to do so, as the dismal record of a number of the Army of Tennessee's generals would amply prove.

Davis refused Bragg's request, and the probable reason was that chief among the army's officers of questionable value was Davis's old friend and West Point crony, Leonidas Polk. Having resigned from the army on graduation from West Point thirty-five years before, Polk had made a career as an Episcopal clergyman and for a number of years before the war had been bishop of Louisiana. He was smooth, ingratiating, and persuasive, but as a general headstrong and incompetent. He was also the Army of Tennessee's senior major general, second in rank only to Bragg himself. Sizing up Polk, Bragg had written to Davis that William J. Hardee was his only competent major general. Because Polk and Hardee were the only officers of that rank in the Army of Tennessee, the implication was clear and Davis did not miss it. In responding to Bragg's request to purge the army of what Bragg called "dead-weight" Davis let it be known that he considered himself bound by law to respect everyone's seniority. Clearly, the president would protect his crony Polk, and Bragg would have to keep the generals he had.[5]

The campaign proved one of tantalizing opportunities and repeated frustrations for Bragg. He won the race with Buell for a position controlling the road to the latter's base at Louisville. According to "the book," he now had the Union general in a very bad way indeed. Buell was supposedly obligated to make a desperate effort to restore his theoretically severed line of communication. As it turned out, however, the stolid Northern commander was packing along enough supplies to feed his army for a considerable length of time. Bragg, on the other hand, was gathering his supplies from the countryside as he marched. Among the friendly population of the Nashville Basin, where he had originally hoped to bring Buell to bay, Bragg might have been able to draw supplies for a prolonged stay in one place, but in Kentucky, where the population averaged neutral at best, he could not. He dared not attack Buell without the aid of Smith's troops, and Smith seemed to have errands of his own farther east, around Lexington, and was in no hurry to join Bragg. With his army running out of food, Bragg had to retreat toward Smith's position in the heart of the bluegrass region.[6]

That finally brought his forces into contact with those of Kirby Smith and ended the divided command arrangement. It also gave Buell unimpeded opportunity to restore his communications and proceed with the campaign at his own speed and with all the advantages he could bring to bear, primarily numbers. Confederate success in the campaign now hung entirely on the prospect of massive recruitment among Kentuckians, to which Kirby Smith had pegged his hopes at the outset. By this time, however, it was appearing more and more a forlorn hope. Some Kentuckians may have responded enthusiastically to a flamboyant cavalry raid, but almost all of them who meant to fight for the Confederacy were already in its ranks and had been there for some time. Recruiting was practically nil. In short, Kirby Smith, dragging a reluctant Bragg behind him, had bet the campaign on Kentucky's rising and had lost.

Bragg had only one more expedient to try. The governor of Kentucky's pro-Confederate shadow government had accompanied Bragg into the state and the general now proposed to set up the state government in order to operate the Confederate conscription act. Perhaps Kentuckians would shoulder Southern muskets whether they were willing or not. Then, however, Buell put his ponderous force into motion. Hoping to hold the state capital, Frankfort, Bragg made plans to strike one of the separate columns of Buell's advancing army. The plan promised a limited but impressive Confederate success, but it was thwarted when Polk balked and refused to carry out Bragg's orders. That left Bragg no choice but to retreat.[7]

The campaign's great battle, Perryville, was anticlimactic, coming as Bragg lashed out at one of the several tentacles with which Buell continued to grope for him through the bluegrass region. A confused affair on both sides, Perryville was a tactical success for the Confederates but not on a big enough scale to open any new strategic possibilities against Buell's superior numbers. Bragg continued his retreat back into Tennessee.[8]

He found there a maelstrom of savage criticism. Generals like Smith and Polk blamed Bragg as a fig leaf to cover their own failures. Confederate Kentuckians, who were an influential clique within the army's officer corps, hated Bragg for saying what they did not want to hear: Kentucky had chosen Union or neutrality. Rather than accept that, the Kentucky clique howled for Bragg's removal. Still other officers, such as Hardee, fell under the influence of the malcontents, particularly the plausible and insinuating Polk. For public, press, and politicians, it was enough simply that Bragg had presided over a losing effort. Robert E. Lee and Albert Sidney Johnston had each in turn become press whipping boys under similar circumstances and Bragg had no prewar reputation to compare with theirs.

Bragg's situation was difficult. He had become a political liability to the administration and his ability to lead within the army was potentially impaired by the distrust or hatred of those he commanded. He might get one more chance.

To be sure, Bragg himself was far from blameless in the debacle that had by this time all but ruined his military career. An ideal general would have reconciled himself far more quickly to the inevitabilities presented him by Davis and would have turned large powers of intellect and fortitude to the task of overcoming and making the best of them. No one, not even the present writer, has ever suggested that Bragg was anything like an ideal general. Unlike his eastern counterpart, Robert E. Lee, Bragg showed a serious inability to adjust to serious disappointments. In the face of the confusing command situation in Mississippi, he could have pressed Davis for clear instructions and, if they were still lacking, perhaps issued orders to Van Dorn as he thought fit, hoping Davis would approve. He could have proceeded much the same way with Smith, issuing firmer orders despite his lack of formal authority and putting Smith's promise of obedience to a more rigorous and repeated test. Perhaps he would have complied. Most important, Bragg could have tried his best to make use of the generals he was forced to live with, putting the incompetent ones where they could do the least harm, perhaps kicking Polk upstairs into a harmless but honorable position as second in command. None of these solutions would have solved all his problems, or even the biggest ones, but they could perhaps have made his situation somewhat better. As it was, Bragg's behavior tended to aggravate the problems with his generals. On the eve of departure for Kentucky, he roundly and publicly criticized one of his generals as "an old woman, utterly worthless." Questioned privately about the statement by a concerned friend, Bragg insisted that it was no more than the truth. "I have but one or two fitted for high command, and have in vain asked the War Department for capable people," Bragg complained. "The Government is to blame for placing such men in high position." All that was true enough, but not especially helpful.[9]

Bragg seems to have made some effort to overcome the defects of his own personality. Kirby Smith in particular noticed that even after he had criticized Bragg extensively and to his face, the general behaved with remarkable courtesy toward him. In a letter to his wife, Smith wrote that Bragg "spoke kindly to me & in the highest terms of praise and admiration of my 'personal character and soldierly qualities'—I was astonished." Perhaps Bragg reckoned he was merely giving credit where credit was due; at any rate, a more personable and politically astute demeanor at all times would have been extremely useful in making the best of Bragg's bad situation.[10]

Despite the vocal public criticism of Bragg and intense complaints from Polk and Kirby Smith, Davis retained Bragg in command of the Army of Tennessee. A successful new campaign would be vital to Bragg for restoring his badly tarnished reputation and recovering the confidence of his army. During the late fall of 1862, influential Tennessee politicians were calling loudly for the recapture of Nashville, and that pressure at least partially set the objective for Bragg's winter campaign.

Nashville was already well on its way to being the continent's most heavily fortified city and was held by a large army. Storming the city would therefore be folly. Bragg hoped to accomplish his purpose in another way. Establishing his army at Murfreesboro, about thirty miles southeast of Nashville, he threatened the new Union commander, William S. Rosecrans, into keeping his army concentrated around the Tennessee capital while Bragg's cavalry ranged around the city, gathering supplies for the Army of Tennessee and cutting its opponent's supply routes except the Cumberland River. If Bragg's plan worked, Rosecrans would come out of the Nashville fortifications to meet Bragg in the open. Bragg would then ambush him and destroy his army in a complete victory that would give the Confederacy Nashville and much more.[11]

As it turned out, Rosecrans proved all but impervious to goading, either by Bragg or his own impatient superiors. But other events combined to lure him out of the Nashville lines. A Union army under Ulysses S. Grant threatened Vicksburg, Mississippi. Concerned that the Confederate force there under John C. Pemberton would be unable to stop Grant, Davis pressured newly appointed Western theater commander Joseph E. Johnston to shift troops from Bragg to Pemberton. Johnston objected, correctly, that Bragg's troops could not reach Pemberton in time to make a difference, but he and Bragg both held out hope of stopping Grant by means of cavalry raids against his supply lines. Unconvinced, Davis traveled west himself, visited Bragg's army, was highly impressed, and personally gave the order to send 10,000 of Bragg's troops—a quarter of his infantry—to Pemberton. "Fight if you can," he told Bragg, "and fall back beyond the Tennessee [River]" if necessary.[12]

Military secrecy was virtually nonexistent in the Civil War, and word of the depletion of Bragg's army was soon in the newspapers, and the newspapers in the hands of Rosecrans, who promptly took advantage of the situation by marching on Murfreesboro. Bragg thus got his chance to strike Rosecrans in the open, but with a serious disadvantage in numbers. True to the president's instructions to fight if he could, Bragg attacked just outside Murfreesboro at dawn on the last day of 1862. He achieved tactical surprise, wrested the initiative from his more numerous adversaries, and crumpled the entire Federal right, nearly cutting it off from its base at Nashville. More or less abysmal performances by division commanders John P. McCown, Benjamin F. Cheatham, and John C. Breckinridge, combined with the absence of those 10,000 men, put complete success just out of Bragg's reach. Still, he had punished Rosecrans far worse than Lee and Jackson would combine to punish Joe Hooker four months hence at Chancellorsville. The difference, however, was that Hooker lost his nerve and retreated, leaving the Southerners to claim a victory. Rosecrans did not, and the superior size of his force meant that Bragg, whose Sunday punch had failed to put his opponent on the canvas, would ultimately have to give way. That became even more apparent when an attack Bragg ordered on January 2 ended in fiasco, leaving everyone with an even worse taste of what had at first appeared a successful battle. The next day, at the urging of his generals, Bragg withdrew another thirty miles or so to the vicinity of Tullahoma, Tennessee.[13]

It is hard to say what Bragg could have done that would have substantially altered the outcome of the campaign. Shunting aside inadequate generals, as Lee did in Virginia, had not been an option open to Bragg, so the miscues of incompetent officers were unavoidable in the western army. The loss of a quarter of his infantry on the eve of the battle left Bragg without the manpower to make his first day's success decisive, and that had been Davis's doing. To add frustration to the affair, the troops had indeed, as Johnston predicted, been too late to influence the outcome in Mississippi and, true to Johnston's and Bragg's word, the cavalry raids had successfully turned back Grant's advance. True, Bragg's handling of the botched attack on the final day of the battle had been less than inspiring, but even then it is hard to suggest any viable alternative for him other than retreat. Finally, far from falling back all the way to the Tennessee River as Davis had suggested might be necessary, Bragg had surrendered only a few dozen miles of ground and taken up a strong position behind a chain of hills, known as the Highland Rim, near Tullahoma.[14]

Yet the outcome of the battle at Murfreesboro all but ruined Bragg as an army commander. In the words of historian Grady McWhiney, it "destroyed Bragg's usefulness as a field commander." Although Bragg would continue to make the Army of Tennessee as well equipped and disciplined as a Confederate army was likely to be and continue to make excellent strategic assessments and decisions, his stock with many of his generals had fallen to the point that he could no longer lead effectively. Too many of his generals distrusted or hated him and would find reasons not to carry out his orders promptly and fully. If that had been the worst of the problems with Confederate command in the West, Davis's situation would have been easier. The grim truth was that by this time the South's western generals had developed a corrosive, self-destructive group personality, and winning their trust and hearty cooperation would have been more than almost any general could do. Later that year, even Lee, with his towering reputation, did not believe he would have been able to command the "cordial cooperation" of the Army of Tennessee's generals. For Bragg, the army was now a snake pit, and the snakes were aroused.[15]

Braxton Bragg was simply not the man to tame them. Stung by intense criticism both inside and outside the army, including newspaper articles berating him for retreating against the advice of all his generals, Bragg did something foolish. Wanting reassurance and moral support, he turned to the least likely quarter to get it: his generals. He composed a circular to them asking (1) if they had advised retreat from Murfreesboro, and (2) if they had lost confidence in him. His staff was appalled and persuaded him to delete the second question. Some wording in the note's concluding sentences, however, still implied as much and Bragg's enemies within the officer corps were only too happy to construe it that way, announcing that they and the army had indeed lost confidence in him and that he ought to resign. They had a point, but it was not one that Bragg was likely to take well under the circumstances.[16]

Word of this mess got back to Jefferson Davis, who was at a loss to know "why General Bragg should have selected that tribunal and have invited its judgments upon him." The president ordered Johnston to resort to Tullahoma at once. Johnston seems to have been genuinely impressed with Bragg's administration of the army as well as its organization and drill. He also had an uncanny knack for sensing exactly what Davis wanted him to do—and doing the opposite. Johnston thus reported back to Richmond that Bragg was doing a fine job and should be retained. Furthermore, if Bragg were replaced, Johnston did not want the job. Davis had indeed intended to replace Bragg with Johnston and was highly irritated at Johnston's contrariness, especially since the latter had been complaining for months that he did not want the theater command he held but instead desired command of an individual army. Davis tried to maneuver around Johnston's refusal by giving orders for Johnston to send Bragg to Richmond. That would put the reluctant general in command of the Army of Tennessee in effect, without any formal assignment. Johnston replied that Bragg's wife, who had been staying just behind the army's lines, was dangerously ill, perhaps dying, and that it would be cruel to order Bragg away then. That was true enough, but if Davis had been more resolute he could have issued an order relieving Bragg of command but allowing him to stay with his wife. Instead, the president simply waited. By the time Elise Bragg was out of danger, Johnston himself was ill and wrote Davis that he could not allow Bragg to go to Richmond, since then there would be no one to command the army. Once again, Davis proved insufficiently resolute. He simply allowed Bragg to remain in command of the Army of Tennessee by default. The decision was underlined when in May 1863 Davis ordered Johnston to visit the other sector of his department, Mississippi, where even more pressing dangers were afoot.[17]

Bragg thus served out the final six months of his tenure as Army of Tennessee commander, including his last three campaigns, as a general disliked by many of his subordinates and distrusted by his commander in chief. Davis would be in the position of supporting a general whose very presence in command was against his better judgment. Bragg was still a capable commander, with excellent strategic sense, yet his effectiveness was ruined because too many of his officers would disobey his orders or carry them out halfheartedly and without trying to understand their purpose. Davis had fatally crippled Bragg in his two campaigns at the head of the army—in Kentucky by leaving him a fragmented command system that included incompetent officers, and at Murfreesboro by removing a quarter of his combat strength. Bragg was simply not a good enough general to overcome those problems or to inspire the devotion of a large number of his officers. Davis had also contributed to the fatal undermining of Bragg in a more general sense by leaving Leonidas Polk in the army. The conceited, incompetent, but smooth and very persuasive former bishop persistently spread the poison of discontent within the army, weakening Bragg's ability to lead.

That weakness appeared in glaring form when Rosecrans advanced in late June 1863. Bragg had planned to block Rosecrans with Hardee's corps and swing Polk's corps over to strike the Federals in flank. The plan was thoroughly practical and promised impressive results, but by this time relations between Bragg and many of his top generals, Polk and Hardee included, had deteriorated to the point of breakdown. The Army of Tennessee's commander and his two top lieutenants were hardly on speaking terms. Polk and Hardee thus did not understand Bragg's plan or did not want it to succeed, and wished to avoid any contact with the enemy so long as Bragg remained in command. In meetings with Bragg, they not only advised retreat but urged it vehemently, with Polk all but browbeating Bragg to turn the army's back on the enemy. Bragg reluctantly followed their advice in falling back from the Highland Rim to Tullahoma and then farther to the Elk River. When he appeared inclined to turn and offer battle there, Hardee wrote a confidential note to Polk with a thinly veiled suggestion that they consider mutiny and the removal of Bragg from his command rather than meet the enemy with him at their head. Whether they actually would have acted in that manner remains a moot point; within hours of Hardee's note, Bragg again acquiesced to continued retreat, first to the foot of the Cumberland Mountains, and then over them to Chattanooga on the Tennessee River. A powerful Confederate army commanded by a skilled strategist had suffered an almost complete failure to function—indeed, had been virtually removed from the chessboard of the war's operations—by the breakdown in relations between its commanders and some of his top subordinates.[18]

This fiasco of Confederate command was repeated six weeks later when Rosecrans renewed his advance, this time skillfully using the mountainous terrain of southeastern Tennessee to turn Bragg's position in. Bragg had to abandon the gateway city of East Tennessee and fall back into Georgia. This time, however, he had been strengthened by reinforcements from Mississippi and Virginia and turned on his pursuer. By skillful maneuvering and excellent use of deception, Bragg twice got his army into position to crush the isolated elements of the pursuing Union army piece by piece. On both occasions, Bragg's generals simply refused to carry out his orders to attack. Having convinced themselves that Bragg was an idiot, they had come to believe that any movement he ordered was likely to be ill-advised if not disastrous. So, with every advantage of position and numbers on their side and with positive orders from Bragg to launch an attack, Polk, Thomas C. Hindman, and Daniel Harvey Hill took counsel of their fears, hung back in fear of nonexistent Federal reinforcements lurking beyond the horizon, and so let pass not one but two of the war's most spectacular opportunities for a resounding—and cheap—victory.

Rosecrans pulled his army together and began to slide

back toward Chattanooga and out of Bragg's carefully laid trap. The only hope now of a truly decisive Confederate victory lay in cutting the Federals off from Chattanooga. That Bragg attempted on September 19 and 20, 1863, near Chickamauga Creek. Incredibly, his effort was hamstrung by another failure to carry out an order, this one to Polk and calling for a "day-dawn" assault on the key northern sector of the Union lines. The attack went in three hours late, after the Federals had entrenched and brought up reinforcements. They butchered the advancing Southerners, although one of their officers observed that had the attack come at dawn his men could not have withstood it. When the other end of the Union line broke, the Confederates were able to end the battle on a victorious note, but they did so by driving the defeated Federals toward Chattanooga rather than cutting them off from it; thus, their success was doomed to be a hollow one. The Army of Tennessee was in no condition to renew the struggle or undertake vigorous pursuit. Bragg knew it and so followed the retiring Federals at a cautious pace.

Once the euphoria of Chickamauga's tactical success had worn off and the strategic barrenness of the battle became apparent throughout the Confederacy, yet another wave of criticism burst on Bragg. The denunciations became still louder when Bragg finally moved decisively against the chief demoralizer of the army's officer corps and ordered Leonidas Polk relieved from duty. Again Davis demonstrated that his loyalty to Polk would take precedence over all other considerations, including the maintenance of good discipline in the army. Declaring Bragg's action illegal, he set it aside and would have forced Polk on Bragg again had not the former refused to serve under him. Bragg quite properly asked Davis to relieve him from command of the Army of Tennessee, but again the president refused. By this time relieving Bragg would in all probability have meant appointing Johnston to take his place, and events during the second half of 1863 had made that general even more repugnant to Davis than before. Instead, Davis undertook to retain Bragg and finally, now that it was too late, accorded him limited support in purging his army of those generals who were disrupting its command system—including some who had recently gotten up a petition calling for his removal. He demoted Simon B. Buckner from corps to division command and sent away D. H. Hill and effectively demoted him from lieutenant general to major general. Bragg also reshuffled the army's brigades and divisions to break up pernicious cliques, but these actions were too little, too late.

Rosecrans was a beaten man after Chickamauga and pulled his army into Chattanooga, abandoning key ground needed to secure the Union supply line to the city. Bragg accepted the gift happily and established an effective siege of the city and the Union army in it. Yet he was trying to fight with an army that was not fully in his control. Resourceful and resolute action by the new Union commander, Ulysses S. Grant, bid to reopen the supply line to the city. Trying to respond, Bragg was crippled by the balky uncooperativeness—even high-handed disobedience—of yet another of his subordinates who thought himself a better strategist than Bragg, this time, James Longstreet, a recent transfer from Virginia.[19]

Bragg soon found a way to get rid of Longstreet, giving him command of a key expedition that represented Bragg's last hope of retaining the strategic initiative, a bid to clear the Federals out of Knoxville and thus make possible a massive Confederate turning movement against Grant like the one that had discomfited Buell just over a year before. Longstreet showed no understanding of Bragg's plan and little zeal to accomplish it. The initiative went to Grant, who launched a devastating serious of assaults in late November that culminated with the Confederate rout at Missionary Ridge, which Bragg called his own "shameful discomfiture." Bragg renewed his request to be relieved of command, and this time Davis complied. Braxton Bragg never again commanded a major army.[20] The final verdict on Bragg is an equivocal one. He was an excellent administrator, organizer, and strategist. He had considerable talent as a general—far more than his critics then or since have given him credit for. Yet at the same time he lacked two important attributes as a general: the ability to adjust rapidly to the frustration of his plans and, more important, the ability to inspire admiration, respect, and obedience even when his army did not achieve success. These shortcomings prevented him from surmounting the difficult circumstances into which Davis repeatedly thrust him.

In Bragg, Davis squandered a major potential asset. In a cause that suffered a lack of generals with the skill, training, and strength of character to lead large armies in desperate battles, Davis had in Bragg a serviceable, useable general. Bragg was no Robert E. Lee, or anything of the sort, but such military paragons are never common. Davis needed to win the war using at least several men of lesser abilities, and Bragg was, in many ways, one of the more promising candidates to be one of those lesser but still vital contributors to Confederate victory. Had Davis wisely and vigorously supported Bragg, placing him from the outset within a sound command system along with good officers, he might have been able to make of the dyspeptic general a commander as successful as the Confederacy needed him to be. His failure to do so, and Bragg's inability to overcome the difficulties this created, combined to play an important part in the fatal deterioration of Confederate command in the West and to final defeat in the war.

5

The General Whom the President Elevated Too High: Davis and John Bell Hood

HERMAN HATTAWAY

On July 11, 1861, Major John Bell Hood rode out of camp accompanied by about eighty troopers, trying to find and, if possible, capture some of the "thieving Yankees" who occasionally left their base at Newport News to pillage nearby farms. A group of Federals tried to ambush Hood's column and he responded by quickly dismounting some of his men and sending them forward. A forty-five-minute firefight ensued before the Yankees were defeated. Hood led his mounted troopers in a charge that inflicted a complete rout, captured two officers and ten enlisted men, and killed at least two of the enemy. Hood reported that the thicket was so dense that he did not know how many the enemy detachment had numbered, or if his men possibly had killed any more than the two they found and buried before returning to camp. The Confederates lost but one horse.[1]

From this first encounter, Hood rose to be the last of Jefferson Davis's full generals, attaining an army command in late August 1864. The rank would not be permanent, for the Confederate Senate later affirmed that the promotion had been only a temporary one. Although Hood failed officially and otherwise in army command, he was a better general than many historians and students of the Civil War have indicated. Hood simply rose too high, out of his element, above his level of competence—which maximally was at division command.

Hood was born in Owingsville, Kentucky, on June 1, 1831, and graduated from West Point in 1853—forty-fifth in his class of fifty-two: not a very serious or distinguished student. He also had 196 demerits, just four short of expulsion for inadequate military correctness and deportment. He served first in California and then Texas—becoming a Texan by choice. He resigned his commission as a first lieutenant of cavalry in the United States Army after Sumter and was commissioned first lieutenant of cavalry in the Confederate States Army. His first duty sent him to Kentucky on a recruiting mission. On his return, he reported to Major General Robert E. Lee in Richmond, who told him he would instruct the cavalry units then assembling in camps at Yorktown. Before summer came in 1861, Major Hood commanded all the cavalry on the York River.

Then came his first encounter with the enemy. His superior, John B. Magruder, in a report to Lee, called the skirmish "a brilliant little affair." A delighted Lee forwarded Magruder's report to Jefferson Davis. So began the association between soldier and president. By October 1, 1861, Hood rose to the rank of colonel and to the command of the Fourth Texas Infantry Regiment.

Any number of factors might have played a role in Hood's rise: a West Point training, an impressive physical size, association with Texas, and—possibly—personal recommendations from Albert Sidney Johnston, Hood's old commander in the Second United States Cavalry, as well as from Hood's distant relative, Gustavus Woodson Smith.

Later that fall, Hood's regiment was combined with the other Texas units in Virginia to form a brigade. Its commander, Louis T. Wigfall, resigned from the army early in 1862 to take a seat in the Confederate Senate. Hood then took command of the Texas Brigade as a brigadier general.

Hood's promotion, in the words of his best biographer, Richard M. McMurry, was "the major mystery of his career."[2] Although Hood had been a competent regimental commander, he had done nothing to distinguish himself. In promoting Hood, Davis jumped him over two senior colonels (James J. Archer of the Fifth Texas and William T. Wofford of the Eighteenth Georgia). One might speculate that two factors may well have played a role in Davis's decision. Neither Archer nor Wofford were West Point graduates, and Davis *always* gave preference to Academy men for high-level military appointments. *And* the command of Hood's old regiment went to one of Davis's friends.

Hood's promotion to brigadier general set the stage for his emergence as a major figure in the Confederacy. He eventually distinguished himself on a dozen battlefields with the Army of Northern Virginia. Within six months he garnered the attention of just about everyone. During the summer of 1862, he became "the gallant Hood of Texas" and was regarded as one of the bright hopes of the Confederacy. The successes he achieved at the head of what came to be known as "Hood's Texas Brigade" paved the way for his promotions to higher commands.[3]

The first known meeting between Hood and Jefferson Davis occurred on May 22, 1862. Davis had ridden out to observe an expected attack by Major General Gustavus W. Smith's wing of the Army of Northern Virginia upon the enemy, near the Chickahominy River. The Confederate president sought someone to give a summation of developments and found Hood. "He told me he did not know anything more than that they [the Confederates] had been halted," Davis wrote to his wife, Varina. Asking where Smith was, Hood "replied he believed he [Smith] had gone to a farm-house in the rear, adding that he thought he was ill."[4] McMurry suggests that Davis rode off, perhaps concluding that General Joseph E. Johnston had bungled the planned attack. The commander in chief's distrust of Johnston would loom large in Hood's future. In his biography of Davis, historian William C. Davis suggests that at this meeting "perhaps the sad-eyed young general's [Hood's] calm impressed the president."[5] In any event, Davis would play an ever growing role in nurturing Hood's career throughout the war.

Johnston was wounded and obliged to relinquish command of the army, and on June 1, 1862, Davis gave the command to Robert E. Lee. As a brigade commander, Hood played no role in helping to develop Lee's plans. Hood did, however, fight well, garner much attention and praise, and distinguish himself. When, in October 1862, James Longstreet and Thomas J. "Stonewall" Jackson were elevated to be lieutenant generals, George Pickett and Hood filled the vacated major generalcies, the latter assigned a division commanded under James Longstreet.[6] At Gettysburg, Hood was severely wounded in the left arm, thereafter losing all use of the limb. Until that time, his performance in the battle had been spectacular. Even the visiting Englishman from the Coldstream Guards, Arthur James Lyon Fremantle, paid Hood "a very handsome compliment."[7]

On the retreat into Virginia, Hood remained at Staunton

under the care of Dr. John Darby, the surgeon attached to Hood's division. Details on Hood's life for the ensuing few weeks are skimpy, but by early September he was in Richmond. There was never much doubt that he would return to duty. Meanwhile, Brigadier General Micah Jenkins was in command of Hood's division—but the officers regarded Jenkins as incompetent, and they talked Hood into returning to the division for the Chickamauga campaign—although he did not need much persuasion.

On September 18, 1863, he joined his division in the woods along Chickamauga Creek, just in time to lead them in the battle that was shaping up. Again, typically, Hood performed boldly and well—until he was struck in the right leg by a bullet. He fell from his horse into the arms of an aide. Hood refused to leave the field until he was sure his men were driving the enemy; once in the care of surgeons, his damaged limb was amputated at the thigh.

Word was sent to Richmond in battlefield dispatches on September 20 and 21, 1863, that Hood had been wounded in the Battle of Chickamauga. On the twenty-second, a rumor—apparently started in Atlanta and repeated by newspapers throughout the Confederacy—asserted that he had died. One grieving Richmond diarist noted that "his loss is a severe one, second only to that of Jackson." Lee wrote that he "mourn[ed] for our brave Hood," but Jefferson Davis got word to him the next day that the rumor was false: Hood was recuperating.[8]

By October 8, Hood was asking when he might return to duty. He could sit up and hoped soon to be ambulatory on his crutches, and he was much interested in army politics. By late October he felt able to travel. He went first to Atlanta, later to Wilmington, and finally to Richmond, where he spent three months during the winter of 1863–64. By early January, when he could once again ride a horse, President Davis frequently invited him to go on excursions about the city. Much gossip centered on the obvious friendship between the two. Despite the disparity in their ages, Davis and Hood were soul mates, of a sort. Both were romantically attached to the values of the Old South and both admired, perhaps even envied, qualities they saw in each other. Of course, each had something tangible to offer the other: Davis was having trouble with his popular image, while Hood was an immense favorite with the public; Hood was severely wounded and possibly elicited genuine sympathy from Davis; and, as for Hood, the president was a valuable ally if Hood's ambitions for higher rank and further command were to be fulfilled.

Historian McMurry points out that "for the rest of his life," Hood's "physical mobility would be severely limited" and admits that there also "was the possibility that the wounds altered Hood's psychological makeup in a significant manner." But McMurry opines that there were no major changes in the behavior that Hood had manifested in "a reasonably consistent pattern that ran through his entire life."[9]

Again, as after Gettysburg, there seems never to have been any doubt that Hood would return to active duty and this time be promoted as well. Right after the Battle of Chickamauga, both Longstreet and Bragg had recommended Hood's promotion and President Davis on October 29 noted that he would promote Hood to lieutenant general. There was brief consideration of giving Hood a departmental command, perhaps that of the Trans-Mississippi, but it seemed most appropriate that he fill a corps command in the Army of Tennessee.

Because there was no open slot for another lieutenant general, Davis withdrew Daniel H. Hill's nomination to the Senate for that rank and substituted Hood's. The only known official inquiry into Hood's fitness for the field came with casual questioning, to which Hood replied that all he needed was a small carriage and all of his former staff officers, who knew his manner and approach. The Senate confirmed the promotion on February 11, 1864, with date of rank to be September 20, 1863—the day he had sustained his wound at Chickamauga.

Numerous historians have concluded that during the winter of 1863–64, Hood nurtured a close friendship not only with Davis, but also with Braxton Bragg—who was brought to Richmond early in 1864 as the president's military advisor. This, in turn, leads them to the assertion that Hood later was an administrative spy in Joe Johnston's army. Some have even suggested that there was a Davis–Bragg–Hood cabal working to undermine Johnston and to pave the way for Hood's taking over the command. McMurry, however, insisted that "there is little real evidence to substantiate these charges" and a careful look afresh at the evidence reaffirms his conclusion.

An administrative spy? Well, maybe. But only because Davis treasured having minute information about what was going on in the Confederacy's armies. Lee knew this and fulfilled Davis's yearnings; Joseph Johnston preferred keeping his cards close to the chest. And, in any case, if it were anything, it was only a Davis–Hood cabal, for Bragg did not reach Richmond until shortly before the time Hood left. Finally, the very idea of a Davis involvement in some scheme to risk the well-being of a major army (and probably the very survival of the Confederacy itself) in order to undermine Johnston is *absurd*.

It is, however, more difficult to delineate the precise nature of the Davis–Hood relationship. Beyond doubt they were close. Davis and Hood socialized much. The general once escorted Mrs. Davis and they sat at a small table talking for more than an hour after the others had left the room. At least once Hood borrowed Davis's carriage, and at least once

Hood sat in the president's pew at church—with the president helping the unsteady cripple down the steps afterward.

Clearly, Davis and Hood discussed various strategic possibilities and what might be done militarily. Hood praised the vain Davis in just the right ways, once urging that Davis take personal field command: "I would follow you to the death!" he asserted.[10] The two agreed that the South needed somehow to seize the initiative. Doubtless, Davis's assessment of Hood's military insights and capacities increased during this period.

Hood garnered the adulation and admiration of a wide array of folk. He even received as a gift from General Beauregard in the spring of 1864—a cane carved from Fort Sumter's flagstaff that had been shot down during the 1863 siege.[11] Davis was one of the general's genuine admirers, but he had great political reasons for attaching himself to the war hero.

But was Hood trying to apple-polish? Especially to apple-polish Davis? Mary Chesnut, who saw a lot of "Sam" Hood—as his friends called him ever since West Point, although no one could remember why—liked him a lot, and noted in her diary: "General Hood's an awful flatterer." Hood told Davis things that Davis liked to hear. But was Hood fawning over Davis with his own gain mainly in mind? That is impossible to know for certain, but his best biographer wrote: "Hood was a naive and romantic man." He, perhaps more so than anyone else in the Confederacy, might simply have been sincere in his praise of Davis. In 1866, when Davis was imprisoned—thus quite without power either to reward or punish—Hood wrote to Stephen D. Lee that Davis was "the greatest man of America—the martyr of modern times."[13]

More important may be the issue of whether the time that Davis and Hood spent together influenced the president's decision to put Hood in command of a corps in the Army of Tennessee. But Davis already had decided to do this, at least as early as October 29, 1863.[14]

Historian Steven Woodworth thinks that Davis made a bad mistake in selecting Hood.[15] Yet, aside from health limitations, experience made him clearly the most qualified of all the Confederate major generals for corps command. He had performed magnificently on every field of battle on which he appeared—except on one occasion when his position had not been directly engaged. He took part in much major combat, often boldly leading his troops, and often turning the tide of battle. Most significantly, too, he had been a major general for sixteen months by the time of his promotion; and, counting time he had served in place of William H. C. Whiting, had actually commanded a division for nineteen months. At Chickamauga he had successfully led a conglomerate command that amounted to a corps. Thus, by all logic—assuming one could accept his health limitations—Hood was the best possible choice.

Woodworth does not agree with this—"While Davis could undoubtedly have done worse than Hood in his selection of a corps commander for the Army of Tennessee, he probably could have done better too"—and points to Alexander P. Stewart and Patrick R. Cleburne. Hood at thirty-three, Woodworth adds, had not "demonstrated a mental and emotional stability beyond his years that might have justified vesting him with such heavy responsibility."[16]

The new lieutenant general wrote his first letter from the field to Davis on March 7, 1864. In it he expressed hope that the Army of Tennessee might be strengthened so that it thus would be enabled to attack the enemy rear. Other letters followed over the course of the next two months. The army, he assured, was in fine condition, but needed more manpower to take the initiative. If it *were* adequately built up, it "should be sufficient to defeat and destroy all the Federals on this side of the Ohio River."[17]

Hood wrote similar letters to Bragg and to Secretary of War James A. Seddon, but Hood's optimism contrasted with Johnston's gloomy assessments of the army's condition and potential. Historian McMurry asserts that "it is impossible to know Hood's motive in writing these letters."[18] It is certainly probable that Davis had asked Hood to write, but, whatever the motivation, Hood's letters precipitated a tense and testy debate between Johnston and the Richmond authorities. Hood's optimistic statements, McMurry admits, were "in character for Hood," but nonetheless, they "smack of sycophancy."[19]

By early April, Hood's letters began to contain stringent criticism of Johnston for his sluggish reluctance to move against the Federals. Some think that this marks the beginning of the effort to remove Johnston from command.[20] Hood certainly was aggressive and itched for action; Johnston was conservative and reluctant to take the offensive. It was Hood's lifelong habit to correspond unofficially without going through channels and, indeed, this was a common practice in the Confederacy. But Hood was not the only general writing critically of Johnston: William J. Hardee, Alexander P. Stewart, and Joe Wheeler all did so, too.

After the Army of Tennessee had retreated to Cassville, Georgia, Johnston perceived a possible opportunity for demolishing Sherman's army. The Union commander was trying another of his typical wide-turning movements and Johnston wanted to slam against one isolated enemy wing, destroy it, and then go after the other. Hood's division was part of the assault force. He discovered that leading a corps was much more complicated than heading up a brigade or division.

Typically careless about details, he neglected to order an adequate reconnaissance. Suddenly, a Union force of undetermined origin and size appeared on his flank and rear. These enemy troops were but a small portion of Sherman's army that had taken a wrong turn and were trying to fumble their way back to the main body, but Hood panicked. He hurriedly pulled his troops back from the planned jumping off point for the intended attack and set them to digging entrenchments furiously—to fend off this "vicious and nefarious" assault force.

Johnston was shocked at first by Hood's report, but soon he, too, was wallowing in doubt and in the end concluded that Hood had perhaps been prudent in calling off the assault. Now, however, Johnston thought the army was in a good position for defense; Hood and Leonidas Polk believed the site was indefensible. They wanted to attack rather than to retreat and did not want to stand pat. Johnston instead elected to pull rearward. And so the campaign went: one retreat after another.

During the actions near Cassville on May 19, and New Hope Church on May 28, 1864, Johnston began to perceive inklings that Hood would not or could not perform at top efficiency. Possibly, too, Hood, seeing Johnston retreat, had grown more openly scornful and abrasive toward his commander. It is certain that they now were no longer as close as they had been when the campaign opened, and their rift soon accelerated. Louis Wigfall, a friend of both Johnston and Hood, visited army headquarters and confided to Johnston that there were rumors in the capital that Davis was planning to replace Johnston with Hood. Not long thereafter, Hood had grown confident enough or angry enough to publicly discuss his disagreements with Johnston.[21]

As the Atlanta campaign unfolded, Davis grew more and more impatient and dissatisfied with Johnston's defense.

Davis finally reached his last straw on July 17, 1864, and ordered Johnston to relinquish his command to Hood. This decision has been one of the most vociferously debated by participants in the war and students ever since. McMurry's analysis is a good one. First, break the matter down into separate questions. Should Johnston have been replaced? Yes; that was justified. Was Hood the best and most logical choice? Given the extant critical situation and the proximity of the army to enemy contact, the new commander had to be with the Army already. The only realistic possibilities were Hardee or Hood. Davis had been pondering these possibilities for a while, and first seemed to have been leaning toward Hardee. On that date, Bragg, whom Davis had sent to visit the army, telegraphed Davis—and then wrote him a long letter—indicating that Hood was very popular with the men and, combined with his known penchant for aggressiveness, his appointment would have a good effect.

The fundamental dilemma that Davis faced was that the Confederacy's manpower pool for top-level commanders was too scanty. No one other than R. E. Lee had demonstrated ability or potential to successfully lead an army against a larger force. Davis took a gamble in elevating a man whose "most conspicuous qualities," to quote McMurry, "were those of the post-1830 South: physical bravery, aggressiveness, superb combat leadership, intuitiveness, emotionalism, impatience, lack of attention to obstacles, planning, and detail. These characteristics made Hood and others of his generation fine regimental, brigade, and division commanders." Woodworth's ultimate assessment of John Bell Hood is that "throughout his military career, Hood walked a fine line between audacity and foolhardiness."[22]

Thus, at the age of thirty-three, Hood became the last and youngest of the eight full generals of the Confederacy. He already had risen "above the level where courage and combat leadership sufficed," to quote McMurry again. And now he was one step above that: he had truly reached a level of incompetence. As Woodworth has suggested, Hood "never really got the knack of handling an army." Yet, given the available talent, the Confederate president could do little else. One division commander summed up the situation well when he wrote on July 18: "Hood has 'gone up like a rocket.' It is to be hoped . . . that he will not come down like the stick. He is brave, whether he has the capacity to Command armies (for it requires a high order of talent) time will develop. I will express no opinion."[23]

Early in August 1864, Hardee asked to be transferred. A series of telegrams were exchanged between Hardee, Bragg, and Davis, prompting Davis finally to say that he was sorry Hardee found his situation in the Army of Tennessee so unpleasant, assuring him that no insult was intended when Hood was promoted over him. Hardee pressed further, saying that his service under Hood was "personally humiliating" and added that Hood had approved his request to leave. Davis then communicated to Hood that "General Hardee's minute knowledge of the country, and his extensive acquaintance with the officers and men of the command, must render his large professional knowledge and experience peculiarly valuable in such a campaign as I hope is before you."[24] Hardee then let the matter drop for the time being, but his resentment toward Hood continued unabated, no doubt weakening the effort to defend Atlanta. But then, historian Albert Castel thinks there was little chance for a successful defense, in any case.[25]

Davis was rightly anxious to keep Hardee with the army because he knew there was a vexatious shortage of officers competent to command a corps. Carter L. Stevenson now headed Hood's old corps, but Hood did not deem him suitable for the job, even temporarily. After conferring with

Hardee and Alexander P. Stewart, Hood put Benjamin F. Cheatham—Hardee's senior division commander—in temporary command of the corps. Hood asked the War Department to send him Mansfield Lovell, Wade Hampton, or Stephen D. Lee—in that order of preference. Lee got the job. Lee was a very able officer and could have been a magnificent division commander—ironically, one of the few command positions he did not hold during one of the Civil War's most remarkable careers, rising through every rank from captain to lieutenant general. But Lee was younger than Hood by one year—both of them were too young either for corps or army command, and Lee had even less experience leading large bodies of troops than Hood had the previous winter when he had been given a corps. Perhaps Patrick R. Cleburne might have been a better choice, but he had gotten ensnared in the army's vicious infighting and politics.

Lee's arrival did not end Hood's problem with command assignments for long: Stewart, wounded on July 20 in the Battle of Ezra Church, was incapacitated for two weeks and thus Cheatham was once again pressed into corps command. This, in conjunction with other calamities—Major General W. H. T. Walker was killed on July 22 and Major General William W. Loring, one of Stewart's division commanders, was seriously wounded at Ezra Church—necessitated other juggling in the command arrangements. Indeed, Hood was constantly obliged to seek adequate leaders to head his divisions, brigades, and regiments. Perhaps Davis might have had keener insight into this problem—but even if he had, he could have done little to facilitate the process.

The historian Charles Fair, in his *From the Jaws of Victory*, observed that it is characteristic of poor generals to denounce subordinates for their defeats. Hood began to display that characteristic in September 1864 after the fall of Atlanta.

Hood wrote Davis, blaming Hardee, and again requested that Richard Taylor be sent to relieve him. When Davis did not immediately respond, Hood wrote another letter thoroughly lambasting Hardee, placing full onus on him for the recent losses and indicating that it was "of the utmost importance that Hardee should be relieved at once."[26]

The second most serious problem Hood had with generals stemmed from the departure in mid-September of Brigadier General Francis A. Shoup. At his own request, Shoup, the army's chief of staff, was relieved. Hood appointed no new chief of staff, and most of Shoup's former duties devolved on Major Arthur Pendleton Mason. Administration in the Army of Tennessee, never exemplary, now fell apart. Poor administration then played a major role in the tragic events that ensued. Perhaps Davis, who of all people cared about administration, might have intervened.

Hood tried to bolster morale by getting the men paid. The president did become involved in this matter, telegraphing Hood on September 17 that a special requisition was being made to pay the army. Hood next addressed the problems of supply, informing Davis that the army was in great need of shoes and clothing. Hood finally issued a circular urging that moccasins be made out of beef hides for the barefooted men. Equally pressing was the problem of ensuring an adequate supply of munitions and possibly securing more artillery pieces as well as horses, saddles, and related equipment. Still, Hood reassured Davis that he intended to be active, that "I shall continue to interrupt as much as possible the communications of the enemy."[27]

Davis seemed to like this plan, and ultimately, McMurry concludes, it "was as sound as anything the Confederates could have devised."[28] Davis also decided to visit the army. Reaching Hood's headquarters at Palmetto, Georgia, on September 25, he spent two days reviewing the troops and talking with various generals. He heard many complaints about Hood—especially from Hardee. But Davis did as much soothing as he could and, as he later described it, he and Hood discussed "the operations which might retrieve what he had lost."[29] Davis also made a change in command arrangements: he created the Military Division of the West— in effect combining two military departments that included Hood's army—and put Beauregard in charge.

Davis did achieve his main goal of raising the army's morale, but he let his elation loosen his tongue a bit too much. In a speech at Columbia, South Carolina, he proclaimed: "His [Hood's] eye is now fixed upon a point far beyond that where he was assailed by the enemy." Sherman read the speech in a newspaper a few days later and proclaimed that "the taking of Atlanta broke upon Jeff. Davis so suddenly as to disturb the equilibrium of his usually well-balanced temper, so that . . . he let out some thoughts which otherwise he would have kept to himself." Sherman now heeded Davis's warning and turned to meet the expected threat to his communications.[30]

Hood, however, soon diverged from the plan that he and Davis had agreed on. Hood decided to abandon Georgia to the Federals and move into Alabama and then Tennessee. He commenced this without first consulting Davis, the War Department, or Beauregard, or even informing them of what he was doing. His plan may have been full of fantasy, but if he moved fast and made no mistakes, it was perhaps as good as anything.

Beauregard raised many objections, and the relationship between him and Hood eventually became abrasive. The Creole did much to facilitate matters and arrange for the army's needs. On Beauregard's insistence, Hood reopened full communication with the War Department and no major objections were lodged against his intentions. Hood wrote to Davis that "should he [Sherman] move . . . south from Atlanta, I think it would be the best thing that could happen for our general good," and added, "Beauregard *agrees with me* as to my plan of operation." Although Bragg advised to the contrary, Davis, with some reservations, approved the movement. Davis, too, was perhaps deluded by Hood's dream.[31] On September 26, 1864, Mary Chesnut recorded that her husband had told her that Custis Lee was urging Davis to replace Hood with Beauregard, but Davis remained undecided about that. Mrs. Chesnut subsequently recorded that in October Davis was again defending Hood's conduct.[32]

Thomas L. Connelly and Archer Jones suggest in *The Politics of Command* that Davis was elated over the launching of a western offensive; indeed "it is not, perhaps, too much of an exaggeration to say that a western offensive had become even more of an *idée fixe* for Davis that it had been [long before] for Beauregard and that Davis, the convert, was more devout than Beauregard, the prophet." In the unfolding of it all, both Beauregard and Davis botched their proper functions. Beauregard ill understood the limits of his authority and therefore showed an almost total lack of initiative in dealing with Hood's Tennessee campaign. Davis, in turn, possessed so intense and ultimately so warped a concern with strategy that it induced him to neglect logistics.[33]

The president urged on Hood the necessity of inflicting defeat on the Federals before their army in the region, into which he would thrust, could be reunited or reinforced. "You may first beat him in detail," Davis wrote, "and subsequently without serious obstruction or danger to the country in your rear advance to the Ohio River."[34] As the campaigns unfolded, Davis gave Hood occasional tactical advice no more. Perhaps the president censured himself privately after the disastrous Battle of Franklin. Certainly, earlier in the war, the Confederate commander in chief would never have allowed any general, even R. E. Lee, to go off on such a solo campaign. As the weeks passed, Davis increasingly doubted Hood's generalship: the president tallied the total casualties Hood suffered in his first ten weeks in command and compared them—unfavorably—with those of Johnston's last ten. That Davis did not interfere shows how tired he was by then. And it is possible Hood had been taking a derivative of laudanum as a painkiller, clouding his judgment. Perhaps, as many historians assert, he had no plan at all.

After the disastrous Franklin and Nashville campaigns were finally over and the army had limped into winter quarters, Hood resigned his command. He made his way to Richmond, where he took a room in the Spotswood Hotel and worked on reports of his campaigns—going as far back as the operations around Atlanta and including some material quite critical of Johnston's conduct before Hood had relieved him. When Hood had first arrived in Richmond, criticism of Davis for having relieved Johnston was rife and there is some credible evidence that Davis used Hood ("perhaps unknowingly," McMurry points out) to bolster Davis's defense against his detractors.[35]

After Hood submitted his reports, there was talk of sending him to a command in western Virginia, but R. E. Lee was averse to that idea, so Hood spent the next six weeks at leisure in Richmond. Hood then requested, and it was agreed, that he be sent to the trans-Mississippi on a fact-finding mission, possibly to probe the feasibility of moving troops across the river. Prior to departing, Hood wrote a touching letter to Davis: "Before leaving for Texas allow me to say that I more than appreciate all of your kindness to me. Please never allow anyone to cause you to think for one moment, that I did not know that you were ever more than ready to assume all responsibility naturally belonging to you.

I know sir you were in no way responsible for my operations whilst Commanding the Army of Tenn. Believe me Sir ever your sincere friend, And I pray God, may ever bless & protect you." In a postscript, Hood added: "I am more content & satisfied with my own [sic] work whilst in command of the army of Tenn, than all my military career in life."[36] Hood was an honest man. He had done the best he could under the circumstances that had prevailed as he had been able to perceive and understand them at the time. He simply had risen two steps beyond his maximal level of competence. The tragedy is not that he could not see this, but that Davis had so thoroughly overestimated Hood's capacity and that the South's resources of command below the very top echelons were so meager.

By October 1865, Hood was back in New Orleans, and—with an extraordinarily early inclination to prepare memoirs—was anxious to begin collecting information about his military career. He submitted a request to Major General Philip Sheridan—Hood's West Point classmate and prewar comrade in the Fourth Infantry, now in command of the Federal forces occupying Louisiana—for permission to visit Davis, then imprisoned at Fort Monroe, Virginia. Sheridan telegraphed President Andrew Johnson requesting approval, but Johnson said no.[37]

Hood continued to gather materials for his memoir for the rest of his life. A major and jolting catalyst appeared in 1874 when Johnston published his own memoir, including much vitriolic criticism of his enemies. Johnston's main target was Davis, but in discussing the 1864 campaign, Johnston depicted Hood as incompetent and blamed his blunders largely for the loss of North Georgia. Hood read and fumed; Johnston either asserted or implied that Hood had often proposed impracticable plans, failed to execute orders, fought foolish battles without authority, generally been a great handicap, and occasionally lied. Hood immediately determined to compose a "Reply to General Johnston." Sherman added more fuel to the fire when the next year he published his memoir, in which he unfavorably contrasted Hood's "rash" behavior with Johnston's "cautious and prudent conduct" and suggested that Hood had "played into our hands perfectly" when he traipsed off to Tennessee, leaving the Federals an open road through Georgia. Hood responded by rounding out his memoir, adding to the "Reply to General Johnston" an expanded defense of his actions and a synopsis of his early military career. This became *Advance and Retreat*, but Hood died of yellow fever in the summer of 1879 before he could find a publisher. Beauregard intervened and arranged for publication in New Orleans in 1880 as an aid to the Hood Orphan Memorial Fund. Although historian Connelly calls Hood's *Advance and Retreat* a "blind, charging attack upon Johnston," it nevertheless provides a partial corrective to Johnston's equally biased reminiscences and is a classic argument for the bold offensive in war.[38]

For his part, Davis remained Hood's loyal supporter. The general had been dead for two years when Davis published his memoirs: *The Rise and Fall of the Confederate Government*. It followed Hood's account of the Tennessee campaign and concluded: "The fidelity and gallantry of that officer and the well-known magnanimity of his character are a sufficient guarantee of the impartiality of his narration."[39]

6

"To Comfort, To Counsel, To Cure": Davis, Wives, and Generals

LESLEY J. GORDON

In 1881 Jefferson Davis dedicated his two-volume *Rise and Fall of the Confederate Government* to "The Women of the Confederacy." He praised them for their piety, patriotism, fortitude, soothing ministrations, "domestic labors," and "zealous faith in our cause."[1] Recently, these Confederate women Davis acclaimed so highly have attracted considerable scholarly attention. There seems a continual flood of published Southern women's personal diaries and memoirs, and Civil War historians have begun to explore more closely ties between the home front and the battlefront. Just as historians now recognize that the Confederacy was not a monolithic, united entity, scholars affirm a variety of female experiences, attitudes, and stories. Sometimes Confederate women were as self-sacrificing and fervently supportive as Davis's tribute maintains, but they could also be bitterly divided and disaffected by the war's demands. Historians have begun to realize that the traditional tendency to separate soldiers' experiences from civilians', especially women, distorts the broader societal impact of civil war.

One way to combine this recent exploration of the private and female side of war with more traditional military approaches is to examine marriages and wives of prominent Civil War leaders. These were powerful men who were fathers and husbands at the same time they were generals and politicians. Wives, particularly Victorian elite women, saw their husbands in a different, and often, more vulnerable light than did other male contemporaries.

This is not to say that historians have entirely neglected wives of Civil War leaders. Steven E. Woodworth's *Jefferson Davis and His Generals*, and his recent *Davis and Lee at War*, for example, mine personal papers and published recollections of generals' wives for insight into leaders' personality and behavior. Woodworth demonstrates repeatedly that generals' wives mattered. He describes Albert Sidney Johnston leaving the army in 1834 because of his wife's poor health, but notes that her death led him back into the ranks; Pennsylvania-born John C. Pemberton, Woodworth states, pledged his allegiance to his wife's native South; and Braxton Bragg's concern for his wife's severe illness was one of the factors that kept him in command after March 1863. Wives could be pleasant distractions. William Hardee's Christmas time wedding in 1862, or Edmund K. Smith's honeymoon in September 1862 were enjoyable interruptions to the frustrating performances and constant backstabbing characteristic of western theater commanders. A wife could serve as a handy name for a gun. In Columbus, Missouri, troops christened a large cannon "Lady Polk" in honor of Leonidas Polk's wife. A wife could also be a liability. John Hunt Morgan, Woodworth contends, "was not his old self" after his marriage. "His marriage," Woodworth writes, "seemed to have taken all the fire out of him." But generals' wives have little individual presence in Woodworth's intensive study of military strategy and male personalities. Sometimes he fails to reveal their first names, but almost always he refers to their appearance.[2]

Appearance mattered to Confederate male elites, but a woman's name, wealth, and status were more important. Romantic love and companionate marriage were increasingly important to Victorian Americans, but for Southern slaveholders the marriage institution continued to reaffirm their intricate system of class, gender, and racial domination. Generals' wives were helpmates, confidants, lovers, and friends. They also could be social, political, and economic assets.

This chapter examines the wives and marriages of five prominent Confederate leaders: Jefferson Davis, Joseph E. Johnston, Braxton Bragg, P. G. T. Beauregard, and Robert E. Lee. Considering these men as husbands, and their wives as individuals, allows a greater understanding of the war's effect on personal relationships. And it provides a greater appreciation of the women sustaining, concerning, and troubling Jefferson Davis and his generals.

Jefferson Davis married Varina Howell in 1845 and quickly introduced her to the life of a public official. During the fifteen years before the Civil War, he served in Congress and as Secretary of War. Varina easily learned the skills of a politician's wife. She attended and held parties and often visited Congress to listen to debates. She befriended Presidents Franklin Pierce and James Buchanan, and charmed John C. Calhoun. Unlike women in her husband's family, Varina was outspoken and opinionated. She made no apologies for her interest in and knowledge of politics and public affairs. Varina once wrote her mother of visiting the House of Representatives where she heard "nothing but empty vapouring about our abilities, or power to whip England."[3]

When his home state of Mississippi seceded from the Union, Davis gave a somber speech and resigned from the Senate in January 1861. One month later he became president of the new Confederate nation. His wife watched his face as he read the telegram bearing the news of his appointment and noted his dour expression. Varina later wrote: "He looked so grieved that I feared some evil had befallen our family. After a few minutes' painful silence he told me, as a man might speak of a sentence of death." She claimed to know immediately that this would be a daunting and difficult task for a man like Jefferson Davis.[4]

Varina Howell Davis proved a perceptive and shrewd judge of her husband from the first day she met him. She summed up his character, clearly seeing the complex man who would perplex historians. Only sixteen at the time, Varina aptly described Jefferson's "uncertain temper" and his tendency to take "for granted that everybody agrees with him when he expresses an opinion." She observed his aloof and sensitive nature, but also saw hints of charm and kindness. Varina discovered the very weaknesses that soured so many of Jefferson's political and military relationships.[5]

Jefferson and Varina were markedly different individuals whose personalities both clashed and complemented each other. The same traits that made Varina Jefferson's greatest defender also strained their marriage. Her sharp wit and strong will clashed with Jefferson's traditional concepts of appropriate female behavior. Their marriage was long lasting, but certainly not free of tension. A forthright, bright woman paired with a sensitive, stubborn man inevitably caused friction.

Despite their different personalities, Varina was the most important woman in Jefferson Davis's life. Although he later dedicated his war memoir to Confederate women, Jefferson Davis had limited direct interaction with other females, especially wives of his generals. The Richmond social scene was one of the few places where women might have the opportunity to meet and converse with the president, but he was not fond of entertaining. His reserved public personality, intense work ethic, and bad health prevented him from frequent socializing. He often came home too exhausted to eat and too preoccupied to sleep. The Confederate president took more pleasure from solitary walks around the city, horseback riding, or spending private time with his family or close friends. News from the front frequently interrupted any attempts he made to relax or socialize. He once remarked to Varina that he could "give entertainments or administer the Government," but could not do both.[6]

Varina, however, already a veteran of the Washington, D.C., social scene, recognized the public role she and Jefferson had as the Confederacy's first couple. She regularly held levees at their Richmond mansion, welcoming the Confederacy's political and military luminaries. Entertaining allowed the savvy and intelligent Varina opportunities to influence and deflect her husband's critics. Thomas Cooper de Leon called her a "politician and diplomat in one." "She was," he recalled, "naturally a frank, though not a blunt woman, and her bent was to kindliness and charity. Sharp tongue she had, when set that way and the need came to use it; and her wide knowledge of people and things sometimes made that use dangerous to offenders."[7] Visitors noted the Davises' lack of pomp and circumstance and excessive luxuries and the ease with which Varina greeted guests. The president's wife regularly had receptions even when noticeably pregnant. The Davis children commonly attended, adding to the informality. At these social gatherings, Jefferson occasionally let down his veil of formality, revealing surprising charm and good humor, especially toward women. His appearances were usually brief.

Public exposure also meant public attack. Gossip was not merely harmless talk; it revealed jealousies and bitter divisions that ate away at the president's popularity and leadership. Some felt Varina was patronizing, others that she was uncouth and coarsely "western." Critics believed that she wrongly opened the Executive Mansion to just "anyone"; others scorned her as "Queen" and "Empress." Mary Chesnut recalled overhearing "some people" bitterly attacking Mrs. Davis and her close clique of female friends as old and unattractive. A Richmond lady declared that although Varina regularly held social levees, she was "chary of the time she allots us." "If King Solomon were to call with the Queen of Sheba on his arm the fraction of a moment after the closing of her reception," this female observer maintained, "he would not be admitted."[8]

Varina endured these assaults on her and her husband with stubborn fortitude, a biting wit, and worrisome frustration. Although she sought to shield her testy and troubled husband, she, too, could be just as sensitive. At times it was more than she could bear.

Through their public and private trials, Varina was vitally important to her husband. He relied on his wife for her social graces, religious faith, and unquestioning devotion. Plagued by poor health and immense stress, Jefferson found relief and release in his wife and children. Most of the war they managed to stay together. When they were apart, their private correspondence demonstrated their love and devotion.

Jefferson confided his fears and hopes to his wife. In the spring of 1862, he faced a particularly dark time. The death of General Albert Sidney Johnston, losses in the West, the abandonment of Virginia's lower peninsula, and New Orleans, all became too much. For two hours he sat in a chair as Varina read to him, reassuring and comforting him. Varina wanted to ensure that her husband had a spiritual outlet for his overwhelming anxieties. With her encouragement, Jefferson Davis agreed to be baptized on May 6, 1862. The president also voiced his deepest professional frustrations to Varina. Jefferson admitted to his wife that he did not always trust the aggressive Robert E. Lee and confessed his wish to take field command. As he anxiously awaited news from Gettysburg, he wrote Varina, "If I could take one wing [of the Confederate army] and Lee the other, I think we could between us wrest a victory from those people."[9]

Contemporaries and historians credit Varina Davis with having significant influence over her husband's political and military decisions, although they differ in assessing the extent of her power. Davis biographer William C. Davis explains a common perception: "When generals' wives fell out with her, the President seemed to fall out with their husbands. Her favorites seemed to become his." In actuality, there seemed little evidence of this, although Confederate leaders like Judah P. Benjamin certainly increased their favor with the president by cultivating the first lady's good will. She was most assuredly his staunchest defender and, when illness occasionally overwhelmed him, his public spokesperson. Historian Joan Cashin deemphasizes Varina's control of her husband's political and military decisions, stating that although Jefferson openly discussed wartime events with her, she merely played a supporting role. Despite her intelligence and verve, Varina stayed confined within traditional modes of white Southern female behavior: loyal wife, nurturing mother, and pious Christian.[10]

Judith McGuire recounted a story in her published Civil War memoirs that demonstrates Varina's important, but largely conventional, role in the Confederate White House. A father came to the Davises' home one evening, desperately begging the president to procure the exchange of his young son taken prisoner at Williamsburg. Mrs. Davis was in the room listening to the conversation and quietly knitting. When Jefferson explained that he would do what he could, Varina offered a personal reassurance: "She said her husband was a father, and would feel deep sympathy; but if, in the pressure of public business, the subject should pass from his mind, she would certainly remind him." She then invited him to tea. Varina's kind words and gestures, most assuredly feminine ones, impressed the troubled parent and eased his anxiety.[11]

As much as Varina's presence smoothed the Confederate president's rough corners, she also added to his own personal distress. Twice he sent Varina and the children away from Richmond so he did not have to worry about his own family's safety.

Varina championed her husband, but she, too, needed support. Jefferson's preoccupation with war and governing compelled her to seek solace from other women. She had a small group of lady friends with whom she could laugh, confide, and find comfort. Her biographer, Joan Cashin, writes that Varina believed there were "deep differences between the sexes and that intimacy between men and women was difficult, if not impossible; she could share her most private thoughts, her inner self, only with other women."[12] By the fall of 1864, many members of the elite fled the besieged Richmond, leaving Varina without her closest confidants. In November 1864, she wrote Mary Chesnut: "I have suffered a good deal from a sense of isolation since you and the Prestons went away."[13]

Varina's alienation worsened during the Confederacy's final days. In May 1865, she and the children fled south to North Carolina. As she prepared to leave, she wrote a short note to General John Preston describing her depression and fear. Jefferson gave Varina a pistol, advising her that death was preferable to capture. On her arrival in Charlotte, diarist and nurse Kate Cummings noted that "scarcely one, in this whole town brave enough to receive the wife of him who but a short time ago 'all delighted to honor,' but now a homeless burden in the land."[14]

It was a painful change for both Davises. Mary Chesnut wrote, "In Washington when we left it Jeff Davis ranked second to none in intellect—maybe first from the South. . . . Now they rave he is nobody—never was." Regarding Varina, Chesnut wrote, "Oh you would think, to hear them, that he found her yesterday in a Mississippi swamp."[15]

When both Lee and Johnston's armies had surrendered, and Jefferson Davis reluctantly realized his nation was no more, he turned again to his wife. He disclosed to Varina that nothing had happened as he had hoped, and could offer little more than his love now that all else was lost. Varina gently assured him: "It is surely not the fate to which you invited me in brighter days, but you must remember that you did not invite me to a great Hero's home, but to that of a plain farmer. I have shared all your triumphs, been the only beneficiary of them, now I am but claiming the privilege for the first time of being all to you now these pleasures have passed for me."[16]

Varina continued to be Jefferson's "all" during his two-year imprisonment at Fort Monroe. She wrote him constantly and, when allowed, visited. Her presence cheered him and his health improved. When Varina was absent, usually to lobby personally for his release, Jefferson's health worsened.

Varina, too, suffered. Her health was never very good, and the emotional turmoil she experienced as the Confederate president's wife, in addition to the loss of three children, took their toll. The Davis marriage entered a particularly difficult time after the war when Jefferson moved onto an estate owned by another woman. Varina was humiliated. Late in Jefferson's life the two strong-willed individuals seemed to reconcile. She survived her husband by sixteen years. Scholars have praised her memoir of the war as a better, more critical and insightful book than her husband's. Near the end of her life she changed her name to "Varina Jefferson-Davis."

Wives of generals could be equally devoted to their husbands, but, like Varina Davis, the war strained and tried their marriages and forever changed their lives. Few of the wives of Davis's most prominent generals came into personal contact with the president themselves; they either preferred to stay close to their husbands' field command or opted to avoid the Richmond social scene altogether, one of the few places they might interact with Davis. In February 1863, one officer's wife commented: "A sort of court is still kept here— but the wives of our great generals are conspicuous by their absences."[17] Lydia Johnston appeared regularly at Varina Davis's social functions during the first several months of war. Once her husband Joseph went west, she went with him.

It is not surprising that Lydia Johnston was initially a common sight at the Davis levees. She and Varina Davis had been close friends before the war and were habitually spotted in antebellum Washington social circles. They shared a clever wit, intelligence, and faithful allegiance to their husbands. When war began, the women were inseparable; Varina referred fondly to her "dear Lydia." In October 1861, the two women were together in a carriage when it flipped, injuring both. Pregnant Varina suffered some minor cuts and bruises, but Lydia had a fractured arm. In June 1862, after Joseph fell seriously wounded at Seven Pines, Varina allegedly opened the Davis home to the Johnstons while the general convalesced.

The Civil War altered Lydia's and Varina's close relationship. Their husbands were never close, but they had much in common. Both were stubborn and proud men who had difficulty communicating and admitting mistakes. Biographers find fault in both Johnston and Davis for causing the breach that so affected the Confederate war effort, but some have hinted that their wives were also culpable. Richmonder Constance Cary alleged that after President Davis removed Johnston from command in July 1864, "People we met said outspokenly that the Executive's animus against Johnston was based upon a petty feud between their wives, who had been daily associates and friends in the old Washington days." Eventually, Lydia had to choose, and her loyalty to her husband took precedence over that of her old and dear friend.[18]

Lydia Mulligan Sims McLane met Joseph E. Johnston at a Christmas party in 1840. She was eighteen, the daughter of wealthy Marylander Louis McLane, a successful politician and businessman. Joseph was thirty-two, a professional army officer with modest financial prospects. They married in 1845, and Joseph gained money, status, but most importantly a soul mate. The formal and sullen Virginian discovered enduring contentment with his wife. Although they never had children, and Lydia suffered from continual poor health, they enjoyed a durable partnership that lasted four decades.

Lydia, like Varina Davis, knew her husband's weaknesses and she, too, successfully utilized her polished social skills to smooth her husband's rough edges. To most observers, Joseph seemed gruff, self-conscious, quick to anger and take offense, but Lydia appeared consistently good-natured and pleasant. She could be publicly cordial even to her husband's worst enemies, although her private letters show she could match, and even surpass, her husband's rancor. Mary Chesnut, the Davises' loyal champion, found Lydia surprisingly witty, kind, and "of good manners," although the women were not friends.[19]

Others recognized the influence Lydia Johnston had on her husband, including, apparently, Winfield Scott. According to

Lydia, Scott personally pleaded with her to persuade Joseph to stay with the United States Army or keep out of the war entirely. Lydia answered: "This is all very fine—but how is Joe Johnston to live? He has no private fortune. And no profession, or no profession but that of arms."[20]

Lydia also keenly perceived that Joseph Johnston and Jefferson Davis would clash. Even while she was still Varina's friend, Lydia predicted that the Confederate president would destroy her husband. As the war progressed, and the two men's relationship soured, she complained that her Joseph was "the victim of the President's persecution" and "shabbily used" by Davis. When she and Varina became permanently estranged, Lydia formed her own clique of female friends to rival the first lady's. Constance Cary recalled that Lydia "had a court of her own, in later days, rather antagonistic to the ruling power of the Confederate White House, it was said."[21]

Lydia's stay in Richmond lasted as long as her husband served in Virginia. When he went west, she followed. She was not always happy with their location, her health was poor, and she missed her friends and family. In addition, Lydia lost much of the material comforts to which she was accustomed as the daughter of privilege and wealth. In Atlanta, her temporary residence was a small house, "furnished with cots, tables and chairs borrowed from the hospitals, and some few articles lent by kind friends in an effort to make the wife of the commanding General a little more comfortable." She once blamed the "horrid Confederacy" for taking everything "but my virtue." She especially regretted losing her clothes. By the end of the war, Lydia Johnston was a refugee in North Carolina, living in someone else's home. Being close to Joseph was paramount: "I am not sorry to go anywhere," she wrote, "to be a little nearer him."[22]

When they were apart, they, like so many other wartime

couples, wrote extensively to make up for their physical separation. Joseph shared private and professional problems with his wife, thoughts that he rarely revealed to anyone else. In May 1864, the pressures of the war weighed especially heavy on the general's mind. Mired in his infamous fight for Atlanta, Joseph described his frustration and painful regret: "There never was a time when the comfort of your love was more necessary to me for I have never been so little satisfied with myself. . . . I have seen so much beautiful country given up. . . . You can not imagine how distressing it is and the same time humiliating to see the apprehension of the people of a country abandoned to the enemy."[23]

Their correspondence shows Joseph surprisingly more moderate and less bitterly resentful toward Davis than his wife. When Johnston and Davis's "paper war" intensified after Vicksburg, Lydia called one of the president's long and stinging missives something "only a coward or a woman would write" and urged Joseph to resign. She again warned her husband that the president would destroy him. But as she told her friend Charlotte Wigfall, Joseph always had the same simple response: "He could. I don't care. My country." Lydia, however, cared immensely. She was so enraged at both Davises, she "could almost have asked God to punish them." In February 1865, her anger toward the president had not abated: "Never will I forgive a man that has crippled such a true soldier."[24]

Despite these seemingly unchristian sentiments of malevolence and vengeance, Lydia Johnston tried to be a pious wife. Like Varina Davis, she worried about her husband spiritually and sought to ensure his salvation. She wrote letters to General and Bishop Leonidas Polk imploring him to do her a "good deed" by baptizing Joseph. Her husband agreed, and the general took time from his pressing military affairs to undergo the holy Christian ritual of sanctification.[25]

During the war's final desperate days, as Joe Johnston neared the end of an inglorious and controversial wartime experience, Lydia gave in to some festering insecurities. In a letter to her husband, she worried that he would no longer find her physically attractive. "Do you not know," Joseph replied, "that I see your face with my heart, and that it is as lovely to me now—that it give me as much happiness to look at it—as it did when you were eighteen?"[26] In the postwar years their marriage remained firm, and when Lydia finally succumbed to illness in 1887, the old general was lost. He died four years later. Johnston biographer Craig Symonds maintains that during those final years of his life, "He could not bring himself to write or speak her name."[27]

Like Lydia Johnston, Elise Bragg was childless and in poor health. And like Lydia, she was wholly devoted to her controversial husband. Brusque, formal, and a harsh disciplinarian to most, Braxton appeared through Elise's eyes loving, devoted, and kind. They, too, enjoyed a lasting partnership despite the strains of war and defeat.

The North Carolinian army officer fell in love with the intelligent, opinionated, engaging, and rich Eliza Brooks Ellis practically at first sight. Elise, the daughter of a wealthy Louisiana planter, was not entirely sure she shared his ardor. Soon after their marriage in June 1849, she confided to a cousin: "You know I censured Col. Bragg for being too cold and reserved a lover. I little knew the depth and affection that was concealed under such an exterior—he is an ardent and devoted husband and fonder of displaying his affection in a thousand little tendernesses than even myself." Elise and Braxton's marriage was a remarkably strong and equal partnership. Through constant illnesses, extended absences, public attacks, and military failures, Braxton remained wholly devoted to Elise. "I am lost without you, dear wife," Braxton once wrote.[28]

Elise provided respectability and wealth, but she also gave Braxton his greatest happiness. Elise stayed close to Braxton through much of the Civil War. While he commanded in the western theater, her frequent visits markedly changed the formal and stiff atmosphere of his quarters. When he resigned in the wake of his humiliating defeat at Missionary Ridge, he turned to Elise for solace. She soothed his broken spirit and nurtured his exhausted body. When he went to Richmond to serve as Davis's military advisor in 1864, Elise accompanied him. They spent evenings alone, enjoying their privacy and intimacy away from Richmond's active social scene.

When they were apart, the Braggs, like the Johnstons, wrote each other frequently. Their wartime correspondence reveals Braxton fully describing military matters and Elise responding freely with advice and suggestions. At one particularly bleak time during the war, she blasted western Confederate troops: "If our soldiers continue to behave so disgracefully we women had better take the field and send them home to raise chickens."[29] She was not above criticizing her husband, as she did after his failed Kentucky campaign in the fall of 1862. Historians have viewed her opinions with mixed feelings. Bell Wiley praised her "perceptive observations," musing, "If Elise Bragg rather than Braxton should not have worn the general's star."[30] Judith Hallock believes Elise's censure of the War Department in 1863 "hit the mark."[31] Grady McWhiney, however, criticizes her for basing her views on "whim or rumor." He wonders if she biased Braxton against Tennessee troops and counseled him to invade Tennessee from Chattanooga.[32] Whether Elise directly influenced her husband's military decisions, she indirectly influenced his wartime career and performance. Her dangerous bout with typhoid in March 1863 kept Braxton in command longer than President Davis originally intended. When

Joseph Johnston realized how ill Elise was, he declined notifying the embattled Bragg that he must relinquish command and return to Richmond. Certainly Joe Johnston's devotion to his own sickly wife added to his sympathy for Bragg's situation. The delay turned to weeks, and the hapless Bragg remained in command. At other times during the war, observers noted that before he initiated an attack, he made sure she had enough time to escape any potential danger. In 1865, when Fort Fisher, North Carolina, fell to the enemy, Bragg sought to strengthen Confederate morale by keeping his wife nearby.

Elise believed in her husband's military abilities. In March 1862, she criticized "the President's favorite," Albert Sidney Johnston, and "egotist" Pierre G. T. Beauregard as less talented men than her husband. Despite the increased apprehension it would cause her, she wished Davis would appoint Braxton commander of the Confederate western forces. Not for personal reasons, she explained, "but because I truly feel, and the President knows, and *has acknowledged* you are the only one capable of managing volunteers." A few days later she reiterated her views: "Can Mr. Davis still remain impassive and still infatuated with Johnston? I have a great mind to go to him myself and tell him the plain unvarnished truth."[33]

Elise Bragg's defiance lasted throughout the war. When Union troops seized her and Braxton in Washington, Georgia, she verbally blasted her captors with angry epithets while hurriedly tearing up military dispatches. During their travel north, a corporal described Braxton as "pleasant company, but reserved and very much a gentleman." Elise, however, "had nothing to say . . . she had expressed her opinion to the Yanks an hour before."[34]

Elise played the untraditional and notably masculine role

of military counsel, but also the more acceptable and feminine parts as wifely nurturer. Despite her own weak constitution, Elise fretted constantly about Braxton's poor health and depressed spirits. War's brutality troubled her deeply. One contemporary commented that Mrs. Bragg worried "a good deal whenever she hears of the necessity of shooting any of the men, and pleads for them when she can."[35]

Braxton Bragg died suddenly and quietly in 1876. His beloved Elise survived until 1908.

Like Jefferson Davis, Braxton Bragg, and Joe Johnston, Pierre G. T. Beauregard was sensitive to criticism and loath to admit mistakes. His wartime marriage serves as a striking contrast to the marriages of these other leaders. His wife is a shadowy figure in the Civil War narrative.

Little is known about Caroline Deslondes Beauregard except that she, like Pierre, was a member of a prominent Creole Louisiana planter family. Beauregard's biographer T. Harry Williams argues that Pierre never loved Caroline the way he did his first wife, Marie Laure Villere, to whom he was married for nine years. Williams contends that Caroline was either beautiful or "plain and plump," and implies that the marriage's main advantage was in providing Pierre with a politically powerful brother-in-law, Senator John Slidell. The second marriage was childless, and Pierre's military duties kept him absent from their Louisiana home for extended periods of time.[36]

Beauregard's Civil War experience began early with the firing on Fort Sumter in April 1861. He continued to play leading roles in the unfolding drama while his wife Caroline remained out of the spotlight. Although he allegedly wrote her regularly, he never visited. Caroline's health failed, and when New Orleans fell to the Union in 1862, she stayed behind enemy lines.

Meanwhile P. G. T. Beauregard launched his controversial Civil War career far from his wife. Rumors of excessive entertaining and infidelity began to swirl. Although his own health was poor, he had a penchant for fine champagne and festive balls. There was a constant stream of visitors at his headquarters, especially young women. He also maintained correspondence with a number of female admirers, including the novelist Augusta Evans, with whom he seemed especially close. In one letter to a male friend, Beauregard admitted that Evans was a woman whom "it would not do for me to see too often, for I might forget 'home and country' in their hour of need and distress."[37]

All the time Beauregard enjoyed his lady fans, his wife remained alone and ill in occupied New Orleans. At one point Union General Benjamin "Beast" Butler offered Beauregard a pass through the lines to visit his sick wife. Beauregard apparently took no notice of the invitation and told no one of the offer.

Mary Chesnut provided some insight into the Beauregard marriage. She wrote in her diary on May 29, 1862: "Beauregard's wife is still in New Orleans and he gnashes his teeth. She will not leave a doctor who (only one in the world) understands her case." Beauregard, a man who brooded and complained, and felt wildly unappreciated by the Confederacy, seemed to behave similarly in his marriage. Davis and Johnston also had tender egos, but their wives were there to soothe and make them feel whole again. Caroline's stubborn defiance, however, seemed to exacerbate her husband's professional frustrations. "He never had much brains—eh?" Chesnut wrote, "And now he is losing his heart. Wife won't come away from New Orleans. But they say she is dead, poor thing—second wife too."[38]

In March 1864, Caroline did die. In a letter to his wife's

sister, Pierre wrote: "My Poor Caroline must have often asked herself on her bed of pain if she would ever see me again, and, more than once in her agony, her wandering thoughts must have directed themselves toward these battle lines in order to bid me an eternal good-bye. I well know that her beautiful soul, her generous and patriotic heart preferred the salvation of the country to the joy of seeing me."[39]

Beauregard later described himself in the third person quietly mourning his wife: "He had borne his affliction not only like a Christian but with all the fortitude of a soldier, none but his own military family being able to detect any sign of grief in the countenance of the bereaved husband."[40]

Rumors quickly spread that Beauregard's desertion and neglect contributed to her death. A Northern-based newspaper in New Orleans was especially virulent in attacking the general for not just "plotting for the destruction of his country, but deserting his invalid wife for years together, and leaving her dependent upon others for those acts of kindness and support that should be given by a husband." The *Richmond Enquirer* reprimanded the Northern press for its poor taste, but mainly defended Caroline as innocent and virtuous and too weak to have left the city. The paper explained: "The devotion of this lady to her husband, her love for him, was such that she would not allow her family to communicate to him her critical position."[41] Beauregard, a man constantly conscious of his public image, was outraged. He angrily fought the accusations, emphasizing his patriotism and her "hallowed grave." He wanted her headstone to read: "The Country comes before me."[42]

Thousands attended Caroline's funeral, including a large number of women. Confederate newspapers heralded her as the model silent, suffering, general's wife. "Mrs. Beauregard's devotion to her husband could not be exceeded," a Richmond paper declared. "She shared his joys and sorrows in her every thought." The paper predicted: "When the history of this war is written, instances of as remarkable virtue, fortitude and devotion in woman will be illustrated as any that have come to posterity in the story of the Grecian States."[43]

After the war, John Esten Cooke asked Beauregard if he could include Caroline's story in a book called *Heroic Women of the South*. Beauregard rejected the request, explaining that he would accept the honor "with pleasure if the one I love so dearly had done more than pray and suffer in silence for the success of our sacred cause." Instead, he felt that "heroic women" who "devoted their time and labor to assisting and taking care of the sick and wounded—besides encouraging the fainthearted," were more worthy of inclusion.[44]

We have a somewhat similar story with Robert E. Lee and his wife, Mary Custis. Like Beauregard, he seemed to be happiest when away from his wife. He talked of his "military family" in the field, and even when within a few miles of her residence, Lee repeatedly pleaded duty kept him away. His most recent biographer, Emory Thomas, maintains that Robert always felt frustration with the sickly and spoiled Mary, the adopted granddaughter of George Washington.

Robert married Mary in 1831, a match that ensured him wealth, property, and reaffirmed his family name, tarnished by his once heroic, but later hapless, father. Mary was allegedly not very attractive or engaging—a dramatic contrast to her handsome and dashing army husband. Extended separations became a consistent factor in their marriage. His army assignments, and her poor health and repeated pregnancies, regularly kept them apart. The Civil War did little to change the basic dynamics of the Lee marriage.

Although her husband would become one of the Confederacy's greatest heroes, war brought many difficult changes to his wife. In 1861 she was uprooted from her childhood home at Arlington and made one of the South's many refugees. She felt outraged and humiliated, but her husband exhorted her to accept the loss as God's will. Julia Gardner Tyler met Robert Lee in June 1861, and heard him describe Mary's escape from northern Virginia, her illness, and trials. "He spoke," Tyler noted, "very calmly and indifferently of the desecration of his home at Arlington and the flight of his invalid wife."[45]

By the time the war began, Mary had given birth to seven children, and her health was terrible. Mary Chesnut described Lee's wife as "martyr to Rheumatism" who "rolls around in a chair. She can't walk." Mary Lee realized her pitiful state and lamented: "Poor lame mother—I am useless to my children."[46]

Mary, like many Confederate women, desperately wanted to feel useful. To contribute to the war effort, and no doubt to gain some attention from General Lee, Mary embarked on a nearly obsessive knitting campaign. Indeed, much of the Lees's wartime relationship revolved around her knitting and his counting socks and mitts. This mundane exchange seemed to allow the invalid Mary to reach out to her husband and his beloved army, an army to which Robert gave much more of his energy, affection, and love than to his wife.

During the first several months of war, while Robert was in Richmond, Mary scrambled to avoid capture in and around northern Virginia. She finally settled in Richmond in June 1862, not having seen her husband for over a year. Soon after her arrival in the city, Robert wrote, "I am strongly tempted to go in to see you." He explained: "My constant duties alone prevent, & preparations for the anticipated movement of troops will detain me." For the next four years, Robert used the same excuse, rarely seeing his wife and daughters although they were always relatively close to his command.[47]

Mary and Robert corresponded regularly and, like other generals, Robert mixed personal and professional matters in his letters. He worried about her health and safety in the Confederate capital and assured her that he wished he could see her. His increasingly important military responsibilities, he told her, precluded him from writing more often or visiting her. "You forget," he wrote in March 1863, "how much writing, talking and thinking I have to do, when you complain of the interval between my letters. You lose sight also of the letters you receive." Two months later he chided: "I see you are relapsing into your old error, supposing that I have a superabundance of time and have only my pleasures to attend to." Robert also divulged to his wife his military hopes and frustrations, occasionally revealing more to her than he did in his official reports to Richmond. Frequently his letters to his wife echoed the same language and sentiments as those he sent to the president or the War Department. In the aftermath of his defeat at Gettysburg, for example, Robert stated: "The army has laboured hard, endured much and behaved nobly. It has accomplished all that could have been reasonably expected. It ought not have been expected to have performed impossibilities or to have fulfilled the anticipations of the thoughtless and unreasonable." Five days later his letter to Davis had a similar ring, although he took all the blame for the defeat.[48]

Emory Thomas argues that Lee preferred the company of women to men, although not necessarily the company of his ailing wife. Robert did carry on a number of flirtatious relationships with young women throughout his married life, and during the war he continued correspondence with several ladies. The vivacious and outgoing Constance Cary once asked Mary Chesnut if "God [was] to take poor cousin Mary

Lee—she suffers so—wouldn't these Richmond women campaign for Cousin Robert?" Cary added, "In the meantime Cousin Robert holds all admiring females at arm's length."[49]

The Lees were notably absent from Richmond's social scene. Robert remained at the front and Mary's illness confined her at home. The death of their daughter Annie also dissuaded the Lees from public entertaining. Some contemporaries believed that Mary disapproved of parties, balls, and dinners during wartime: "Mrs. Lee felt a sense of impropriety in the suggestion that the wife and daughters of the commanding general of half starved armies himself sleeping always in a tent and living on ascetic fare, should take the lead in any entertainments of a social sort." Mary's knitting became well known and was a striking contrast to other elite ladies's activities. A Confederate officer's wife wrote in 1863: "Mrs. Lee is never seen at receptions. She and her daughters spend their time knitting and sewing for the soldiers, just as her great-grandmother, Martha Washington, did in '76 and General Lee writes that these things are needed." While Varina Davis and other prominent politician's wives held parties and receptions, Mary Lee preferred quiet industry.[50]

One Richmond female observer claimed in her postwar recollections that besides the knitting, bandage making, and other industrious activity that Mary Lee conducted, she also offered a place for people, especially women, to come and find a sympathetic ear. Sally Nelson Robins recalled the Lees' home being a "common meeting place" where "people came to talk of victory or sorrow; they could stay here if they had nowhere else to go; they gathered here to work, the disheartened came for comfort from the tender, loving wife of the commander in chief. Mourning mothers came to her in their agony; wives of heroes brought their joy over recent success; friends came without ceremony." The Richmond house

Mary Lee rented became a sort of mecca for the Confederate faithful.[51]

Jefferson Davis commended Confederate women for their patriotic zeal, and fortitude. A wartime poem similarly extolled Southern ladies:

> Up and down, through the wards, where the fever
> Stalks noisome, and gaunt and impure,
> You must go, with your steadfast endeavor
> To comfort, to counsel, to cure!
> But strength will be given to you
> To do for these dear ones what woman
> Alone in her pity can do.[52]

Wives of generals were not always heroic; like the men they married, they were complex individuals with strengths and weaknesses. They did not always endure the war and its deprivations bravely without complaint. But they, like their famous husbands, found their lives forever changed by these horrific four years. Civil War catapulted Jefferson Davis, Joseph Johnston, Braxton Bragg, P. G. T. Beauregard, and Robert E. Lee into new positions of leadership, but it also brought daunting challenges and responsibilities. Their wives shared in their successes and defeats, but also experienced prolonged absences and intensive public scrutiny. Sometimes it was too much to bear, and they became angry and desperate. Varina Davis, Lydia Johnston, and Elise Bragg publicly and unashamedly championed their husbands and stayed close to their men throughout the conflict. Caroline Beauregard and Mary Lee, hindered by ill health, struggled to regain their soldier-husband's attention, but failed. Robert Lee and P. G. T. Beauregard became consumed by war, professional ambitions, and the attentions of younger women. They left their suffering wives behind.

These women's wartime stories illustrate both traditional and untraditional modes of female behavior. In the midst of war, they tried to be pious, loving, and supportive helpmates, but they were often savvy and outspoken military advisors. Varina Davis, Lydia Johnston, and Elise Bragg gave their husbands personal and professional guidance and reassurance; Mary Lee provided Robert unquestioning stability and many well-knit socks. When the war ended, and these men faced humiliating and emasculating defeat, their wives stood faithfully by to try and make them feel whole again.

7

The Image of Jefferson Davis as Commander in Chief

HAROLD HOLZER

On the eve of the first battle of the Civil War, the wife of a Confederate general worried that President Jefferson Davis seemed "greedy for military fame." She took pains to record the concern in her diary. The journal was not published for another forty-four years, and, revealingly, when it finally appeared, the critical comment was expunged. By then, Davis had lost a war but gained an enduring military image. Powerful enough to inhibit criticism, and satisfying enough to please even the "greediest" of vainglorious leaders, that image owed much to the medium of popular prints.[1]

Americans living in today's millennium-eve, image-saturated, Internet-downloaded culture long ago lost the taste for stiff, static portraits of elected leaders and battlefield heroes. We no longer decorate our homes with such pictures. We no longer display them to signify our patriotism or politics. Originally published in large format to dominate the family parlor in places of honor above the hearthstone, the surviving nineteenth-century pictures have been relegated now to public and private collections, where they are often considered the stepchildren of more "important" relics of the period. Such prints are usually reproduced today—if they are reproduced at all—as tiny illustrations in history books, billboards reduced to little more pictorial impact than postage stamps.

It is almost impossible now to appreciate how such prints once dominated family homes. After all, most of us no longer have hearths, and parlors have been replaced by family rooms or dens whose principal visual decoration is the TV set: why settle for a single picture when one has a remote control and eighty channels to zap? The print has gone the way of the antimacassar and the whatnot, lost in the realm of misty folklore. It is easy to forget what such graphics once meant to their proud owners.

As a case in point, most modern Americans confronting the signature image of the 1997 Civil War Institute session would probably fail to comprehend the composition or even recognize the characters. It is familiar only to students of the Civil War. And even we have taken it for granted for too long. A close look at the two-by-three-foot original will reveal a surprisingly rich image that might well qualify as the signature image of the brief, golden age of Confederate printmaking.

The untitled lithograph presents the high military command of the Confederate States of America posing in impressive, if unlikely, unity. Here, together in art as they never were in life or camp, are Robert E. Lee, "Stonewall" Jackson, Joseph E. Johnston, P. G. T. Beauregard, and a host of other great chieftains. And significantly, occupying the place of honor in the central space of the composition, is the Confederacy's commander in chief, Jefferson Davis.

True, the image has achieved some ubiquity, serving to illustrate countless modern magazines and history books. But more often than not, it is identified only as a wartime picture of Davis and his commanders. In fact, it is much more. This is not a mere illustration, but an emblematic Confederate image, and as such its original meanings are well worth recalling. The longtime absence of analysis is attributable at least in part to the fact that the original lithograph bears no specific copyright date. How can we know for certain what it was meant to convey if we do not know when it was published? Fortunately, the picture does bear clues about its origins. A close look reveals troops marching in the distance. Background figures study war maps, or keep watch on distant enemies through a telescope. From these incidental scenes we may infer that the picture was created after the real fighting of the Civil War began. From the original national flag flying at the left, we may also conclude safely that the war had begun only recently. That sense is reinforced by the print's cast of characters, which includes such soon-to-be forgotten early war heroes as George N. Hollins and Ben McCulloch. But the strongest arguments for the print's early appearance are the old-army blue of the "Confederate" uniforms worn by the principal subjects as well as the portraits themselves— most of which became outdated as soon as formerly clean-shaven generals began growing whiskers on campaign. Finally, since the lithograph's caption does reveal that it was published in both Paris and New York, it is reasonable to conclude that the print of Davis and his generals was issued before the blockade inhibited imports and before the irrevocability of disunion closed Southern markets to Northern publishers.

By assigning the print the date of early fall, 1861, its original message becomes clearer. Undoubtedly, it was intended not just to portray current celebrities or decorate domestic wall space, but to evoke national pride in a new nation's new military leaders, principally its commander in chief, whose dominance is suggested by his central position in the print. Here was an image designed to help reassure an infant state that its fight for independence was in capable hands. It may well have succeeded.

But its triumph as an early icon of the Confederacy may be attributable in part to its most unrealistic and mystifying feature, one that is seldom acknowledged, much less explained, in its current uses: the fact that it portrays Jefferson Davis in full military regalia, complete with cape, sword, epaulets, and braid, a commander in chief in literal as well as symbolic command. It was the first of many.

There is no evidence in the entire literature of the Civil War to suggest that Davis ever wore such attire as Confederate president. But that only makes more profound what the costume suggests about Civil War printmaking, the Southern audience for the graphic arts, and the image of Jefferson Davis himself. This lithograph may represent the first manifestation of a powerful and enduring icon: that of Jefferson Davis as a wholly military president, personally directing his generals and his armies, assuming full and courageous responsibility for defending secession, slavery, and the Southern way of life. This is more than a picture; it is a touchstone.

Whether Davis was qualified to assume active military command—and whether, indeed, he truly exercised such prerogatives—are subjects that have been debated by historians for generations. What has seldom been examined—and deserves more active consideration—is the *image* of Davis as commander in chief: its rise, its fall, and its rise again. In an age in which pictures were precious and their display signified the deepest beliefs of their owners, such images influenced the formation of public opinion. Today they can still tell us much, not only about their publishers and their subjects, but their patrons as well.

Ironically, the earliest images of the Confederate president, like the print of Davis and his generals, were Northern in origin. This is hardly surprising, since American printmaking by 1860 was largely centralized in the major publishing centers of the North: New York, Boston, Philadelphia, Chicago, and Cincinnati. Fortunately for Southern print-buyers, Northern-based printmakers were motivated by profit, not politics. Davis was newsworthy, and newsworthy portraiture made money. An early indication of this wholly commercial focus could be glimpsed in the edition of *Frank Leslie's Illustrated Newspaper* dated just five days after Abraham Lincoln took his oath of office as President of the United States.

Under the page-one headline, "Our first Portrait of the President," the editors proudly announced its newest Lincoln woodcut, boasting: "Great labor and care have been bestowed upon its preparation, and we feel assured that as . . . a life-like portraiture [sic] of the man who has been chosen to fill the highest office in the gift of the people at a time of great trouble and difficulty, it will be conceded by all to be unequaled in excellence and truthfulness." Yet the engraving that appeared beneath those words showed not Abraham Lincoln but Jefferson Davis, "first president of the new Southern Confederacy." The highly touted engraving of Lincoln was inexplicably relegated to the centerfold. Whether this amounted to an embarrassing publishing gaffe or constituted proof that Davis's ascent fascinated more Northerners at the time than Lincoln's, this is how the new Confederate president was introduced in the graphic arts.

For as long as they were able to do so without appearing unpatriotic, Northern publishers of separate-sheet display prints echoed *Leslie's* acknowledgment of Davis's new prominence. The New York lithographers Jones & Clark, for example, quickly adapted the same photographic model as *Leslie's* had consulted for a handsome 1861 portrait, presenting the potential enemy of the Union in an entirely sympathetic manner—no doubt casting a mercantile eye toward Southern audiences who still enjoyed access to Northern products.

Such considerations clearly also mattered to the anonymous artist who crafted the group portrait of Davis and his generals. But that print was different. It did not present Davis in benign, newsworthy portraiture, but as a man of war—a rallying symbol to one section of the country and a genuine threat to the other. The notion that Davis was not only a political, but a military, leader represented a claim that could hardly be made with equal conviction by those depicting the new, quintessentially civilian president of the United States.

Other evidence abounded. Printmaker C. P. May offered *The Officers of the Confederate States Army & Navy*, which placed a Davis portrait among those of his uniformed military leaders, with nothing in either its caption or design specifically to justify his inclusion. And New York photographer Charles H. Fredericks achieved the same intriguing ambiguity with his composite *carte-de-visite* for family albums, *Fifty One Portraits of the Confederate Army & Navy*, showing Davis in the midst of an assembly of thirty-seven military officers and only fourteen fellow civilians (among whom were quasimilitary figures like the captured Confederate emissaries John Mason and John Slidell, and Roger A. Pryor, who was believed to have fired the first shot on Fort Sumter). Davis's civilian patina was quickly vanishing, a development that both he and his admirers probably welcomed. After all, when William L. Yancey delivered his memorable introduction of the new Confederate president—declaring that "the man and the hour have met"—he went on, in a nearly forgotten coda, to enlarge on his enthusiasm by pointing out that Davis was not only a "statesman" and a "patriot," but, crucially, a "soldier."[2]

The new commander in chief had come by his military reputation honestly—and, many agreed, heroically. First came a West Point education. Richmond matron Constance Cary Harrison probably spoke for an entire generation of Southerners when she later recalled: "At the time we knew him, everything in his appearance and manner was suggestive of such training." Davis's reputation owed as much to action as to appearance. He fought in the Black Hawk War, the same conflict in which his Union counterpart, Abraham Lincoln, experienced, in his own description, only "bloody struggles with the musquitoes." And Davis went on to glory in Mexico, as colonel of the First Mississippi Rifles at Monterey and Buena Vista. There, a young fellow officer named Jubal Early was first "struck with his soldierly bearing." Mrs. Harrison noticed the very same "soldierly bearing" in 1861 Richmond, adding that the supposedly civilian chief magistrate "was always clad in Confederate gray" that resembled a uniform, and rode horseback "with a martial aspect." Little had changed since Mexico.[3]

Davis's long service record was enough to convince many Southerners—including Davis himself—that his proper place in a war for independence was in military, not civil, command. For one thing, as historian Ludwell Johnson has observed, Davis appeared to have "believed he was" nothing less than "a military genius." Notified that he had been chosen president of the new Confederacy, Davis's first reaction was reportedly the wistful comment: "I would love to head the army." By preference, he maintained, "I was a soldier," insisting: "I thought myself better adapted to command in the field." Davis seems to have accepted the presidency still believing that the honor was only "temporary" and that he would soon be able to resign to take command of Mississippi troops. An admirer from Georgia explained: "He realized . . . that a military life would be far better for him and more according to his own desires."[4]

Some thought him capable of even broader military responsibility. A full two months after his inauguration, the fiery secessionist Edmund Ruffin remained convinced that Davis should "assume military command" of the entire army, "for the salvation of our cause." Varina Davis excitedly reported around the same time: "There is a good deal of talk here of his going to Richmond as commander of the forces," adding, "I hope it may be done." As historian Stephen Woodworth has put it, "The expectation and confidence of the South in its new president's military leadership could not have been more obvious."[5]

Newspapers of the day fueled the growing enthusiasm for the military president. To the Richmond *Dispatch*, Davis seemed "a tower of strength with the iron will . . . of Andrew Jackson," another war hero who became a president. In the worried words of the *Cleveland Plain Dealer*, he loomed to Northerners as a "genuine son of Mars," the Roman god of war. Many Southerners came quickly to see him as the direct descendant of at least a demigod. It would not be lost on citizens of the Confederacy that as a former military commander elected the first president of a new country battling for its independence, Davis represented the second coming of the father of his country. As the Richmond *Enquirer* put it, "The mantle of Washington falls gracefully on his shoulders."[6]

This was too evocative a sentiment for picture-makers to ignore, and it is likely that they not only reflected but helped build it. Engravings and lithographs endorsed the growing sense that in Davis's Washingtonian ascent history was repeating itself. Richmond printmakers Hoyer & Ludwig produced one print pointedly captioned, *Jefferson Davis, First President of the Confederate States of America*. And New Orleans publisher A. E. Blackmar offered a Davis portrait as the cover illustration on sheet music for a celebratory new march evocatively entitled *Our First President Quickstep*. As Davis hastened to the new Confederate capital of Richmond, one newspaper reported that his imminent arrival had understandably "infused a martial feeling in our people that knows no bounds."[7]

The enthusiasm was such that General Leonidas Polk remained convinced up to a month before the Battle of Bull Run that "Davis will take the field in person when the movement is to be made." Polk would be proven right, if not in reality, at least in popular prints. To paraphrase William L. Yancey, the man and his iconographical hour met in July 1861. Just as news reached the Confederate capital that a great fight was about to take place near Manassas, Davis left Richmond for the front. Wrote the excited Confederate war clerk John B. Jones: "I always thought he would avail himself of the prerogative as commander-in-chief, and direct in person the most important operations in the field. I . . . believe he will gain great glory in this first mighty conflict."[8]

Three days later, the Confederate president's wife proudly announced: "A great battle has been fought—Jeff Davis led the center, Joe Johnston the right wing, Beauregard the left wing of the army." A Southern newspaper echoed her view, lauding Davis as "our noble warrior president."[9]

Printmakers provided the visual accompaniment to this burgeoning legend: pictures that could be proudly displayed in patriotic homes to attest to the commander in chief's heroism. Perhaps with earlier prints of Washington as an equestrian hero much in mind, Richmond's Hoyer & Ludwig issued *President Jefferson Davis Arriving in the Field of Battle at Bull's Run*. Portraying Davis on horseback and in full uniform with epaulets, it conveyed the unmistakable impression that the commander in chief had been personally responsible for the Confederacy's first great military triumph.

In his friendly postwar biography, Frank H. Alfriend left no doubt that Davis's "presence on the field [at Manassas] was the inspiration of unbounded enthusiasm among the troops, to whom his name and bearing were the symbols of victory." Alfriend insisted: "While the struggle was still in progress, it was his privilege to witness the flight, in utter confusion and dismay, of the Federal forces." By this time, however, the myth of Davis's supposedly pivotal arrival at Manassas had been completely deflated. His admirers learned within weeks that Davis got to the scene after the fighting was almost over and was actually told at first that his army had been whipped. Of course, he wore no uniform that day. Commandeering a horse, he rode out to the field, where he first learned that Union, not Confederate, forces had been routed. Davis himself would later claim, quite carefully, only that during his ride he observed "here a musket, there a cartridge-box, there a blanket or overcoat," the authentic marks of sudden retreat.[10]

That a more heroic version of his participation at first prevailed—and for a time persisted—is evident in Northern-made graphics as well. One comic print by an unknown lithographer, *The Battle of Bull's Run*, was designed principally to lampoon the hapless Union forces who had fled in retreat. But visible in the distance were the commanders of the Confederate triumph, all on horseback, observing, and presumably directing, the victory, as modern generals were required to do from afar on vast fields of action. Close inspection of these vignettes reveals not only Johnston and Beauregard in the saddle, but also the man whom Varina Davis claimed led the center wing of the army: her husband. The caption clearly identified the command sites as: "Beauregard's Headquarter [sic]," "Johnston's Headquarter," and "Jeff. Davis Headquarter."

Eventually, even the stubbornly loyal war clerk John B. Jones admitted that "the battle had been won, and the enemy were flying from the field before the president had appeared." Jones conceded further that the confusion was caused, at least in part, by a dispatch from the front sent by Davis himself. From this, Jones "conceived the idea that he . . . had directed the principal operations in the field." In short, the commander in chief had directly influenced the advancement of his martial image—an image, the surviving pictorial evidence suggests, that was immediately accepted North as well as South and perhaps in Europe. Years would pass before a resentful General Johnston complained that "in fact, the fighting had ceased before" Davis ever reached the troops. "When the President wrote," Johnston icily suggested, "he had forgotten." Another eyewitness, Captain John Imboden, recalled seeing "a gentleman on horseback, who was lifting his hat to everyone he met." Unknowingly testifying to the impact of the earliest Davis pictures, Imboden recalled: "From the likeness [sic] I had seen of President Jefferson Davis, I instantly recognized him." Reputation and recognition conveniently converged for Davis at Bull Run, leaving quite a few others besides Imboden dutifully impressed. Printmakers gave credit to Davis for leading a battle he arrived too late even to witness. The impact of their work was nearly indelible.[11]

Several years later, when artist W. B. Cox concocted his own version of *The Heroes of Manassas*, Davis remained highly visible, shown riding alongside Beauregard, Jackson, and Johnston. In Cox's picture, the battle was still raging, exemplified by the fuse of a Union bomb burning menacingly nearby. This suggested that like his commanders, the commander in chief had subjected himself to genuine physical danger at Bull Run. True, the 1863 painting was never adapted by a Confederate engraver or lithographer; the Southern printmaking industry was by then fading, and Northern printmakers were no longer creating heroic portraits of the Confederate enemy. The painting was eventually copied by a Lynchburg, Virginia, photographer. In both painting and mass-produced photo, the Confederate gray worn by president and generals seems almost indistinguishable. From the

Cox picture alone, it would be difficult for any viewer to tell whether Davis was in uniform or in mufti at Bull Run. But a viewer would certainly infer that he was very much part of the action. Davis's military image was only growing stronger. The increasing vitality of that image was precisely what a nation, trying to be born in war, needed.

And so, to Confederates, Davis remained a symbol of early battlefield glory, his image, in a typical portrait print, plausibly perched atop cannons, flags, and ammunition to suggest a confluence of civil and military power. In Europe, as demonstrated as early as May 1861, in a caricature of *The American Gladiators* for London *Punch*, Davis was viewed as an identifiable symbol of Confederate military authority even before Lincoln earned similar recognition: the *Punch* woodcut featured a recognizable portrait of Davis, but pictured his Union counterpart as a generic, decidedly un-Lincolnesque gladiator. By the time *Punch* showed the two presidents again in the 1863 caricature, *The Great Cannon Game*, their struggle reduced to a metaphorical billiard match, Lincoln had come into his own as a comic, if not terribly commanding figure. Even so, his character was made to sourly acknowledge Confederate military superiority by declaring of Davis: "Damn'd if he ain't scored again."

To Union print patrons, Davis graduated from curiosity to dangerous foe. Boston lithographer Louis Prang portrayed him in 1862 in another military group portrait, but now all the characters were bluntly identified in the title as *Enemies of Our Union*. The special threat that Davis now seemed to pose to the North was reflected in such prints as *The Soldier's Song—Unionism vs. Copperheadism*. The image left no doubt but that the Confederate leader, portrayed as a snake coiled around a southern palmetto tree, was a formidable enough foe to require armed soldiers, soaring eagles, and loaded cannon to dislodge him, and to confront the Copperheads the print claimed he inspired. As an impassioned verse beneath the image charged, Davis and his supporters now seemed

> Fit associates for arch-traitors—
> Lucifer, and Iscariot old,
> Arnold, who sold his native land—
> Betrayed his cause for British gold!

To several printmakers, the dangerous Davis operated under the influence of Satan himself. In the 1862 lithograph, *The Emblem of the Free*, lithographer Benjamin H. Day showed a sleeping Davis dreaming of the patriots of Valley Forge, clutching the flag he had dishonored while being implored to remember the Revolutionary martyrs by the ghost of George Washington, viewed now as his critic, not his predecessor. Unmoved, Davis will succumb to the temptations of a winged Lucifer. Printmaker Louis Hough similarly depicted Davis preparing to greet his "faithful ally," the Devil, but accoutered him in a saber and spurs to discredit (but thereby acknowledge) his military image.

It is surely proof of Davis's durable image as a military figure—particularly, by this time, in the embattled North—that an 1863 lithograph by Oliver E. Woods of Philadelphia, *The Pending Conflict*, represented the Union merely as an anonymous soldier under frontal attack from the Rebels and subject to sniping at the rear by a copperhead snake. He resembles no Union celebrity of the day. Representing the Confederacy, on the other hand, was a clearly identifiable Davis—flatteringly dressed in full military regalia. The appearance of such a print two years into the Civil War suggests that, for a surprisingly long time, the North failed to strip Jefferson Davis of his potent image as military figure.

Even when assailing him, Northern printmakers seemed invariably to concede his military credentials. Currier & Ives's *Breaking That "Backbone,"* for example, was designed to suggest new hope for the Union cause, but suggested too that only when Lincoln armed himself with the potential military impact of the Emancipation Proclamation did he begin posing a genuine threat to Davis and the impervious monster of secession. An inventive "trick" print of 1861 confronted Davis's martial reputation with artistic ingenuity and sharp wit, but in so doing implicitly confirmed how seriously Davis was then regarded as a military threat—for why else parody him? Examined right-side-up, the print depicted *Jeff Davis Going to War*, dressed in hilariously excessive armor. But upside-down, the print presented the opposite image. "Jeff. Subdued" was a haggard army mule about whom an accompanying verse declared:

> . . . When he hears the cannon roar,
> And views the dying in his gore,
> His courage fails and then, alas!
> He homeward travels like an ass

Only after 1863 did Davis finally stop hearing "the cannon roar" in Northern-made period prints. With the bloody conflict continuing to extract unprecedented sacrifice, Davis was finally assigned less glory and more blame. The comic but brutal *Jeff Davis on His Own Platform* may have been the first print to show him going to the gallows for treason. It would not be the last. And even in this print he was shown wearing the kind of Phrygian cap that Alexander the Great had worn. In both victory, as the representative military man, and in defeat, portrayed as a traitor at his hanging, Davis from the beginning of the war to its end had come to symbolize the Confederacy itself.

There would be no pro-Davis response from what was left of the Confederate printmaking industry that had introduced Davis's military image in the first place. Chronic shortages in talent and supplies eventually strangled Confederate

Printmaker unknown, *[Jefferson Davis and His Generals]*, lithograph
published by Goupil & Co., Paris, and Michael Knoedler, New York,
ca. 1861. (Portrait File. Miriam and Ira D. Wallach Division of Art,
Prints and Photographs. The New York Public Library, Astor, Lenox,
and Tilden Foundations)

Printmaker unknown, *President Davis, First President of the New Southern Confederacy*, woodcut engraving on cover of *Frank Leslie's Illustrated Newspaper*, March 9, 1861. (Fort Wayne, Indiana, Lincoln Library and Museum)

(Below) C. P. May, *The Officers of the C.S. Army & Navy*, composite photographs issued as a lithograph, New York, ca. 1861. (Washington, D.C., Library of Congress)

Hoyer & Ludwig, after
J. Wissler, *Jefferson Davis, First
President of the Confederate
States of America*, lithograph
published by Tucker & Perkins
& Co., Augusta, Georgia,
1861. (Richmond, Virginia,
Eleanor S. Brockenbrough
Library, The Museum of
the Confederacy)

(Below) A. E. Blackmar &
Bro., *Our First President
Quickstep*, illustrated sheet-
music cover, New Orleans, ca.
1861. (University of Virginia)

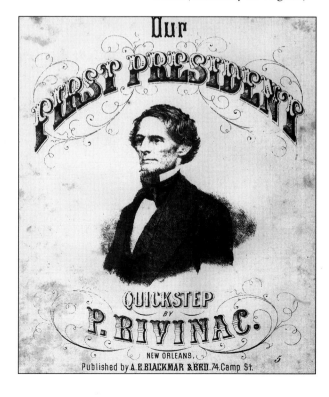

Printmaker unknown, *The Battle of Bull's Run*, detail (above) of lithograph (below), ca. 1861. (Washington, D.C., Library of Congress)

W. B. Cox, *The Heroes of Manassas*, oil on canvas, ca. 1863–1865. (West Point Museum, U. S. Military Academy)

L. Prang, *Enemies of Our Union*, lithograph, Boston, 1862. (Washington, D.C., Library of Congress)

Smith & Swinney, *The Soldier's Song—Unionism vs. Copperheadism!*,
lithograph with verse caption, Cincinnati, 1864. (Washington, D.C.,
Library of Congress)

(Opposite, above) B[enjamin H.]. Day [Jr.], *The Emblem of the Free*,
lithograph published by Samuel Canty, New York, ca. 1862. (Washington, D.C., Library of Congress) *(Opposite, below)* L. Hough or Haugg,
*The Southern Confederacy a Fact!! Acknowledged by a Mighty Prince
and Faithful Ally*, lithograph, Philadelphia, 1861. (Washington, D.C.,
Library of Congress)

THE EMBLEM OF THE FREE.

WITH ORIGINAL MUSIC.

The Traitor's Dream, by Samuel Canty.

Mr MOB LAW   Sec TOOMBS.   JEFF. DAVIS.   Vice Prest STEPHENS.   THE PRINCE TO HIS CABINET:
Chief Justice.   Genl BEAUREGARD.   Truly! Fit representatives of our Realm.

THE SOUTHERN CONFEDERACY A FACT !!!

ACKNOWLEDGED BY A MIGHTY PRINCE AND FAITHFUL ALLY.

J Hannis Publ. 600 Chestnut Str Philada 3d Story

Oliver Evans Woods, *The Pending Conflict*, lithograph, Philadelphia, 1863. (Washington, D.C., Library of Congress)

(Below) B[enjamin H] Day [Jr.], *Breaking That "Backbone,"* lithograph, published by Currier, & Ives, New York, ca. 1862–63. (Washington, D.C., Library of Congress)

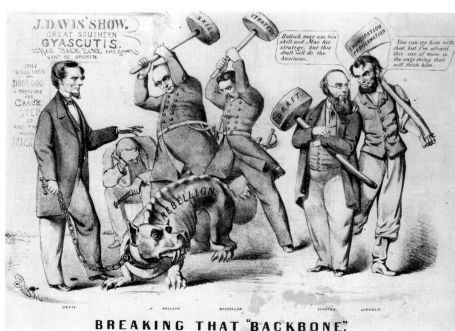

Jeff. Davis going to War.

AN
Jeff. returning from War

E. Rogers, *Jeff. Davis going to War./Jeff. returning from War
An [Ass].* Lithograph, Philadelphia, 1861. (Washington, D.C.,
Library of Congress)

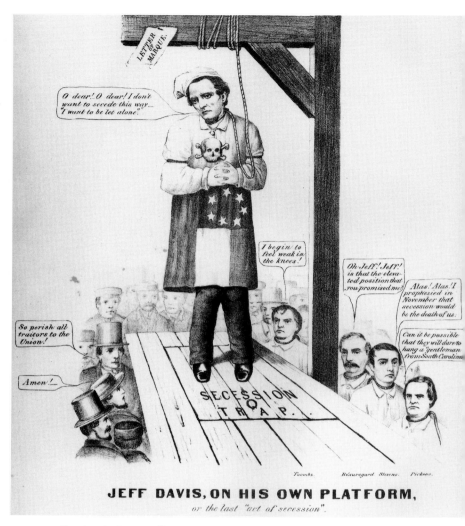

JEFF DAVIS, ON HIS OWN PLATFORM,
or the last "act of secession".

Currier & Ives, *Jeff Davis on His Own Platform, or the last "act of secession,"* lithograph, New York, ca. 1861–62. (Washington, D.C., Library of Congress)

(Opposite, above) Currier & Ives, *"Your Plan and Mine,"* lithograph, New York, 1864. (Washington, D.C., Library of Congress) *(Opposite, below)* Joseph E. Baker, *Jeff's Last Shift*, lithograph, published by J. H. Bufford, Boston, 1865. (Fort Wayne, Indiana, Lincoln Library and Museum)

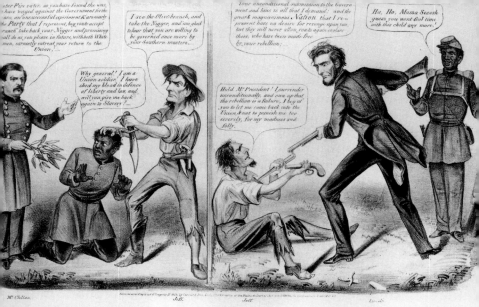

"YOUR PLAN AND MINE".

JEFF'S LAST SHIFT.

CAPTURE OF JEFF DAVIS, MAY 10TH 1865, AT IRWINSVILLE, GA.

A "SO CALLED PRESIDENT" IN PETTICOATS.

THE LAST ACT OF THE DRAMA OF SECESSION.

Kimmel & Forster, *The Outbreak of the Rebellion in the United States 1861*, lithograph, New York, 1865. (Fort Wayne, Indiana, Lincoln Library and Museum)

(Opposite, above) Gibson & Co., *A "So Called President" in Petticoats*, lithograph, Cincinnati, 1865. (Washington, D.C., Library of Congress)
(Opposite, below) Gibson & Co., *The Last Act of the Drama of Secession*, lithograph, Cincinnati, 1865. (Washington, D.C., Library of Congress)

THE LAST OFFER OF RECONCILIATION

Dedicated to the Memory of our most lamented late President Abraham Lincoln

JEFFERSON DAVIS AND HIS CABINET

With General Lee in the Council Chamber at Richmond

F. Gutekunst, *Jefferson Davis and the Confederate Generals*, phototype, published by Dr. J. Olney Banning & Son, Philadelphia, 1890. (Gettysburg National Military Park)

(Opposite, above) Kimmel & Forster, *The Last Offer of Reconciliation, In Remembrance of Prest. A. Lincoln, "The Door is Open for All,"* lithograph, published by Wm. Vought, New York, 1865. (Fort Wayne, Indiana, Lincoln Library and Museum) *(Opposite, below)* Thomas Kelly after an original engraving of "The First Reading of the Emancipation Proclamation Before the Cabinet" by A. H. Ritchie, *Jefferson Davis and His Cabinet. With General Lee in the Council Chamber at Richmond,* lithograph, New York, 1866. (Washington, D.C., Library of Congress)

James A. Wales, *A Dead Hero and a Live Jackass*, woodcut engraving published in Puck, New York, June 22, 1881. (Photo by Brian Campbell Fischer, courtesy Roger A. Fischer)

publishing. Artists and printmakers were conscripted into mil-itary service or assigned to government printing. As for raw materials, an agent for the Marietta Paper Mill admitted in 1863, "I have on hand a few bundles of paper . . . and this will be the last for some time . . . we have strained every nerve to supply, now all our hands are taken. . . . You know Paper Makers are not to be had in the South." Another Georgia mill, leveled by a fire, took to advertising openly for recy-clables: "old ledgers, old cash books, old journals, old bank books, of any kind either all written over, partly written over, or not written over at all." But there was nothing available, not even for government presses "urgent for paper."[12]

The ready supply of ink dried up, too. Southern printers were forced to experiment with shoe black, fig juice, pome-granate, and other inadequate substitutes. One observer vividly remembered such a futile effort (including with his recollection a protypical racial comment):

> There was a large room in the building set apart for that pur-pose, and in it benches were set up with slabs to grind up lamp black. The varnish was made up in a large iron kettle and the litho[grapher]s had to take turns superintending it. They were assisted by darkies who were nearly all slaves. It was quite a sight to see about twenty of them stripped to the waist, mixing and grinding ink. Of course, the ink was only half ground and it was with some difficulty that we could print and keep it on the stone.[13]

Those scarce printmaking elements that could be salvaged in the war-ravaged Confederacy were directed to "official" publishing: the making of currency, and stamps—many of which bore the likeness of Jefferson Davis, but in a form too crude (and, of course, too tiny) to inspire. Publication of votive prints for home display ended. The standard reference for Confederate publishing during the war lists a total of

9,497 titles issued between 1861 and 1865. But among these are only some fifty-five pictorial prints—and this meager list includes sheet-music covers and maps. Under such hardship, the most alluring military image could not survive, much less thrive.[14]

Even the region's sole pictorial newspaper, the *Southern Illustrated News,* suspended publication. Its maiden issue had vowed that "our engravings and biographical sketches of the distinguished men connected with the present struggle will . . . be continued from week to week until completed." Even the rival *Frank Leslie's Illustrated Newspaper* was moved to comment favorably: "The South is . . . resolved to have pictures of its own. By one bound it leaps to the dignity of an illustrated newspaper." But the *Southern Illustrated News* focused its coverage on field commanders, inexplicably failing in its entire two years of existence to produce a single portrait of Jefferson Davis. By the time editors realized the omission, if they ever did, it was too late to remedy it. The paper's 1862 editions are filled with unanswered pleas for "sketches of Scenes and Incidents connected with our army." So desperate did the newspaper become for images its artists could reproduce that one advertisement pleaded with "the relatives of officers in the army" to send new "Pictures of our Generals." The demise of the *News* signaled the death throes of the entire Southern print publishing industry.[15]

Another sign of the demise of Confederate printmaking came in late 1862 and early 1863 when a French-born Richmond artist named L. M. D. Guillaume executed a series of equestrian portraits of six Confederate heroes. On the painter's mind from the outset was the notion of selling the resulting pictures to a printmaker for mass reproduction for a wide public. Indeed, Guillaume eventually sold rights to the series for $2,000 to the very same publishers who had had issued the print of Davis and his generals back in 1861. But the project died aborning. Confederate audiences were denied the opportunity to own copies of what turned out to be an inspiring series: portraits of Robert E. Lee, "Stonewall" Jackson, Joseph E. Johnston, P. G. T. Beauregard, John Singleton Mosby, and their commander in chief, Jefferson Davis. Guillaume portrayed Davis atop a handsome white charger, a military aide in the background, fully reflecting the view expressed by a contemporary that the president's "name and bearing" continued to be "the symbols of victory" even after victories stopped occurring. This time, however, few viewers would see evidence of the visual approbation.[16]

With the Confederate printmaking industry in ruins, no working engravers and lithographers were on hand to record Davis's persistent activism as a commander. Ready to "take the field" again at the Seven Days' Battles in 1862, Davis rushed to the Peninsula. As the Battle of Mechanicsville raged on June 26, General D. H. Hill was shocked to see "President Davis and staff" hurrying past them, "going 'to the sound of the firing.'" Davis came under "a terrific fire" that day, according to General James Longstreet. "The Federals doubtless had no idea that the Confederate President" was "receiving point-blank shot from their batteries." Ordered to safety by a worried Robert E. Lee, Davis and his party retreated only as far as a nearby stream where, "concealed from Lee's repelling observation" by a high bank and thick bushes, he remained to watch "while the battle raged." Mrs. Davis proudly boasted: "The President was on the field every day during the seven days' fight and slept on it every night." Ultimately, Union forces retreated from the vicinity of Richmond and the Confederacy was saved. Here surely was the stuff of heroic portraiture: imagine a picture of a president riding bravely, unharmed, through a barrage of enemy shelling. But his triumph came too late for Davis to be honored by the moribund Confederate graphics industry. It was not that

Davis seemed unworthy of such tributes. Robert E. Lee met the same iconographical fate and for the same reason: notwithstanding his growing fame, with Confederate publishing suspended, Lee would never once be honored in a single separate-sheet wartime print. Ironically, the disintegration of Confederate printmaking—its growing inability to comment pictorially on current events once shortages of paper, ink, and artists began crippling the publishing industry—may have served later to protect Davis's image in the graphic arts. Confederate printmakers could never counter their early outpouring of heroic portraits with critical pictures that might have reflected Confederate dissatisfaction with Davis once the war began going badly. Print production vitality declined just as Davis's reputation did; the president did not escape political blame, but he did escape pictorial blame.[17]

Davis went on to make appearances at Murfreesboro and Vicksburg, although one contemporary claimed that the president did not witness "either of the battles." Later he traveled to Chattanooga as well. Constance Cary Harrison insisted that Davis's "own inclination" remained "to be with the army, and at the first . . . sound of a gun, anywhere within reach of Richmond, he was in the saddle and off to the spot." Biographer William C. Davis put it more succinctly, observing that Davis simply "could not stay off the battlefield." But Confederate printmakers could no longer so depict the peripatetic commander in chief. General Beauregard, for one, was probably pleased. He dismissed the importance of such personal appearances, insisting to the end that Davis had been an inadequate, albeit very public, commander in chief. "We needed for President," he insisted, "either a military man of a high order, or a politician of the first class without military pretensions." Davis's bravery, Beauregard believed, was overridden by his poor management. "It is but another of the many proofs," he concluded, "that timid direction may readily go with physical courage."[18]

Physical courage, however, does inspire heroic portraiture, and Jefferson Davis inspired his share before economic as well as political factors conspired to end such portrayals at home. Printmaking did continue to thrive in the North long after it withered in the South. But there, Davis's military image was dealt another blow in 1864—this time for the opposite reason: political, not economic. That year, Davis's Union counterpart was challenged for reelection by George B. McClellan, a former general running on a peace platform. Pro-Lincoln images began portraying Lincoln as the more warlike of the two candidates, often inserting Davis as the symbol of an unpatriotic Democratic peace platform and, therefore, as a silent but influential force behind the McClellan candidacy. The message was simple: a vote for McClellan was a vote for Davis.

For such prints, the once-military image of Davis was radically altered. Discarding the neatly uniformed character from the earlier prints that acknowledged his war record, printmakers usually portrayed Davis as a prototypical evil plantation master, wearing a ridiculously large hat and carrying a whip and a dagger, with the hopelessness of his cause represented by his ragtag trousers and shredded shoes.

In prints such as the Currier & Ives election caricature, *Your Plan and Mine*, the Democrats' campaign against Lincoln was personified by precisely such a Davis figure about to reenslave a black soldier who had earned his freedom by fighting for the Union. Now Lincoln, not Davis, seemed the bold military figure. To illustrate the contrasting Republican plan, the print showed Lincoln holding a defeated Davis at bayonet point, declaring: "The great & magnanimous nation that I represent have no desire for revenge."

American printmakers *did* harbor a desire for revenge—pictorial revenge—especially if it was profitable. When the opportunity arose to shatter what remained of Davis's military image, they seized it with vigor. That opportunity arrived on May 10, 1865, when Davis was captured in Irwinsville, Georgia, after throwing on his wife's raincoat and shawl to elude his pursuers. On June 3, less than four weeks later, *Frank Leslie's Illustrated Newspaper*—the same journal, ironically, that had introduced Davis so respectfully in its cover portrait some four years earlier—proposed in another front-page woodcut that Davis had attempted to evade capture by donning a dress and bonnet.[19]

In only a few weeks, an extraordinarily prompt response by mid-nineteenth-century standards, publishers of separate-sheet prints contributed dozens of variations on this theme, depicting "Jeff's Last Shift," "Our Erring Sister Caught at Last," "The Chas-ed 'Old Lady' of the C.S.A.," or "A so-called President in Petticoats," to name a few titles that appeared. All the lampoons shared a determination to humiliate by exaggeration. And with no Confederate printmaking industry to respond to the assault, the Davis image crumbled, the once-imposing commander reduced to a national joke, the once-convincing martial pretense destroyed by the charges of cowardice and, worse, feminine disguise. (In sharp contrast, Robert E. Lee, was dramatically rescued from image oblivion and transformed into a postwar icon.)[20]

In one hoopskirt-and-bonnet print, the cartoon character of Davis would refer to his new, emasculated image a "blessing in disguise." But the real Davis insisted in his autobiography that the widely accepted libel was a lie. In a sense, it hardly mattered; the damage was done in a seemingly unending array of caricatures, in all of which the once-proud figure was shown running from his captors, skirts flying to reveal the masculine clothing he had allegedly tried to conceal.

The abundance of these prints must surely have encouraged a collective sigh of relief—fueled by robust laughter—in a North whose citizens had become accustomed to images that for four years had made Davis out to be a thoroughly manly, indeed threatening figure. The once-dangerous "traitor," who seemed in earlier prints a fit candidate for execution by hanging, now emerged as a contemptible comic figure seeking to evade capture by abandoning masculinity and, with it, honor.

As portrayed in successively exaggerated graphics, in separate sheet prints, *carte-de-visite* photographs, sheet music, comic pamphlets, and in cartoons in the illustrated press, the thoroughly humiliated president was shown in hoopskirts or petticoats, wearing a (sometimes feathered) bonnet, even daintily waving a fan. Beneath each disguise was the easily identifiable Davis, sporting his familiar goatee, and revealed to be wearing riding boots adorned with spurs, looking almost like a man imitating a man impersonating a woman.

Thus ridiculed in images that emphasized gender confusion and mocked his reputation as a man of military bearing and honor, Davis not only lost his iconographic reputation, but in the bargain, as historian Nina Silber has pointed out, invited deprecation of the entire Southern aristocratic class as well as the image of much-vaunted Southern womanhood. It should not be overlooked that Davis's "petticoat" image also proliferated alongside—and stood in sharp contrast to—the postwar image of another famous Confederate, Robert E. Lee. At the same time they were flooding the market with "hoopskirt" caricature, Northern printmakers were concurrently issuing scenes, many overblown, of Lee's dignified surrender to Ulysses S. Grant at Appomattox. Such prints invariably depicted Lee as gallant in defeat, if only to make the victorious Union general seem greater for having defeated such a worthy man. By comparison, Davis's image was left in ruins. The iconographical miracle was that it could recover and flourish as it ultimately did.[21]

One northern printmaker—Gibson & Co. of Cincinnati—ventured to portray Davis's escape in heroic terms. Its lithograph of *The Last Act of the Drama of Secession* showed not the president's capture but the beginning of his flight. Sympathetic as it was, the print, clearly aimed at Davis's admirers in the economically strained postwar South, could hardly counter the sheer volume of comic renditions. But it did presage an astounding image revival. Gibson's Davis was shown bidding farewell to military, not civilian, aides. A color bearer rides nearby, and soldiers' tents can be seen in the distance. Davis's departure is viewed as an altogether military operation. It is easy enough to imagine that the corner edge of his wife's handkerchief, into which she weeps as she stands nearby, is not a handkerchief at all, but an epaulet on Davis's shoulder. The military image was being reborn in defeat.[22]

With the restoration of peace, and the reopening of an image-hungry Southern marketplace, many Northern printmakers resumed treating pro-Confederate themes sympathetically. Once the Confederate cause was lost, images bruised by war were quickly repaired. Davis's was no exception. White Southerners again began yearning for his portraits virtually as soon as Davis was shackled by his captors at Fortress Monroe. After that, Davis seemed a living martyr to the cause, suffering for the collective sins of the Southern people and manfully enduring punishment at the hands of military authorities as a military prisoner of war—a far better image than that of a fleeing coward in drag.

Some Northern-made graphics, like the retrospective history print *The Outbreak of the Rebellion*, went so far as to suggest, by relegating Davis to the distant background, that he had played only a minor role in secession and war. A companion print, *The Last Offer of Reconciliation*, went even further, placing the disgraced Confederate president on an equal footing with the now-enshrined Lincoln, thus achieving for Davis the same kind of reflected glory that Lee attained in Appomattox pictures designed principally to celebrate the man who vanquished him, Ulysses S. Grant.

In the heated new competition to create heroic pictures for postwar Southern audiences, Davis's image renaissance might take unusual forms. One print owed its creation to, of all things, A. H. Ritchie's seemingly incompatible engraving of *The First Reading of the Emancipation Proclamation Before the Cabinet*, which achieved huge popularity in 1866. That same year, a New York lithographer named Thomas Kelly boldly stole the design, switched a few of its characters, and issued the result as a supposedly "new" group picture of Lincoln and his cabinet meeting in a war council with General Grant.

At the same time, in an obvious effort to adapt the pirated design for Southerners, too, Kelly created yet another version of the image by superimposing the heads of Confederate officials on the bodies of Lincoln's ministers. The result was a vivid, if awkward, portrait of Davis and *his* Cabinet, meeting with Lee. Such a depiction of the grand Lee reporting to his commander in chief could not help but provide renewed evidence that Davis had maintained his authority over the Confederate military during the war. Surely lost on such sympathetic viewers was the fact that the entire ensemble was actually portrayed in Abraham Lincoln's cabinet room, and that the document Davis was shown clutching in his hand was arguably Lincoln's greatest military order—of all things, the Emancipation Proclamation.

Davis's image as commander in chief came full circle two years before the appearance of his controversial memoirs. In 1879, the living symbol of the Lost Cause was compellingly presented in an updated adaptation of the old group portrait of the commander in chief with his military staff. Published in Philadelphia, the new edition, *The Generals of the Confederate Army*, presented sixteen wartime heroes, five more than in the 1861 original, substituting for some of the earlier military celebrities the commanders who won fame later in the war. Appropriate Confederate gray uniforms at last replaced the earlier, incongruous Union blue. The portrait of Lee was finally made to resemble the white-bearded figure now familiar to Northern and Southern audiences alike. Even the Confederate flag was updated. But there, in the very center of the scene, still occupying center stage, still inexplicably uniformed, and still clutching a telescope through which he presumably oversaw the actions of his lieutenants, was the military figure of Jefferson Davis, now in majestic revival. Eighteen years after the outbreak of war and the original appearance of this image—fourteen years since his humiliation at Irwinsville—Davis proved he had effectively outlived both the death of Southern printmaking and the devastating blow that Northern cartoonists had dealt to his image after his capture.

There was still dissent, of course. The late-century pictorial magazine *Puck* compared him unfavorably with the mythologized Lincoln in a brutal cartoon entitled "A Dead Hero and a Live Jackass," published in 1881 in response to the appearance of Davis's *Rise and Fall of the Confederate Government*. He could hardly compete with a saint. And, of course, this dissent reflected the struggle over the meaning of the Civil War and the terms of reunion. Such pictorial response was to be expected in an atmosphere of growing competition for national memory and a struggle to comprehend the meaning of both the Civil War and the terms of reconciliation.[23] But Davis's stubbornly enduring image as a military hero lasted to 1890, when yet another Philadelphia publisher issued a final print of *Jefferson Davis and the Confederate Generals.* Although the printmaker did not attempt to portray Davis in uniform, he did place him in the foreground of the picture in the dominant position; the others in the room, including Lee, were made to face him and thus implicitly defer to his stature as commander in chief. Davis not only outlived his contemporaries, he was presented in this particular group portrait as outranking them eternally as well.[24]

The Davis military image survived, setbacks notwithstanding, for as long as the fashion for separate-sheet prints themselves endured in American homes. Originally, two rival Davis images had battled for preeminence: the Southern military image of a battlefield hero on the order of George Washington and the various Northern military images of a dangerous, satanically influenced tyrant, a cockaded buffoon, an emasculated coward, or an armed plantation overseer. Many of these images—both Southern and Northern, celebratory and assaultive—were military. Davis's original martial image faded only with the death of Southern printmaking around 1863. His Northern-made military image died with his capture in 1865, but was later reintroduced for repatriated Southern white audiences.

In the end, the heroic military image, rather than the comic one, prevailed because Northern commercialism, combined with rekindled dominant Southern patriotism and sympathy for the living symbol of the Lost Cause, proved powerful enough to inspire a Davis revival after his militancy ceased to be a threat to the Union. In effect, the image of Davis as a commander in chief did not die at all—it went into an iconographical coma. It returned because white Southern audiences demanded it.

Some historians have questioned the very existence of such nationalistic feelings in the Confederacy. In the words of the four scholars who wrote *Why the South Lost the Civil War*, it was only a "dream." Historian Frank Vandiver has argued further that Davis seems today a "leader without legend." But such comments fail to recognize powerful evidence of a sustained Southern yearning to celebrate, and later to recall, Davis as a commander in chief. It is no coincidence that more plaques, memorials, and monuments honor him than honor any other American "president"—save for George Washington and Abraham Lincoln. And it is surely no accident that the three principal equestrian statues built after the war in downtown Richmond portrayed Lee, Jackson, and Davis (as they would be later on the gigantic side of Stone Mountain in Georgia). The three constitute the military trinity of Confederate memory. Alone among them, Davis survived most of the century, a living memorial to the Lost Cause, "traces of his military service still showing in his carriage" at age eighty.[25]

The Davis renaissance peaked in 1886, when the old man himself undertook a rigorous tour to dedicate Confederate monuments and speak out again, unrepentantly, about the Cause. Crowds cheered him wherever he went. D. H. Hill heard one of the ovations and admitted, "We ought to honor him to honor ourselves." Printmakers did precisely that, often in terms that surely seemed gratifyingly military to the president who had wanted only to be a general.[26]

A centennial assessment of Davis in a 1908 edition of the *New York Times* acknowledged his persevering military image: "He had given the best proofs of capacity for the art of war." White Southerners seemed to agree, and prints showing a uniformed president undoubtedly inspired such memories. The art of war had in turn proved its own capacity to keep that image alive.[27]

In 1922, fifty-seven years after the end of the war, surviving Confederate veterans held a sentimental reunion in Richmond. An artist named Margaret Dashiell was on hand to paint a watercolor of those ancient survivors—most now hobbled and stooped—as they gathered in small groups to exchange fading memories. The old soldiers chose to encamp that day at the one site that seemed irresistibly to beckon them for this final call to arms. Appropriately, Dashiell's painting showed them clustered outside the former White House of the Confederacy. What better place to sound the trumpet for the last time than the grounds of the residence of their old commander in chief? After Gettysburg, a frustrated Davis had confided to his wife: "If I could take one wing and Lee the other, I think between us we could wrest a victory from these people." Sixty years later, perhaps remembering the popular pictures that had so convincingly testified to his military prowess, his old admirers may have still believed him.[28]

8

Was the Best Defense a Good Offense? Jefferson Davis and Confederate Strategies

JAMES M. McPHERSON

IN NARRATIVES of their campaigns written years after the Civil War, Generals Joseph E. Johnston and Pierre G. T. Beauregard agreed that the Confederacy should have won the war. The Southern people, wrote Johnston, were "not guilty of the high crime of undertaking a war without the means of waging it successfully." And Beauregard insisted that "no people ever warred for independence with more relative advantages than the Confederates."[1]

If readers somehow failed to get the message, Johnston and Beauregard spelled it out: the blame for failure lay on the shoulders of their commander in chief, Jefferson Davis. To such accusations, leveled in private as well as in public, during the war as well as after it, Davis did not deign to reply directly in the 1,200 pages of his own postwar account of *The Rise and Fall of the Confederate Government*. Instead, he declared loftily, he would tell the truth in full confidence "that error and misrepresentations have, in their inconsistencies and improbabilities, the elements of self-destruction, while truth is in its nature consistent and therefore self-sustaining."[2]

In the spirit of this indirect exchange, Davis's relationships with his generals have framed much of the analysis of the reasons for Confederate defeat. His feuds with Johnston and Beauregard, his supposed favoritism toward Braxton Bragg and John Bell Hood—or alternatively, according to Steven E. Woodworth, his failure to sustain Bragg and his fatal refusal to jettison Leonidas Polk—are often portrayed as major causes of disasters in the western theater, where the Confederacy lost the war. At the same time, Davis's personal rapport with Robert E. Lee, for which most historians give Lee the principal credit, helps explain the Confederacy's relative success in that theater. The "dysfunctional partnership" between Davis and Johnston, maintains Craig Symonds, "was an unalloyed disaster for the cause they served" and responsible in large measure "for the failure of the Confederate war effort." In the end, this and other rifts between Davis and his western-theater generals more than outweighed the positive results gained by the "powerful team" of Lee and Davis.[3]

The focus on the interpersonal relations between Davis and his generals in much historical writing reflects another facet of a larger tendency in the scholarly literature to emphasize internal divisions as the principal causes of Confederate defeat—divisions of race, class, gender, and region. I have written elsewhere that such "internal" explanations sometimes suffer from the "fallacy of reversibility"—for the North experienced equal if not greater internal divisions that came close, at times, to crippling the Union war effort.[4] The same point can be made about Lincoln and his generals. If Davis had Joe Johnston, Lincoln had George McClellan and

George Meade; if Davis had Beauregard, Lincoln had Fré-
mont; if Davis looked bad by sticking too long with Bragg—
or if we go along with Woodworth, by sticking too long with
Polk and other corps commanders in the Army of Tennessee—Lincoln looked bad by successively appointing and then
dismissing Pope, Burnside, and Hooker over the course of a
year during which the morale of the Army of the Potomac
sank to a point perilously close to collapse.

Although the personalities and the relationships among
the commanders in chief and their principal army commanders in both Union and Confederacy had an important impact on the outcome of the war, a focus on strategy rather
that personalities might yield better understanding. Several of
the other chapters in this volume, especially those by Emory
Thomas, Craig Symonds, and Steven Woodworth—drawing
on books they and others have written in recent years—offer
a number of important insights into strategy as well as personalities.

To appreciate these insights, a review of the larger context
of Confederate military strategy will prove helpful. Over the
last two millennia, studies of military leadership have usually concentrated on victorious generals and their strategies.
One thinks of Hannibal, Julius Caesar, Alexander the Great,
Marlborough, Frederick the Great, Napoleon, Wellington,
von Moltke. In the case of the American Civil War, the focus
of much professional study of strategy and leadership, particularly by British military historians but also by some Americans, has been on Grant, Sherman, and Lincoln. One thinks
of J. F. C. Fuller and John Keegan on Grant, Basil H. Liddell
Hart on Sherman, Colin Ballard on Lincoln, and also of
T. Harry Williams, Kenneth P. Williams, Herman Hattaway,
and Archer Jones. The purpose of such studies has often been
to derive some positive lessons, some formula for success
from their campaigns.

Two exceptions to this emphasis on victors are the numerous studies of German generals and their strategies in both world wars and studies of Confederate generals in the Civil War, especially Robert E. Lee and Stonewall Jackson. These exceptions, however, go at least partway toward proving the rule; that is, even though the Germans and the Confederates lost their wars in the end, they won a good many victories along the way and exhibited a strategic or tactical brilliance in the process that has made their campaigns a fit study to divine the secrets of their success—and perhaps also of their failures.

So often cited is Karl von Clausewitz's dictum that war is the continuation of politics by other means that it has become almost a cliché. Because of its familiarity, however, we sometimes gloss over the distinction that Clausewitz drew between politics and other means while blurring the continuity between them. To unpack the meaning of Clausewitz's aphorism, let us distinguish between two kinds of strategy: *national* strategy, the shaping and defining of a nation's political goals in time of war; and *military* strategy, the ways in which armed forces are used to achieve those goals. A crucial branch of military strategy is *operational* strategy, the planning of a specific operation or campaign to carry out the larger military strategy. In the United States, national strategy is defined by the president and Congress; military strategy is carried out by commanders of the armed forces. The president plays a key role in formulating both kinds of strategy as head of state and commander in chief. He serves as the intermediary between the government and the armed forces, conveying the national strategy to his generals while communicating to Congress and people the ability of the armies to achieve those goals.

In theory there should be a congruity between national and military strategy. That seems an obvious commonsense observation. But in practice, military strategy in many wars has diverted from national strategy. Wars have a tendency to take on a character and momentum that become increasingly incompatible with the original national strategy. And in many wars, sharp disagreement about war aims develops within the polity, giving military commanders mixed and confusing signals about national strategy, which inhibits their ability to devise an appropriate military strategy. That is what happened to the United States in Vietnam. In other wars, conflict between national strategy as defined by civilian leadership, and military strategy as defined by generals, can cause a nation to fight at cross purposes. In the Korean War, President Harry Truman insisted on a limited war, while General Douglas MacArthur wanted to fight an unlimited one. Truman finally had to fire MacArthur, producing a sense of frustration among many Americans who, like MacArthur, desired to overthrow Communism in North Korea and perhaps in China as well.

The experience of Vietnam as well as of American military intervention in Lebanon during the 1980s and Somalia during the 1990s led Colin Powell, as chairman of the joint chiefs of staff, to develop the "Powell Doctrine," which is essentially a formula for clarity of national strategy and congruity between it and military strategy. According to the Powell Doctrine, before the United States undertakes a military action abroad, there must be a clearly defined national purpose supported by the polity and a precise military strategy to accomplish that purpose, no more and no less. The Gulf War, the intervention in Haiti, and, more debatably, that in Bosnia, are fruits of the Powell Doctrine.

The most successful wars in American history have been those with a close congruity between national and military strategy. The national strategy in the Revolution was American independence; the military strategy achieved this goal, no more and no less. The national strategy in the Mexican War was the Rio Grande border for Texas and the acquisition of New Mexico and California; when these were achieved, the United States stopped fighting. In World War II, the national strategy was not merely the liberation of Europe and Asia from Fascist conquest but the overthrow of Fascist governments in the Axis nations themselves. This required a military strategy of total war and unconditional surrender; that is precisely what the Allies carried out. In the Gulf War, the national strategy was to drive Iraq's army out of Kuwait; when that was done, the coalition forces stopped fighting.

In the Civil War, the Northern national strategy expanded as the war went on, from a limited war to restore the status quo antebellum to an unlimited one to destroy slavery and the social order it sustained, in order to give the United States that new birth of freedom Lincoln invoked at Gettysburg. Lincoln's genius as commander in chief was his ability to shape and define this expanding national strategy and eventually to put in place, after three rocky years, a military strategy and military leaders to carry it out.[5]

Jefferson Davis as commander in chief suffers by comparison with Lincoln, in part because the Confederacy lost the war and in part because of his flaws of personality and leadership. Davis was thin-skinned and lacked Lincoln's ability to work with critics for a common cause. Lincoln was reported to have said of McClellan in the fall of 1861 that "I will hold McClellan's horse if he will only bring us success."[6] It is hard to imagine Jefferson Davis saying the same of Joseph E. Johnston. Because of dyspepsia and neuralgia that grew worse under wartime pressures, Davis was wracked by pain that exacerbated his waspish temper. Even his wife Varina noted that "if anyone disagrees with Mr. Davis he resents it and ascribes the difference to the perversity of his opponent."[7] Lincoln was more eloquent than Davis in expressing his country's war aims, more successful in communicating them to his people. Nothing that Davis wrote or spoke during the war has resonated down through the years like the peroration of Lincoln's first inaugural address, the peroration of his annual message to Congress on December 1, 1862, the Conkling letter of August 26, 1863, the Gettysburg Address, or the second inaugural.

In his first message to the Confederate Congress after the outbreak of war, however, Davis did define clearly and concisely the Confederate national strategy: "We seek no conquest, no aggrandizement, no concession of any kind from the States with which we were lately confederated; all we ask is to be let alone."[8] This was a thoroughly *defensive* national strategy. It was grounded in an important fact, so obvious that its importance is often overlooked: the Confederacy began the war in firm control of nearly all the territory it claimed. This is rarely the case in civil wars or revolutions, which typically require rebels or revolutionaries to fight to gain control of land or government or both. With a functioning government and a strong army already mobilized or mobilizing in May 1861, the Confederacy embraced 750,000 square miles in which not a single enemy soldier was to be found save at Fort Monroe at the mouth of the James River and Fort Pickens on an island off Pensacola. All the Confederacy had to do to win the war was to defend what it already had.

The nearest comparison was the United States on July 4, 1776. And Davis, like the leaders of that first American war of secession, seems initially to have envisaged a "thoroughly defensive, survival-oriented" military strategy, in the words of Steven Woodworth, that would be consistent with his thoroughly defensive national strategy.[9] Like the Roman General Quintus Fabius in the Second Punic War, or George Washington in the American Revolution, or the Russian General Mikhail Kutuzov in 1812, such a survival-oriented strategy would trade space for time, keep the army concentrated and ready to strike enemy detachments dangling deep in Confederate territory, and above all avoid the destruction or crippling of the main Southern armies. Such a defensive strategy of attrition might wear out the will or capacity of the enemy to continue fighting, as the Americans and Russians had done in 1781 and 1812.

What matter if this Fabian strategy yielded important cities and territory? Americans in the Revolution lost New York, Philadelphia, Charleston, Savannah, Williamsburg, and Richmond, yet won their independence in the end. On one occasion during the Civil War, Jefferson Davis articulated such a strategy. "There are no vital points on the preservation of which the continued existence of the Confederacy depends," he maintained. "Not the fall of Richmond, nor Wilmington, nor Charleston, nor Savannah, nor of all combined, can save the enemy from the constant and exhaustive drain of blood and treasure which must continue until he shall discover that no peace is attainable unless based on the recognition of our indefeasible rights."[10]

But Davis said this in November 1864. Perhaps he was right then, for by that time the crucible of war had forged a fierce Confederate nationalism that had sustained the will to fight despite the loss of territory and cities—although not for long after the subsequent loss of the cities named by Davis. In 1861, however, Confederate nationalism was still fragile. The states had seceded one by one on the principle that the sovereignty of each state was superior to that of any other entity. The very name of the new nation, the *Confederate* States, implied an association of still sovereign states. This principle was recognized in the Confederate Constitution, which was ratified by "each State acting in its sovereign and independent character."[11] Davis also bowed to the concept of state sovereignty in his policy of brigading Confederate troops by states—something infrequently done in the Union army. Given the existence of this initial provincialism, if Davis had tried to pursue a purely Fabian strategy in 1861 by concentrating Confederate troops in Virginia and Tennessee, for example, and leaving other areas to fend for themselves, the Confederacy might have fallen to pieces of its own accord. Popular and political pressures compelled Davis to scatter small armies around the perimeter of the Confederacy at a couple of dozen points in 1861.

The danger of such a dispersal, labeled by T. Harry Williams as a cordon defense and by Craig Symonds as an extended defense, was that an enemy superior in numbers and resources might break through this thin gray line somewhere, cutting off and perhaps capturing one or more of these small armies and penetrating as far into Confederate territory as if it had been left undefended.[12] That is precisely what happened in late 1861 and early 1862 in western Virginia, Missouri and Arkansas, Kentucky and Tennessee, coastal North and South Carolina, southern Louisiana, even northern Mississippi and Alabama. In a rare confession (made in a private letter), Davis wrote in March 1862: "I acknowledge the error of my attempt to defend all of the frontier."[13]

He need not have been so hard on himself. Under the circumstances of 1861, he had little choice. The governors of North and South Carolina, or Mississippi and Arkansas and Alabama, not to mention the citizen soldiers from those states who had sprung to arms to defend home and family, would not have allowed him to strip their states of troops to fight in Virginia or Tennessee. This parochialism (if that is the correct word) would remain a problem for Davis and the commanders of his principal armies during most of the war. But the experiences of 1861 and early 1862 did drive home the lesson of a need for some degree of concentration to meet the main enemy threats.

Underlying this principle of concentration was the advantage of interior lines. From 1861 to 1864 the Confederates repeatedly used their interior lines in both the Eastern and Western theaters to achieve at least a partial concentration to strike invading enemy armies. The first and one of the most famous examples was the transfer by rail of most of Joseph Johnston's small army from the Shenandoah Valley to Manassas in July 1861 to repel Irvin McDowell's attackers at Bull Run and drive them in a rout back to Washington. Nine months later, when faced with a buildup of McClellan's forces on the Peninsula, the Confederates again used interior lines to transfer most of Johnston's army from Centreville to Yorktown. As Craig Symonds points out, this campaign revealed a difference between Davis and Johnston concerning the relationship between interior lines and concentration. Davis retained part of his concept of an extended defense, desiring to leave a substantial force on the Rappahannock to protect that region against Union forces south of Washington. Johnston wanted to concentrate nearly all Confederate units in Virginia against McClellan, as near to Richmond as possible, even at the risk of yielding northern Virginia, the Shenandoah Valley, and the Peninsula temporarily to the enemy. After disposing of McClellan, Johnston said, the main Confederate army could then recapture these other regions.[14]

That is what eventually happened in the summer of 1862, but not under the command of Johnston, who was wounded at Seven Pines and replaced by Robert E. Lee on June 1. Part of the army of 90,000 men that Lee concentrated in front of Richmond by the last week of June 1862, the largest single Confederate army of the war, was drawn from the Shenandoah Valley. During the previous two months, Stonewall

Jackson had brilliantly executed another operation that emulated a successful American strategy in the Revolution: a concentration of superior numbers in a mobile force to strike separated enemy outposts or detachments. George Washington had done this at Trenton and Princeton, and other American commanders had done the same in the Carolinas during the Revolution; Jackson borrowed a leaf from their book and struck smaller Union detachments at McDowell, Front Royal, and Winchester and then turned on his pursuers to check them at Cross Keys and Port Republic.

Jackson then became part of Lee's concentrated army that drove McClellan away from Richmond in the Seven Days—although Jackson himself did not perform up to expectations in that campaign. In the next one, however, he exceeded expectations. Jackson carried out Lee's bold exploitation of interior lines to concentrate against Pope along the Rappahannock as McClellan was withdrawing from the Peninsula. Using a favorite strategic operation of Napoleon, *les manoeuvres sur la derrière*—a wide flanking movement to get into the enemy's rear—Jackson then marched around Pope's flank, destroyed his supply base at Manassas, and held out until the Confederates reconcentrated to win the second battle of Manassas.

Confederates in the western theater also practiced the strategy of concentration in 1862. After the Federals had broken through the cordon defense of the other Johnston—Albert Sidney—at several points in Kentucky and Tennessee, and had captured 20 percent of his troops at Fort Donelson, Johnston retreated all the way to Corinth, Mississippi. There he concentrated his scattered forces for a counterthrust at Shiloh. Although this effort did not produce a Confederate victory and it cost Johnston his life, Shiloh nevertheless set the Federals back on their heels for a time. The Confederate Army of Mississippi, now commanded by Beauregard, was finally forced to evacuate Corinth at the end of May 1862, just as Joseph Johnston's army in Virginia had evacuated Yorktown several weeks earlier. But these retreats set the stage for offensive operations later in the summer under new commanders (Lee in Virginia and Bragg in Kentucky) that took the armies across the Potomac and almost to the Ohio River by September.

These campaigns accomplished a startling reversal of momentum in the war. They also represented a new phase in Confederate strategy, which has been variously labeled as offensive–defensive, offensive–defense, or defensive–offensive. Davis himself described it as offensive–defensive and contrasted it with what he called "purely defensive operations."[15] This confusion of nomenclature perhaps reflects a confusion about the precise nature of this strategy and about whether Davis favored it, opposed it, or both favored and opposed it at different times with varying emphasis on the offensive or defensive parts of it, according to circumstances.

The effort to sort out these variables is hindered by the failure of the principals—Davis, Lee, Beauregard, Bragg, and others—to define systematically what they meant by offensive–defensive, or purely defensive. We must tease out the meaning by a study of what they said and did in particular campaigns. One way to approach this matter is by way of an analogy from football, in which any coach would agree that the best defense is a good offense. Lee knew nothing about modern American football (and sports are not the moral equivalent of war), but he would have understood the slogan. Indeed, he could almost have invented it. "There is nothing to be gained by this army remaining quietly on the defensive," he wrote on the eve of the Gettysburg campaign. "We cannot afford to keep our troops awaiting possible movements of the enemy. . . . Our true policy is . . . so to employ our own forces, as to give occupation to his at points of our selection." A year later, Lee told Jubal Early that "we must destroy this army of Grant's before he gets to the James River. If he gets there, it will become a siege and then it will be a mere question of time."[16]

One source of confusion about the meaning of an offensive–defensive strategy sometimes results from a failure to distinguish between strategy and tactics. When Davis or Lee or any other commander spoke of the offensive–defensive— or words to that effect—were they referring to strategy, or tactics, or both? They did not always offer a clear answer. Several combinations of offensive or defensive tactics and strategy are possible; Lee's campaigns demonstrated all of them. The Seven Days and Gettysburg illustrate the operational offensive in both strategy and tactics, but the Seven Days served the defensive purpose of relieving the threat to Richmond. Fredericksburg was a defensive battle in both strategy and tactics. Antietam culminated an offensive campaign, but the Confederates fought there mainly on the tactical defensive. Second Manassas was part of an operational offensive and was both defensive and offensive in tactics. From Spotsylvania to the end of the war, Lee's army fought almost entirely on the defensive both strategically and tactically, although Jubal Early's raid down the Valley and into Maryland was an offensive operational diversion in aid of an essentially defensive strategy in Virginia. The same variables characterized western campaigns and battles. The first day at Shiloh was a Confederate offensive both strategically and tactically, as was the second day at Chickamauga. Every battle in the Vicksburg campaign was defensive both in strategy and tactics for the Confederates, as was every one of Johnston's fights in the Atlanta campaign. When Hood succeeded Johnston, he promptly launched three tactical offensives to serve the strategic defense of Atlanta. Hood's later invasion of Tennessee was an operational offensive that came to grief both in the tactical offensive at Franklin and the tactical defensive at Nashville.

What determined these variables was the strategic and tactical situation at a given time and place in the war. When Davis contrasted the offensive–defensive with the purely defensive, he was probably speaking of both strategy and tactics in different combinations according to circumstances. Failure to sort out these circumstances and the variables that resulted accounts for much of the confusion and ambiguity about Confederate strategy.

Emory Thomas and Steven Woodworth have both clarified and muddied these waters in their recent books and in Thomas's chapter in this volume. Both authors detect a significant difference of emphasis between Davis and Lee, neatly spelled out by Woodworth in his book with the double-entendre title *Davis and Lee at War*: "For Davis, the war could be won simply by not losing, for Lee . . . it could be lost simply by not winning." That is why Davis seemed at times to favor what he called "purely defensive operations," a Fabian strategy that would conserve the Confederacy's resources and armies while compelling the enemy to consume his resources and armies by repeatedly attacking, thereby suffering heavy casualties and eroding the will of the Northern people to sustain an increasingly costly effort to destroy the Confederacy.[17]

Yet from the time Lee took command of what he renamed the Army of Northern Virginia, Davis apparently approved all of the general's operations that have come to be known by the label of offensive–defensive: the attack on McClellan in the Seven Days, the shift of operations to northern Virginia culminating in Second Manassas, the invasion of Maryland, the counterthrust against Hooker at Chancellorsville followed by the invasion of Pennsylvania, and even the detachment of Early to raid down the Shenandoah Valley to the very outskirts of Washington. And let us not forget the western theater, or theaters, where Sidney Johnston and Beauregard launched an offensive at Shiloh, Bragg and Kirby Smith invaded Kentucky, and Bragg subsequently counterattacked Rosecrans at Murfreesboro and Chickamauga, Hood counterattacked Sherman around Atlanta and then launched raids against Sherman's communications in north Georgia preparatory to an invasion of Tennessee, while Sterling Price moved north in an extraordinarily ambitious invasion of Missouri.

If Davis opposed these offensives, we have little record of it and we do have plenty of evidence for his approval, especially of Lee's operations and those of Hood. With respect to Davis's cordial relations with Lee, both Thomas and Woodworth have suggested that Lee charmed and smooth-talked Davis into such support so skillfully that "Davis was unaware of the difference between himself and Lee"; indeed, the "difference was not apparent during the war" and has also escaped most historians.[18] Thomas finds the "dissonance" between Davis and Lee most salient in Lee's two most ambitious offensive efforts to conquer a peace, the invasion of Maryland in September 1862 and the invasion of Pennsylvania nine months later. Yet, curiously, Thomas also notes that Davis "was delighted with Lee's invasion of Maryland."[19] If so, that helps explain why their dissonance was not apparent to Davis at the time or to most historians since. In any event, it is quite true that in the Gettysburg campaign Davis held some troops in the Richmond area instead of combining them with brigades from North Carolina under the command of Beauregard to carry out a diversionary action near Culpeper to draw Federal forces away from Pennsylvania, as Lee requested. Davis did so for the very good reason that as Lee headed north, 16,000 Union troops on the Peninsula under General John A. Dix were threatening Richmond from the east in a brief campaign that has been all but ignored by historians, while Beauregard had his hands full dealing with a major Federal effort against Charleston. Although Davis and Lee appeared to be in accord on most matters of strategy, Thomas and Woodworth are, nevertheless, onto something in their focus on areas of disagreement. As Thomas puts it, the difference in strategic outlook was a "subtle" matter of which word should receive the greater emphasis in the concept of an offensive–defensive strategy.[20] But there is an unacknowledged irony here, if Woodworth is correct that Davis really preferred a "thoroughly defensive, survival-oriented grand strategy." These words describe Joseph Johnston's strategy almost perfectly. But, of course, it was with Johnston that Davis quarreled most bitterly. So thoroughly defensive and survival-oriented was Johnston's strategy in the Atlanta campaign that Richard McMurry was not being altogether facetious when he said that Johnston would have fought the crucial battle of that campaign on Key West.[21] If Davis's choice of Hood to replace Johnston is any clue to his strategic leaning, it was more to the offensive than defensive, for Hood was one of the most offensive-minded of those generals who came up under Lee's tutelage.

A related issue in a discussion of Confederate strategy concerns the East versus West debate. In May 1863, the top Confederate brass confronted a crucial decision about allocation of resources and effort between East and West. Lee had just won a justly renowned victory at Chancellorsville. But the Confederacy faced a dangerous situation at Vicksburg and in middle Tennessee. Longstreet and others proposed the detachment of two divisions from Lee's army to reinforce Bragg for an offensive–defensive against Rosecrans, which might also relieve the pressure against Vicksburg. In such a scenario, Lee would clearly have to remain on the defensive–defensive in Virginia, a prospect he did not relish.

Instead, he counseled Davis to turn him loose on an offensive into Pennsylvania while the western armies remained on the defensive–defensive. The result was the loss of Vicksburg and middle Tennessee while the Army of Northern Virginia limped home after suffering a crippling 25,000 or more casualties at Gettysburg.

Was this a strategic blunder or bad luck? Was Lee's preoccupation with Virginia a consequence of parochialism that limited his vision to the East while the war was being lost in the West? Did his preference for both an offensive strategy and offensive tactics, especially at Gettysburg, bleed his army to death? Did Lee gain too much influence over Davis on these matters, to the detriment of a sound strategic vision for all theaters that would have conserved Confederate manpower and eroded the Northern will through a defensive strategy of attrition before the Confederates in 1864 were forced by circumstances to such a strategy?

These are important questions, and several influential historians have answered them in the affirmative.[22] But ultimately these questions are unanswerable. We just don't know what would have happened if Longstreet had taken two divisions to Tennessee in May 1863, if Lee had not invaded Pennsylvania, or if Lee himself had gone west to take command in that troubled theater as Davis asked him to do in August 1863 and again after the debacle at Chattanooga in November.

What we do know is that Lee was far from alone in perceiving Virginia as the most important theater. Most people in North and South alike, as well as European observers, shared that view. While it may be true that the Confederacy lost the war in the West, it is also clear that Lee's victories came close on several occasions to winning it in the East, or at least staving off defeat. The Confederacy tottered on the edge of disaster when Lee took command on June 1, 1862, with the enemy six miles from Richmond and a huge amount of the western Confederacy under Union control after a long string of Northern victories in that theater. Within a month, Lee's offensive–defensive in the Seven Days had dramatically reversed the equation in the eyes of most observers, whose view was focused on Virginia. This almost-universal fixation on the eastern theater was what prompted Lincoln's lament on August 4, 1862, to Count Agénor-Etienne de Gasparin, a pro-Union French aristocrat: "It seems unreasonable that a series of successes, extending through half-a-year, and clearing more than a hundred thousand square miles of country, should help us so little, while a single half-defeat should hurt us so much."[23]

During the next two months, Lee and Jackson's offensive-defensive strategy came close to winning European diplomatic recognition. Antietam prevented that, but Confederate successes during the next nine months, again mainly in the East, reopened the question and so discouraged many Northern voters with the prospect of ever winning the war that the Copperheads made great gains and potentially threatened the Lincoln administration's ability to continue the war. Lee and his offensive–defensive strategy appeared invincible. Gettysburg proved that it was not, but the lingering legacy of invincibility made Meade so cautious that the Army of the Potomac accomplished little for the next ten months.

Again, in the summer of 1864, it was mainly Lee and his army who nearly caused the North to throw in the towel and forced Lincoln to conclude in August that he would not be reelected and the Union might not be preserved. To be sure, Lee's strategy as well as tactics were now defensive, but the event that did more than anything else to convince many Yankees of the war's hopelessness was an offensive stroke— Early's raid to Washington. As late as February 1865 Secretary of War Edwin M. Stanton and Senator Charles Sumner agreed that "peace can be had only when Lee's army is beaten, captured, or dispersed." So long as that army remained "in fighting condition, there is still a hope for the rebels," but "when Lee's army is out of the way, the whole Rebellion will disappear." And so it proved; Appomattox was the actual, if not literal, end of the war.[24]

A final observation. The subject of this volume is Davis and his generals. That is entirely appropriate. Yet there is an inevitable tendency in such a volume to get so wrapped up in the subject at hand as to neglect part of the context. In the discussion of whether Davis's relations with Johnston, Beauregard, Lee, Hood, or Bragg helped or hurt the Confederate cause, whether more emphasis on the West or a more Fabian defensive strategy might have won the war, we sometimes forget that such matters did not occur in a vacuum. An enemy was out there with command relationships and strategies of his own that both shaped and responded to Confederate command relationships and strategy.

Two anecdotes in conclusion will make this point. In the wilderness on the evening of May 6, 1864, a Confederate attack on the Union right rolled up that flank and routed two brigades. A Union officer rode up to Grant's headquarters and told the general in chief in a panic-stricken voice that all was lost, Lee was in his rear and the Army of the Potomac was doomed. Grant replied in disgust: "Oh, I am heartily tired of hearing what Lee is going to do. Some of you always seem to think he is suddenly going to turn a double somersault, and land in our rear and on both of our flanks at the same time. Go back to your command, and try to think what we are going to do ourselves, instead of what Lee is going to do."[25]

The second anecdote concerns Gettysburg. Several million words, or so it sometimes seems, have been written about which Confederate general was responsible for losing the battle: Lee because of overconfidence, aggressive tactics, or mismanagement; Stuart because of his absence; Ewell because of his failure to attack Cemetery Hill on July 1; or Longstreet for his lack of enthusiasm and promptness in the attacks on July 2 and 3. It was left to George Pickett to fill the void left by these various interpretations. When someone thought to ask Pickett after the war who he thought was responsible for the Confederate defeat at Gettysburg, he reflected for a moment before replying: "I always thought the Yankees had something to do with it."[26]

Notes

Introduction

1. Genl. Robert E. Lee to Jefferson Davis, July 4, 1863; Dunbar Rowland, ed., *Jefferson Davis, Constitutionalist: His Letters, Papers, and Speeches*, 10 vols. (Jackson: Mississippi Department of Archives and History, 1923), 5:535–36; J. C. Pemberton to Jefferson Davis, July 10, 1863, *The War of the Rebellion: A Compilation of the Official Records of the Union and Confederate Armies*, 128 vols. (Washington, D.C.: GPO, 1880–1901) ser. 1, vol. 24, pt. 3, p. 1000; Davis to Pemberton, Care Genl. J. E. Johnston, July 14, 1863; Rowland, ed., *Jefferson Davis, Constitutionalist*, 5:547–48.

ONE: *A Fatal Relationship: Davis and Johnston at War*

1. For an historiographical survey of the Davis–Johnston feud, see the Bibliography.

2. The probably apocryphal fistfight between Davis and Johnston was reported in Robert McElroy's biography, *Jefferson Davis, the Unreal and the Real* (New York: Harper and Brothers, 1937), 1:19. For the conduct records of both Davis and Johnston at West Point, see USMA Post Orders, vol. 3 (1823–25), and the USMA Register of Cadet Deficiencies, RG 404, ser. 101, 2:409.

3. For Davis's early life, and the development of his personality, see William C. Davis, *Jefferson Davis: The Man and His Hour* (New York: HarperCollins, 1991), especially 52–86, 96–107.

4. "Report on the Claim, April 15, 1858, of Lt. Colonel Johnston, 1st

Cavalry, to the rank of Brevet Colonel," Joseph E. Johnston Collection, box 1, folder 3, Earl Gregg Swem Library, College of William & Mary, Williamsburg, Virginia.

5. Davis, *Jefferson Davis*, 334; Craig L. Symonds, *Joseph E. Johnston: A Civil War Biography* (New York: W. W. Norton, 1992), 112–24.

6. Davis's appointments are in the *Journal of the Congress of the Confederate States of America, 1861–1865* (Washington, D.C., 1904–05), 1:461. The act on which Johnston based his argument for seniority was "An Act to Provide for the Establishment and Organization of the Army of the C.S.A.," Mar. 6, 1861, which is printed in United States War Department, *The War of the Rebellion: A Compilation of the Official Records of the Union and Confederate Armies*, 128 vols. (Washington, D.C.: Government Printing Office, 1881–1901; hereinafter *OR*), ser. 1, 1:127–31. Johnston's letter of complaint is dated Sept. 12, 1861, and is printed in *OR*, ser. 4, 1:605.

7. Davis to Johnston, Sept. 14, 1861, *OR*, ser. 1, 1:611.

8. Symonds, *Joseph E. Johnston*, 140–48.

9. Memorandum of G. W. Smith, Oct. 1, 1861, *OR*, ser. 1, 5:885–86.

10. Johnston to Lee, Mar. 27, 1862, and May 9 and 10, 1862, all in *OR*, ser.1, 11(3):405, 502–3, 506.

11. Symonds, *Joseph E. Johnston*, 148–50.

12. Johnston to Lee, Apr. 22, 1862, *OR*, ser. 1, 11(3):456.

13. Johnston *implied* an early evacuation in a series of letters to Lee, but was typically imprecise. See Johnston to Lee, April 24, 27, 29, 1862, all in *OR*, ser. 1, 11(3):461, 469. Davis's telegram to Johnston, dated May 1, 1862, is in *OR*, ser. 1, 11(3):485. Johnston's defensive reply, also dated May 1, 1862, is in Braxton Bragg Papers, Western Reserve Historical Society, Cleveland, Ohio.

14. Johnston to Wigfall, Nov. 12, 1863, Wigfall Family Papers, Library of Congress, Washington, D.C.

15. Johnston to Lydia Johnston, May 8, 1862, McLane-Fisher Family Papers, box 6, Maryland Historical Society, Baltimore.

16. On the Battle of Seven Pines, see Clifford Dowdey, *The Seven Days: The Emergence of Lee* (Boston: Little Brown, 1964). Dowdey is very hard on Johnston and claims that "no action of the war was planned with such slovenly thinking or prepared so carelessly" (p. 84). Steven Newton is much more favorable to Johnston in his recent book *Joseph E. Johnston and the Defense of Richmond* (Lawrence: University Press of Kansas, 1998). Contemporary accounts are flawed by after-the-fact hindsight, but include G. W. Smith, *The Battle of Seven Pines* (Dayton, Ohio: Morningside Bookshop, 1974 [first published in 1891]) and Johnston's own self-serving and

combative account "Manassas to Seven Pines," in *Battles & Leaders of the Civil War*, 2:211. A detailed and readable account is by Stephen Sears, *To the Gates of Richmond: The Peninsula Campaign* (New York: Ticknor & Fields, 1993).

17. Dabney H. Maury, "Interesting Reminiscences of General Johnston," *Southern Historical Society Papers* (1890), 18:180–81.

18. For a discussion of the political aspect of the Davis–Johnston feud, see Craig L. Symonds, "No Margin for Error: Civil War in the Confederate Government," in Steven E. Woodworth, ed., *The Art of Command: Facets of Civil War Generalship* (Lincoln: University of Nebraska Press, 1998), 1–16. On the relationship between Johnston and Wigfall, see Alvy King, *Louis T. Wigfall: Southern Fire-Eater* (Baton Rouge: Louisiana State University Press, 1970), and Thomas L. Connelly and Archer Jones, *The Politics of Command: Factions and Ideas in Confederate Strategy* (Baton Rouge: Louisiana State University Press, 1973), as well as Symonds, *Joseph E. Johnston*, 175–84.

19. Josiah Gorgas, *The Civil War Diary of Josiah Gorgas*, edited by Frank Vandiver (Tuscaloosa: University of Alabama Press, 1947), 50.

20. Johnston to Lydia Johnston, May 31, 1864, McLane-Fisher Family Papers, box 6, Maryland Historical Society, Baltimore.

21. Joseph E. Johnston, *Narrative of Military Operations* (Bloomington: University of Indiana Press, 1959 [first published 1874]), 318.

22. *Journal of the Congress of the Confederate States of America*, 4:453–54, 7:463.

23. Davis Memo, Feb. 18, 1865, *OR*, ser. 1, 47(2):1304–11.

24. Special Orders No. 3, and Lee to Johnston, both dated Feb. 22, 1865, *OR*, ser. 1, 47(2):1247–48; C. Vann Woodward, ed., *Mary Chesnut's Civil War* (New Haven: Yale University Press, 1981), 725, 729.

25. Johnston to Lee, Mar. 23, 1865, *OR*, ser. 1, 47(2):1453–54.

26. Stephen Mallory, "Last Days of the Confederate Government," *McClure's* (Dec. 1900), 240–42.

TWO: *Ambivalent Visions of Victory: Davis, Lee, and Confederate Grand Strategy*

1. Lee's troop strength is from Stephen W. Sears, *To the Gates of Richmond: The Peninsula Campaign* (New York: Ticknor & Fields, 1992), 155–56.

2. Constance Cary Harrison, *Recollections Grave and Gay* (New York: Scribner, 1911), 72–73.

3. The most detailed military biography of Lee remains Douglas

Southall Freeman, *R. E. Lee: A Biography*, 4 vols. (New York: Scribner, 1934–35). See also Emory M. Thomas, *Robert E. Lee: A Biography* (New York: W. W. Norton, 1995).

4. Lee to Annie Lee, Savannah, Mar. 2, 1862, in Clifford Dowdey and Louis H. Manarin, eds., *The Wartime Papers of R. E. Lee* (New York: Bramhall House, 1961), 121–22.

5. Lee to Gustavus W. Smith, Jan. 4, 1863, in ibid., 383–84.

6. See Russell F. Weigley, *The American Way of War: A History of United States Military Strategy and Policy* (New York: Macmillan, 1973), 92–127; Lee to Davis, June 10, 1863, in Dowdey and Manarin, eds., *Wartime Papers*, 508.

7. The standard biography of Davis is now William C. Davis, *Jefferson Davis: The Man and His Hour* (New York: HarperCollins, 1991).

8. See Frank E. Vandiver, *Their Tattered Flags: The Epic of the Confederacy* (New York: Harper's Magazine Press, 1970), 120–21, and Weigley, *American Way of War*, 96–97.

9. Davis to W. M. Brooks, Mar. 13, 1862, in Dunbar Rowland, ed., *Jefferson Davis, Constitutionalist: His Letters, Papers, and Speeches*, 10 vols. (Jackson: Mississippi Department of Archives and History, 1923), 5:216–17.

10. Davis to People, Apr. 4, 1865, in ibid., 529–31.

11. Gary W. Gallagher, ed., *Fighting for the Confederacy: The Personal Recollections of General Edward Porter Alexander* (Chapel Hill: University of North Carolina Press, 1989), 530–33; a slightly different version of this conversation appears in Alexander's *Military Memoirs of a Confederate*.

12. Lee to Davis, Richmond, Apr. 20, 1865, in Dowdey and Manarin, eds., *Wartime Papers*, 939.

13. Jefferson Davis, *The Rise and Fall of the Confederate Government*, 2 vols. (New York: Appleton, 1881), 2:129.

14. Vandiver, *Tattered Flags*, 140.

15. Davis, *Jefferson Davis*, 697.

16. Clement Eaton, *Jefferson Davis* (New York: Free Press, 1977), 245.

17. Archer Jones, *Civil War Command and Strategy: The Process of Victory and Defeat* (New York: Free Press, 1992), 227.

18. Richard M. McMurry, *Two Great Rebel Armies: An Essay in Confederate Military History* (Chapel Hill: University of North Carolina Press, 1989), 138.

19. Douglas Southall Freeman, *Lee's Lieutenants: A Study in Command*, 3 vols. (New York: Scribner, 1942–44), 1:265.

20. Joseph T. Glatthaar, *Partners in Command: The Relationships Between Leaders in the Civil War* (New York: Free Press, 1994), 227.

21. Steven E. Woodworth, *Davis and Lee at War* (Lawrence: University Press of Kansas, 1995), xii.

22. I delivered an abbreviated version of this essay at the Southern Historical Association annual meeting in 1993. The thesis then and here is a theme in my *Robert E. Lee*.

23. Lee to Davis, Aug. 14, 1862, in Dowdey and Manarin, eds., *Wartime Papers*, 254.

24. Lynda Lasswell Crist, Mary Seaton, and Kenneth H. Williams eds., *The Papers of Jefferson Davis*, 9 vols. thus far (Baton Rouge: Louisiana State University Press, 1971–97), 8:339–70.

25. Ibid.; the quotations from Davis to Lee, Aug. 30, 1862, 368; see also Pendleton to Davis, Sept. 13, 1862, ibid., 8:390–91. Lee seemed to like Pendleton, who was an Episcopal clergyman and graduate of West Point, even though Pendleton managed to lose forty-four guns at Shepherdstown, Virginia, in September 1862, and even though he was a notoriously poor preacher. Lee's adjutant Walter Taylor wrote of Pendleton's sermons, "I am not so averse to hearing the General as others but am always sorry to see him officiate, because I know how the soldiers will talk about him." R. Lockwood Tower, ed., *Lee's Adjutant: The Wartime Letters of Colonel Walter Herron Taylor, 1862–1865* (Columbia: University of South Carolina Press, 1995), 186.

26. Lee to Davis, Aug. 30, 1862; Lee to Davis, telegram, Aug. 30, 1862; in Dowdey and Manarin, eds., *Wartime Papers*, 266–68.

27. John J. Hennessy makes a case in his *Return to Bull Run: The Campaign and Battle of Second Manassas* (New York: Simon & Schuster, 1993), 456–62.

28. Lee to Davis, Sept. 3, 1862, in Dowdey and Manarin, eds., *Wartime Papers*, 292–93.

29. Lee to Davis, Sept. 4, 1862, in ibid., 294.

30. Lee to Davis, Sept. 5, 1862; Lee to Davis, telegram, Sept. 6, 1862; and Lee to Davis, Sept. 7, 1862, in ibid., 295–98.

31. Lee to Davis, Sept. 9, 1862, in ibid., 303; James Longstreet, *From Manassas to Appomattox: Memoirs of the Civil War in America* (Philadelphia: Lippincott, 1896), 285; Crist, ed., *Davis Papers*, 8:389n.1.

32. Lee to Davis, Sept. 9, 1862, in Dowdey and Manarin, eds., *Wartime Papers*, 303.

33. Special Orders No. 191; Lee to Davis, Sept. 12, 1862, in ibid., 301–305.

34. Lee to Lafayette McLaws, Sept. 14, 1862; Lee to Davis, Sept. 16, 1862; in ibid., 307–10.

35. Lee to Davis, Sept. 3, 1862; Lee to Davis, Sept. 13, 1862, in ibid., 293–307; Robert K. Krick, "The Army of Northern Virginia in September 1862: Its Circumstances, Its Opportunities, and Why It Should Not Have Been at Sharpsburg," in Gary W. Gallagher, ed., *Antietam: Essays on the 1862 Maryland Campaign* (Kent, Ohio: Kent State University Press, 1989), 55.

36. See Thomas, *Lee*, 261.

37. Lee to Davis, May 30, 1863; Lee to Davis, June 7, 1863; Lee to James A. Seddon, June 8, 1863, in Dowdey and Manarin, eds., *Wartime Papers*, 496, 503, and 505.

38. Lee to Davis, June 18, 1863; Lee to Davis, June 25, 1863, in ibid., 519, 531.

39. Lee to Davis, June 23, 1863; Lee to Davis, June 25, 1863; Lee to Davis, June 25, 1863, ibid., 527–28, 531, 532.

40. Davis to Lee, June 28, 1863, in Crist, ed., *Davis Papers*, 247–48.

41. Postwar account of Major-General Isaac Ridgeway Trimble, *Supplement to the Official Records of the Union and Confederate Armies*, 100 vols. (Wilmington, N. C., 1994), pt. 1, 5:435–36.

THREE: *Jeff Davis Rules: General Beauregard and the Sanctity of Civilian Authority in the Confederacy*

1. Alfred Roman, *The Military Operations of General Beauregard in the War Between the States 1861–1865*, 2 vols. (New York: Harper and Brothers, 1884; reprint, New York: Da Capo Press, 1994), 2:276–79.

2. Dunbar Rowland, ed., *Jefferson Davis, Constitutionalist: His Letters, Papers, and Speeches*, 10 vols. (Jackson: Mississippi Department of Archives and History, 1923), 6:351–56.

3. See William C. Davis, *The Cause Lost: Myths and Realties of the Confederacy* (Lawrence: University Press of Kansas, 1996), chapter 2; Bell Irvin Wiley, *The Road to Appomattox* (New York: Atheneum, 1977), 33–35, 77–121; Grady McWhiney, "Jefferson Davis and the Art of War," *Civil War History* 21 (June 1975): 101–12; James R. Arnold, *Presidents under Fire: Commanders in Chief in Victory and Defeat* (New York: Orion Books, 1994), chapters 6 and 7.

4. Grady McWhiney and Perry D. Jamieson, *Attack and Die: Civil War Military Tactics and the Southern Heritage* (Tuscaloosa: University of

Alabama Press, 1982), 166–67; James I. Robertson, Jr., "Abraham Lincoln and Jefferson Davis: Tragic Presidents," in John Y. Simon and Barbara Hughett, eds., *The Continuing Civil War* (Dayton, Ohio: Morningside, 1992), 39; Allan Nevins, "Introduction" to James D. Richardson, ed., *The Messages and Papers of Jefferson Davis and the Confederacy*, 2 vols. (New York: Chelsea House, 1966), 1:[7].

5. Davis, *Cause Lost*, chapter 2; Arnold, *Presidents under Fire*, chapters 6 and 7; T. Harry Williams, P. G. T. *Beauregard: Napoleon in Gray* (Baton Rouge: Louisiana State University Press, 1955), viii.

6. Archer Jones, ["Review of Steven E. Woodworth, *Davis and Lee at War*"] *Journal of Southern History* 63 (Feb. 1997): 181; John Keegan and Andrew Wheatcroft, *Who's Who in Military History* (London: Routledge, 1996), 24.

7. Steven E. Woodworth, *Davis and Lee at War* (Lawrence: University Press of Kansas, 1995), 74–81; Williams, *Beauregard*, chapter 7; Rowland, ed., *Jefferson Davis*, 5:156–57.

8. William C. Davis, *Jefferson Davis: The Man and His Hour* (New York: HarperCollins, 1991), chapter 13; Beauregard to Roger Pryor, Jan. 20, 1862, P. G. T. Beauregard Papers, Library of Congress.

9. Charles Winslow Eliott, *Winfield Scott: The Soldier and the Man* (New York: Macmillan, 1937), 655–58.

10. Quoted in Williams, *Beauregard*, 112.

11. Ibid., chapters 8, 9, and 10; Lynda Lasswell Crist, Mary Seaton Dix, and Kenneth H. Williams, eds., *The Papers of Jefferson Davis*, 9 vols. thus far (Baton Rouge: Louisiana State University Press, 1971–97), 8:217–18.

12. Ibid., 243–44.

13. Ibid., 253–54.

14. Beauregard to Thomas Jordan, July 12, 1862, P. G. T. Beauregard Papers, Duke University.

15. Crist et al., eds., *Papers of Jefferson Davis*, 8:468–70.

16. Beauregard to William Porcher Miles, Jan. 7, 1863, and Beauregard to James T. Holtzclaw, Sept. 16, 1862, Beauregard Papers, Library of Congress.

17. Raimondo Luraghi, *A History of the Confederate Navy* (Annapolis, Md.: Naval Institute Press, 1996), 4–5, 247.

18. The Federal siege of Charleston is fully described in E. Milby Burton, *The Siege of Charleston, 1861–1865* (Columbia: University of South Carolina Press, 1970), and Stephen R. Wise, *Gate of Hell: Campaign for Charleston Harbor, 1863* (Columbia: University of South Carolina Press, 1994). See also Robert J. Schneller, Jr., "A Littoral Frustration: The Union

Navy and the Siege of Charleston, 1863–1865," *Naval War College Review* 49 (Winter 1996): 38–60.

19. U.S. War Department, *The War of the Rebellion: A Compilation of the Official Records of the Union and Confederate Armies*, 127 vols. and index (Washington, D.C.: Government Printing Office, 1880–1901), series 1, 10:403, 530.

20. Ibid., 546.

21. Beauregard to William Porcher Miles, Dec. 5, 1862, Beauregard Papers, Library of Congress.

22. Steven E. Woodworth, "On Smaller Fields: General P. G. T. Beauregard and the Bermuda Hundred Campaign," in Woodworth, ed., *Leadership and Command in the American Civil War* (Campbell, Cal.: Savas Woodbury Publishers, 1995), 197–230.

23. Beauregard to Charles Villere, Jan. 13, 1863, Beauregard Papers, Library of Congress.

24. Henry Whitney Cleveland, "Robert Toombs," *Southern Bivouac*, 1 (Jan. 1886): 456–57.

25. Williams, *Beauregard*, 113–15, 159–60.

26. [Charles J. Villere,] *Review of Certain Remarks Made by the President When Requested to Restore General Beauregard to the Command of Department No. 2* (Charleston: Evans and Cogswell, 1863), especially 17–19; Williams, *Beauregard*, 164–65.

27. Beauregard to Roger Pryor, Jan. 20, 1862, and Beauregard to Thomas Jordan, Jan. 6, 1867, Beauregard Papers, Library of Congress.

28. Russell F. Weigley, "The American Military and the Principle of Civilian Control from McClellan to Powell," *Journal of Military History* 57 (Oct. 1993): 32–39.

29. Roman, *Military Operations of General Beauregard*, 2:390–95.

30. Michael B. Ballard, *A Long Shadow: Jefferson Davis and the Final Days of the Confederacy* (Jackson: University Press of Mississippi, 1986), chapter 4.

FOUR: *Davis, Bragg, and Confederate Command in the West*

1. Grady McWhiney, *Braxton Bragg and Confederate Defeat*, vol. 1 (Tuscaloosa: University of Alabama Press, 1991; [orig. pub. 1969], 1:260; Dunbar Rowland, ed., *Jefferson Davis, Constitutionalist: His Letters, Papers, and Speeches*, 10 vols. (Jackson: Mississippi Department of Archives and History, 1923), 5:279, 283; U.S. War Department, *The War of the Rebellion: A Compilation of the Official Records of the Union and Confederate Armies*, 128 vols. (Washington, D.C.: Government Printing

Office, 1881–1901; hereinafter *OR*; all volumes cited are from series 1), pt. 2, 17:599, 612.

2. A good example of historians' tendency to represent Bragg as an "old friend" of Davis is found in Thomas L. Connelly's highly regarded study of the Army of Tennessee, *Army of the Heartland: The Army of Tennessee, 1861–1862* (Baton Rouge: Louisiana State University Press, 1967), 182.

3. The fortuitous nature of Beauregard's early successes is demonstrated in T. Harry Williams, *P. G. T. Beauregard: Napoleon in Gray* (Baton Rouge: Louisiana State University Press, 1952), 42–50. For Bragg's early Civil War career, see McWhiney, *Braxton Bragg*, 174–260.

4. Rowland, *Jefferson Davis*, 5:284–85; *OR*, pt. 2, 10:780–86; 16:701–2, 726–27, 731; 17:626, 630, 644–46, 652; 52:324–25; McWhiney, *Braxton Bragg*, 262–71; Ellsworth Eliot, Jr., *West Point in the Confederacy* (New York: Baker, 1941), 384; Joseph H. Parks, *General Edmund Kirby Smith, C.S.A.* (Baton Rouge: Louisiana State University Press, 1954), 198; Connelly, *Army of the Heartland*, 192.

5. *OR*, pt. 2, 16:734–35, 741, 745–46, 751; 17:627–28, 654–55, 658, 667–68; Thomas L. Connelly and Archer Jones, *The Politics of Command: Factions and Ideas in Confederate Strategy* (Baton Rouge: Louisiana State University Press, 1973), 106; Gary Donaldson, "'Into Africa': Kirby Smith and Braxton Bragg's Invasion of Kentucky," *Filson Club History Quarterly* 61 (Oct. 1987): 447.

6. *OR*, pt. 2, 16:741–42, 748–49, 751–53, 768–69, 775–76, 782–83, 799–800, 811, 897; 17:675–76, 683, 685; 52:340; Donaldson, "Into Africa," 451–64; Connelly, *Army of the Heartland*, 195; McWhiney, *Braxton Bragg*, 270–71.

7. Herman Hattaway and Archer Jones, *How the North Won: A Military History of the Civil War* (Urbana: University of Illinois Press, 1983), 252–54; *OR*, pt. 2, 16:775–78, 845–47, 852–54, 859–61, 865–66, 873, 876, 896–97; Donaldson, "Into Africa," 458–59.

8. *OR*, pt. 2, 15:920–21; 16:896–97, 904–05, 912, 1099–1100; Connelly, *Army of the Heartland*, 247, 253; McWhiney, *Braxton Bragg*, 303–11; Joseph H. Parks, *General Leonidas Polk, C.S.A.: The Fighting Bishop* (Baton Rouge: Louisiana State University Press, 1960), 265, 273.

9. Richard Taylor, *Destruction and Reconstruction: Personal Experiences of the Civil War*, introduction by T. Michael Parrish (New York: Da Capo Press, 1995; orig. pub. 1879), 99–101.

10. Parks, *General Edmund Kirby Smith, C.S.A.* (Baton Rouge: Louisiana State University Press, 1954), 245.

11. *OR*, pt. 2, 17:591–92; 20:384–87, 421–23, 492–93.

12. *OR*, pt. 2, 17:781, 793, 800; 20:449–50, 492–93; Rowland, *Jefferson Davis*, 5:294–95, 384; Joseph E. Johnston, *Narrative of Military Operations Directed during the Late War between the States* (New York: Appleton, 1874), 151–52; Thomas L. Connelly, *Autumn of Glory: The Army of Tennessee, 1862–1865* (Baton Rouge: Louisiana State University Press, 1971), 40–42; Parks, *General Leonidas Polk*, 282.

13. *OR*, pt. 1, 20:661, 663–72, 771–79; pt. 2, 463, 468, 479; 20:401; Stanley Horn, *The Army of Tennessee: A Military History* (Indianapolis: Bobbs-Merrill, 1941), 196–200; James Lee McDonough, *Stones River—Bloody Winter in Tennessee* (Knoxville: University of Tennessee Press, 1980), throughout; Connelly, *Autumn of Glory*, 47, 84–85; Christopher Losson, "Major General Benjamin Franklin Cheatham and the Battle of Stone's River," *Tennessee Historical Quarterly* (Fall 1982): 279–80, 286; Hattaway and Jones, *How the North Won*, 320–21; William C. Davis, *Breckinridge: Statesman, Soldier, Symbol* (Baton Rouge: Louisiana State University Press, 1974), 356.

14. In *Autumn of Glory*, 53, Connelly argued that Bragg would not have won the battle even with the extra 10,000 men. His reasoning is that Bragg misused the troops he did have and therefore would have misused any number of additional troops so as to lose the battle regardless of his numbers. Aside from being illogical, this argument overlooks that the misuse of troops Connelly attributes to Bragg was in fact caused by the gross errors of McCown, Cheatham, and Breckinridge.

15. McWhiney, *Braxton Bragg*, 374; Clifford Dowdey and Louis H. Manarin, eds., *The Wartime Papers of R. E. Lee* (New York: Bramhall House, 1961), 642.

16. McWhiney, *Braxton Bragg*, 376–78; *OR*, pt. 1, 20:682–84, 698–99, 701–02; Connelly, *Autumn of Glory*, 74–75.

17. *OR*, pt. 2, 17:813, 816–17, 822; pt. 1, 20:698–99; pt. 2, 476; 23:674, 684–85, 698, 708, 745–46; Rowland, *Jefferson Davis*, 5:418, 420–21; McWhiney, *Braxton Bragg*, 362, 375; Steven E. Woodworth, *Jefferson Davis and His Generals: The Failure of Confederate Command in the West* (Lawrence: University Press of Kansas, 1990), 196–98.

18. *OR*, pt. 1, 23:403, 583–84; pt. 2, 891–92, 954, 948, 950; pt. 1, 24:235; Parks, *General Leonidas Polk*, 315; Connelly, *Autumn of Glory*, 112–34. For a detailed discussion of the feasibility of Bragg's plan for the defense of the line north of Tullahoma, see Steven E. Woodworth, "Braxton Bragg and the Tullahoma Campaign," in *The Art of Command in the Civil War*, Steven E. Woodworth, ed. (Lincoln: University of Nebraska Press, 1998).

19. For a more detailed discussion of the Chickamauga and Chattanooga campaigns, see Steven E. Woodworth, *Six Armies in Tennessee: The Chickamauga and Chattanooga Campaigns* (Lincoln: University of Nebraska Press, 1998).

20. Judith Lee Hallock, *Braxton Bragg and Confederate Defeat*, vol. 2 (Tuscaloosa: University of Alabama Press, 1991), 127–49. Regarding the strategy behind Bragg's detachment of a force into East Tennessee, see Edward Carr Franks, "The Detachment of Longstreet Considered: Braxton Bragg, James Longstreet, and the Chattanooga Campaign," in *Leadership and Command in the American Civil War*, Steven E. Woodworth, ed. (Campbell, Cal.: Savas Woodbury, 1995), 29–65.

FIVE: *The General Whom the President Elevated Too High: Davis and John Bell Hood*

1. U.S. War Department, *The War of the Rebellion: A Compilation of the Official Records of the Union and Confederate Armies*, 127 vols. and index (Washington, D.C.: Government Printing Office, 1881–1901; hereinafter *OR*), ser. 1, 2:298.

2. Richard M. McMurry, *John Bell Hood and the War for Southern Independence* (Lexington: University of Kentucky Press, 1982), 35.

3. Ibid., 26.

4. Dunbar Rowland, ed., *Jefferson Davis, Constitutionalist: His Letters, Papers, and Speeches*, 10 vols. (Jackson: Mississippi Department of Archives and History, 1923), 5:253; Jefferson Davis, *The Rise and Fall of the Confederate Government*, 2 vols. (New York: D. Appleton and Co., 1881), 2:120–22; and McMurry, *Hood*, 40, and 211n5.

5. William C. Davis, *Jefferson Davis: The Man and His Hour* (New York: HarperCollins, 1991), 547.

6. Lynda Lasswell Crist, Mary Seston Dix, and Kenneth H. Williams, eds., *The Papers of Jefferson Davis*, 9 vols. thus far (Baton Rouge: Louisiana State University Press, 1971–97), 8:421, 423n5.

7. C. Vann Woodward, ed., *Mary Chesnut's Civil War* (New Haven: Yale University Press, 1981), 501.

8. Both quotes are in McMurry, *Hood*, 79.

9. Ibid., 84.

10. Ibid., 87.

11. Thomas L. Connelly and Archer Jones, *The Politics of Command* (Baton Rouge: Louisiana State University Press, 1973), 85.

12. Woodward, ed., *Chesnut*, 502–17.

13. McMurry, *Hood*, 87; Hood to Stephen D. Lee, January 9, 1886, Lee Papers, University of North Carolina.

14. McMurry, *Hood*, 88; Davis to Braxton Bragg, *OR*, ser. 2, 52:555.

15. Steven E. Woodworth, *Jefferson Davis and His Generals: The Failure of Confederate Command in the West* (Lawrence: University Press of Kansas, 1990), 302.

16. Ibid., 271.

17. *OR*, ser. 3, 32:606–7.

18. McMurry, *Hood*, 96.

19. Ibid.

20. James Hamilton Eckenrode and Brian Conrad, *James Longstreet, Lee's War Horse* (Chapel Hill: The University of North Carolina Press, 1936), 262.

21. McMurry, *Hood*, 115.

22. Ibid., 123; Woodworth, *Davis and His Generals*, 266.

23. McMurry, *Hood*, 123; Woodworth, *Davis and His Generals*, 288; McMurry, *Hood*, 123.

24. Ibid., 136–37.

25. Albert Castel, *Decision in the West: The Atlanta Campaign of 1864* (Lawrence: University Press of Kansas, 1994).

26. Charles Fair, *From the Jaws of Victory* (New York: Simon and Schuster, 1971), 316; McMurry, *Hood*, 152–53; *OR*, ser. 2, 39:832, 842.

27. *OR*, ser. 3, 38:633; 5:1017, 1023.

28. McMurry, *Hood*, 158.

29. Ibid., 157; Rowland, ed., *Davis Papers*, 7:415; *OR*, ser. 1, 30:805.

30. Herman Hattaway and Archer Jones, *How the North Won: A Military History of the Civil War* (Urbana: University of Illinois Press, 1983), 634; Woodworth, *Davis and His Generals*, 293.

31. John Bell Hood, *Advance and Retreat* (originally published 1880, new edition with introduction by Bruce J. Dinges; Lincoln: University of Nebraska Press, 1996), 273; *OR*, 52:2, 748; Woodworth, *Davis and His Generals*, 295.

32. Woodward, ed., *Chesnut*, 646, 652–53.

33. Connelly and Jones, *Politics of Command*, 169, 188.

34. Rowland, ed., *Davis Papers*, 6:398–99.

35. McMurry, *Hood*, 186–87.

36. Hood to Davis, Davis Papers, Emory University.

37. McMurry, *Hood*, 193.

38. All this is extrapolated from Hood, *Advance and Retreat*, v–xiv.

39. Davis, *Rise and Fall*, 2:573.

SIX: "To Comfort, To Counsel, To Cure": Davis, Wives, and Generals

1. Jefferson Davis, *The Rise and Fall of the Confederate Government*, 2 vols. (New York: Da Capo Press, 1990 [orig. pub. New York: Appleton, 1881]), 1: iii.

2. Steven E. Woodworth, *Jefferson Davis and His Generals: The Failure of Confederate Command in the West* (Lawrence: University Press of Kansas, 1990), examples include 46, 74, 59, 92, 126, 134, 170, 176, 186, 198, 225, 257; Steven E. Woodworth, *Davis and Lee at War* (Lawrence: University Press of Kansas, 1995).

3. Varina Davis to Margaret Howell, Jan. 30, 1846, and Joseph Davis Howell to Margaret Howell, in Hudson Strode, ed., *Jefferson Davis: Private Letters* (New York: Harcourt Brace, 1966), 36, 34.

4. Varina Davis, *Jefferson Davis, Ex-President of the Confederate States of America: A Memoir by His Wife*, 2 vols. (New York: Belford Company, 1890), 2:29.

5. William C. Davis, *Jefferson Davis: The Man and His Hour* (New York: HarperCollins, 1991), 97, 366, 455.

6. Ibid., 448.

7. T. C. De Leon, *Belles Beaux and Brains of the 60s* (New York: Dillingham, 1907), 67.

8. C. Vann Woodward, ed., *Mary Chesnut's Civil War* (New Haven: Yale University Press, 1981), 85, 91, 136; Katherine Jones, *Ladies of Richmond: Confederate Capital* (Indianapolis: Bobbs Merrill, 1962), 149–50.

9. Quoted in Woodworth, *Davis and Lee*, 247.

10. Davis, *Jefferson Davis*, 355, 360, 458; Joan Cashin, "Varina Howell Davis," in G. J. Barker-Benfield and Catherine Clinton, eds., *Portraits of American Women*, 2 vols. (New York: St. Martin's Press, 1991), 1:269.

11. Judith W. McGuire, *Diary of a Southern Refugee During the War* (1867; rpt. New York: Arno Press, 1972), 116–17.

12. Cashin, "Varina Howell Davis," 267.

13. Woodward, ed., *Mary Chesnut's Civil War*, 674.

14. Varina Davis to John Preston, Apr. 1, 1865 in Jones, *Ladies of Richmond*, 268–69; Richard Barksdale Harwell, ed., *Kate: Diary of a Confederate Nurse* (Baton Rouge: Louisiana State University Press, 1959), 280.

15. Woodward, ed., *Mary Chesnut's Civil War*, 746.

16. Jefferson Davis to Varina Davis, Apr. 23, 1865; Varina Davis to Jefferson Davis, April 28, 1865, in Strode, ed., *Jefferson Davis: Private Letters*, 156–59.

17. Jones, *Ladies of Richmond*, 149.

18. Mrs. Burton Harrison, *Recollections Grave and Gray* (New York: Scribner, 1911), 192.

19. Woodward, ed., *Mary Chesnut's Civil War*, 673.

20. Ibid., 187.

21. Lynda Lasswell Crist, Mary Seaton Dix, and Kenneth H. Williams, eds., *The Papers of Jefferson Davis*, 9 vols. thus far (Baton Rouge: Louisiana State University Press, 1971–97), 7: 340n.1. Quoted phrases from Strode, *Jefferson Davis*, 2:456; Craig L. Symonds, *Joseph E. Johnston: A Civil War Biography* (New York: W. W. Norton, 1992), 192; Harrison, *Recollections*, 154.

22. Mrs. D. Giraud Wright, *A Southern Girl in '61: The Wartime Memoirs of a Confederate Senator's Daughter* (New York: Doubleday, 1905), 178; Woodward, ed., *Mary Chesnut's Civil War*, 468; Jones, *Ladies of Richmond*, 56; Lydia Johnston to Charlotte Wigfall, March 16, 1863, quoted in Symonds, *Joseph E. Johnston*, 199.

23. Joseph E. Johnston to Lydia Johnston, May 23, 1864, quoted in ibid., 296.

24. Lydia Johnston to Charlotte Wigfall, Aug. 2, 1863; Lydia Johnston to Charlotte Wigfall, Feb. 19, 1865, quoted in ibid., 220–21, 341.

25. Ibid., 290.

26. Joseph E. Johnston to Lydia Johnston, Apr. 1, 1865, quoted in ibid., 52.

27. Ibid., 379, also 6, 372–73.

28. Elise Bragg to Sarah Butler, June 29, 1849; Braxton Bragg to Elise Bragg, Jan. 9, 1853, quoted in Grady McWhiney, *Braxton Bragg and Confederate Defeat*, 2 vols. (New York: Columbia University Press, 1969), 1:119, 125.

29. Quoted in George Rable, *Civil Wars: Women and the Crisis of Southern Nationalism* (Urbana: University of Illinois Press, 1989), 150.

30. Bell I. Wiley, *Confederate Women* (Westport, Conn: Greenwood Press, 1975), 172–73.

31. Judith Lee Hallock, *Braxton Bragg and Confederate Defeat*, 2 vols. (Tuscaloosa: University of Alabama Press, 1991), 2:86.

32. McWhiney, *Braxton Bragg*, 217–18, 267–68.

33. Elise Bragg to Braxton Bragg, Mar. 3, 1862; Elise Bragg to Braxton Bragg, Mar. 12, 1862, quoted ibid., 207.

34. Hallock, *Braxton Bragg*, 258–59, quote from 259.

35. Harwell, ed., *Kate*, 129–30.

36. T. Harry Williams, *P. G. T. Beauregard: Napoleon in Gray* (Baton Rouge: Louisiana State University Press, 1955), 5, 10, 35–36, 45, 48; Alfred

Roman, *The Military Operations of General Beauregard in the War Between the States, 1861–1865*, 2 vols. (New York: Harper & Brothers, 1884; reprint, New York, 1994), 1: 10; Glenn R. Conrad, ed., *A Dictionary of Louisiana Biography*, 2 vols. (New Orleans, 1988), 1: 54.

37. Pierre G. T. Beauregard to H. H. Dawson, Jul. 15, 1862, quoted in Williams, *P. G. T. Beauregard*, 160. See also 52, 92–93, 99, 171, 259.

38. Woodward, ed., *Mary Chesnut's Civil War*, 352, 468.

39. Pierre G. T. Beauregard to Julia Deslonde, Apr. 2, 1864, quoted in Williams, *P. G. T. Beauregard*, 204.

40. Roman, *Military Operations*, 1:10.

41. *Richmond Enquirer*, Apr. 11, 19, 1864.

42. Pierre G. T. Beauregard to Julian Deslonde, Apr. 2, 1864, quoted in Williams, *P. G. T. Beauregard*, 204–5.

43. *Richmond Enquirer*, Apr. 19, 1864.

44. Pierre G. T. Beauregard to Augusta Evans, Oct. 26, 1866, quoted in Williams, *P. G. T. Beauregard*, 205.

45. Julia Gardner Tyler to her mother, June 16, 1861, in Jones, *Ladies of Richmond*, 65.

46. Woodward, ed., *Mary Chesnut's Civil War*, 450, 569.

47. Robert E. Lee to Mary Custis Lee, June 10, 1862, in Clifford Dowdey and Louis H. Manarin, eds., *The Wartime Papers of R. E. Lee* (New York: Bramhall House, 1961), 190.

48. Robert E. Lee to Mary Custis Lee, Mar. 9, 1863; Robert E. Lee to Mary Custis Lee, May 23, 1863 in Dowdey and Manarin, eds., *Wartime Letters*, 413, 491. Compare Robert E. Lee to Mary Custis Lee, Jul. 26, 1863, and Robert E. Lee to Jefferson Davis, Jul. 31, 1863, in Dowdey and Manarin, *Wartime Papers*, 558, 565.

49. Woodward, ed., *Mary Chesnut's Civil War*, 569.

50. Harrison, *Recollections*, 153; Jones, *Ladies of Richmond*, 149.

51. Quote from Jones, *Ladies of Richmond*, 241–43.

52. "Ladies of Richmond," quoted in ibid., 219.

SEVEN: *The Image of Jefferson Davis as Commander in Chief*

1. C. Vann Woodward and Elisabeth Muhlenfeld, eds., *The Private Mary Chesnut: The Unpublished Civil War Diaries* (New York: Oxford University Press, 1984), 105.

2. Original of the Fredericks *carte-de-visite* in the collection of William Gladstone, West Palm Beach, Florida; William C. Davis, *Jefferson Davis: The Man and His Hour* (New York: HarperCollins, 1991), 306–7.

3. Roy P. Basler, Marian D. Pratt, and Lloyd Dunlap, eds., *The Col-*

lected *Works of Abraham Lincoln*, 8 vols. (New Brunswick, N.J.: Rutgers University Press, 1953–55), 1:510; Charles C. Osborne, *Jubal: The Life and Times of General Jubal A. Early, C.S.A.* (Chapel Hill, N.C.: Algonquin Books, 1992), 28; Robert U. Johnson and Clarence C. Buel, eds., *Battles and Leaders of the Civil War*, 4 vols. (orig. pub. New York: Century, 1888; Secaucus, N.J.; 1991), 2:447.

4. Ludwell H. Johnson, "Jefferson Davis and Abraham Lincoln as War Presidents: Nothing Succeeds Like Success," *Civil War History* 27 (March 1981): 50; Cass Canfield, *The Iron Will of Jefferson Davis* (New York: Harcourt Brace, 1978), 65; Davis, *Jefferson Davis*, 55; Jefferson Davis, *The Rise and Fall of the Confederate Government* (orig. pub. 1881; New York: Da Capo Press, 1990), 1:176, 188, 198, 297; Mildred Lewis Rutherford, *Jefferson Davis, The President of the Confederate States, and Abraham Lincoln, The President of the United States 1861–1865* (Athens, Ga.: United Daughters of the Confederacy, 1916), 8, 22.

5. Steven E. Woodworth, *Jefferson Davis and His Generals: The Failure of Confederate Command in the West* (Lawrence: University Press of Kansas, 1990), 8; Varina Davis to Clement Claiborne Clay, Jr., May 10, 1861, in Katherine M. Jones, ed., *Heroines of Dixie: Confederate Women Tell Their Story of the War* (Indianapolis: Bobbs-Merrill, 1955), 28; Steven E. Woodworth, *Davis and Lee at War* (Lawrence: University Press of Kansas, 1995), 10.

6. Quoted in Woodworth, *Davis and Lee at War*, 6, 9–10.

7. Ibid., 9–10.

8. Davis, *Jefferson Davis*, 346; John B. Jones, *A Rebel War Clerk's Diary at the Confederate States Capital*, 2 vols. (Philadelphia: J. B. Lippincott, 1866), 1:65.

9. Woodward and Muhlenfield, eds., *The Private Mary Chesnut*, 105; Davis, *Jefferson Davis*, 553.

10. Varina Davis, *Jefferson Davis, Ex-President of the Confederate States of America: A Memoir by his Wife*, 2 vols. (New York: Belford Co., 1890), 2:98; Frank H. Alfriend, *The Life of Jefferson Davis* (Cincinnati: Caxton Publishing House, 1868), 305.

11. Jones, *A Rebel War Clerk's Diary*, 1:65; *Battles and Leaders*, 1:244–45, 237.

12. T. Michael Parrish and Robert M. Willingham, Jr., *Confederate Imprints: A Bibliography of Southern Publications from Secession to Surrender* (Austin: Jenkins Publishing Co., n.d.), 12–13.

13. Ibid., 17; Richard B. Harwell, "A Confederate Hell-Box," *Civil War Quarterly* 8 (March 1987): 44.

14. Parrish and Willingham, *Confederate Imprints*, esp. 530–34 (maps and pictorial prints), and 598, 609 (sheet music).

15. *Southern Illustrated News*, Sept. 13, 1862; Oct. 11, 1863; Oct. 4, 1862. Originals in the New York Public Library.

16. Annabel S. Perlik, "Signed L. M. D. Guillaume: Louis Matthieu Didier Guillaume, 1816–1892" (M.A. thesis, George Washington University, Washington, D.C.), 15–16, 61; Alfriend, *Life of Jefferson Davis*, 305.

17. *Battles and Leaders*, 2:352, 448, 499–501; Varina Davis, *Jefferson Davis*, 317.

18. Davis, *Jefferson Davis*, 431; *Battles & Leaders*, 1:226; 2:447.

19. *Frank Leslie's Illustrated Newspaper*, June 3, 1865.

20. See Mark E. Neely, Jr., Harold Holzer, and Gabor S. Boritt, *The Confederate Image: Prints of the Lost Cause* (Charlotte: University of North Carolina Press, 1987), 79–96.

21. Nina Silber, *The Romance of Reunion: Northerners and the South, 1865–1900* (Chapel Hill: University of North Carolina Press, 1993), 30–38; see also Catherine Clinton and Nina Silber, eds., *Divided Houses: Gender and the Civil War* (New York: Oxford University Press, 1992), 284–86.

22. Neely, et al., *The Confederate Image*, 79, 82.

23. See Gaines M. Foster, *Ghosts of the Confederacy: Defeat, the Lost Cause, and the Emergence of the New South* (New York: Oxford University Press, 1987), 72–75; David W. Blight, "'For Something beyond the Battlefield': Frederick Douglass and the Struggle for the Memory of the Civil War," *The Journal of American History* 75 (March 1989): 1167.

24. Roger Fischer, *Them Damned Pictures: Explorations in American Political Cartoon Art* (New Haven: Archon Books, 1996), 180–81.

25. Richard E. Baringer, Herman Hattaway, Archer Jones, and William N. Still, Jr., *Why the South Lost the Civil War* (Athens: University of Georgia Press, 1986), 77; Michael Kammen, *Mystic Chords of Memory: The Transformation of Tradition in American Culture* (New York: Knopf, 1991), 381; Frank E. Vandiver, "Jefferson Davis—Leader Without Legend," *Journal of Southern History* 43 (1977); Canfield, *The Iron Will of Jefferson Davis*, 135. For a good explanation of the impact of wartime deprivation on Confederate nationalism, see Drew Gilpin Faust, *The Creation of Confederate Nationalism: Ideology and Identity in the Civil War South* (Baton Rouge: Louisiana State University Press, 1988), 16–18.

26. Foster, *Ghosts of the Confederacy*, 96.

27. Edward Gary, "Jefferson Davis and His Place in History," *New York Times*, Sunday Magazine section, May 31, 1908, 4.

28. Varina Davis, *Jefferson Davis*, 392.

EIGHT: *Was the Best Defense a Good Offense?*
Jefferson Davis and Confederate Strategies

1. Joseph E. Johnston, *Narrative of Military Operations* (New York: Appleton, 1874), 421; Pierre G. T. Beauregard, "The First Battle of Bull Run," in Robert U. Johnson and Clarence C. Buel, eds., *Battles and Leaders of the Civil War*, 4 vols. (New York: Century, 1888), 1:222.

2. Jefferson Davis, *The Rise and Fall of the Confederate Government*, 2 vols. (orig. pub. New York: Appleton, 1881; reprint New York: Da Capo Press, 1990) 1:321.

3. Craig L. Symonds, Chapter 1 in this volume, 25–26; "powerful team" from Frank E. Vandiver, *Their Tattered Flags: The Epic of the Confederacy* (New York: Harper's Magazine Press, 1970), 140.

4. James M. McPherson, "American Victory, American Defeat," in Gabor S. Boritt, ed., *Why the Confederacy Lost* (New York: Oxford University Press, 1992), 25, 28.

5. James M. McPherson, "Lincoln and the Strategy of Unconditional Surrender," in Gabor S. Boritt, ed., *Lincoln, the War President* (New York: Oxford University Press, 1992), 29–62.

6. Quoted in Shelby Foote, *The Civil War: A Narrative. Fort Sumter to Perryville* (New York: Random House, 1958), 143.

7. Quoted in ibid., 65.

8. Dunbar Rowland, ed., *Jefferson Davis, Constitutionalist: His Letters, Papers, and Speeches*, 10 vols. (Jackson: Mississippi Department of Archives and History, 1923), 5:84.

9. Steven E. Woodworth, *Davis and Lee at War* (Lawrence: University Press of Kansas, 1995), xii.

10. Rowland, ed., *Jefferson Davis, Constitutionalist*, 6:386.

11. Reprinted in Emory M. Thomas, *The Confederate Nation, 1861–1865* (New York: Harper and Row, 1979), 307.

12. T. Harry Williams, "The Military Leadership of North and South," in David Donald, ed., *Why the North Won the Civil War* (Baton Rouge: Louisiana State University Press, 1960), 46; Symonds, Chapter 1, 11.

13. Davis to William M. Brooks, March 15, 1862, in Lynda Lasswell Crist, Mary Seaton Dix, and Kenneth H. Williams, eds., *The Papers of Jefferson Davis*, 9 vols. thus far (Baton Rouge: Louisiana State University Press, 1971–97), 8:100.

14. Symonds, Chapter 1, 12–13.

15. Davis, *Rise and Fall*, 1:314. For "offensive–defense," see Emory M. Thomas, Chapter 2 in this volume, 167; for "defensive–offensive," see

William C. Davis, *Jefferson Davis: The Man and His Hour* (New York: HarperCollins, 1991), 700.

16. Lee to James A. Seddon, June 8, 1863 and Lee to Davis, June 25, 1863, in Clifford Dowdey and Louis H. Manarin, eds., *The Wartime Papers of R. E. Lee* (New York: Bramhall House, 1961), 505, 532; Lee's comment to Early quoted in J. William Jones, *Personal Reminiscences of Gen. Robert E. Lee* (New York: Appleton, 1875), 40.

17. Woodworth, *Davis and Lee at War*, 157; see also Emory M. Thomas, *Robert E. Lee: A Biography* (New York: W. W. Norton & Co., 1995) and Thomas, Chapter 2.

18. Thomas, Chapter 2.

19. Ibid.

20. Ibid.

21. Personal conversation.

22. See especially Thomas L. Connelly, "Robert E. Lee and the Western Confederacy: A Criticism of Lee's Strategic Ability," in John T. Hubbell, ed., *Battles Lost and Won* (Westport, Conn.: Greenwood Press, 1975), 197–214; Grady McWhiney and Perry D. Jamieson, *Attack and Die: Civil War Military Tactics and the Southern Heritage* (Tuscaloosa: University of Alabama Press, 1982); J. F. C. Fuller, *Grant and Lee: A Study in Personality and Generalship* (Bloomington: Indiana University Press, 1957); Alan T. Nolan, *Lee Considered: General Robert E. Lee and Civil War History* (Chapel Hill: University of North Carolina Press, 1991); and John D. McKenzie, *Uncertain Glory: Lee's Generalship Re-Examined* (New York: Hippocrene Books, 1997).

23. Roy P. Basler, Marian D. Pratt, and Lloyd Dunlap, eds., *The Collected Works of Abraham Lincoln*, 9 vols. (New Brunswick, N.J.: Rutgers University Press, 1953–55), 5:355–56.

24. Sumner to John Bright, Feb. 13, 1865, in Beverly Wilson Palmer, ed., *The Selected Letters of Charles Sumner*, 2 vols. (Boston: Northeastern University Press, 1990), 2:268.

25. Horace Porter, *Campaigning with Grant* (New York: Century, 1897), 69–70.

26. McPherson, "American Victory, American Defeat," 19.

For Further Reading: A Bibliography

ONE: *A Fatal Relationship: Davis and Johnston at War*
CRAIG L. SYMONDS

The historiographical debate about the adversarial relationship between Jefferson Davis and Joseph E. Johnston is nearly as confrontational as the contemporary feud, and it began almost the moment the war ended. Both Davis and Johnston wrote personal memoirs and both are still available in modern reprint editions in paperback, although neither is particularly readable. Davis's is by far the better book. Entitled *The Rise and Fall of the Confederate Government* (New York: Da Capo Press, 1990), it appeared in two volumes in 1881. It is a lifeless work, as dry and precise as the man himself, and says relatively little about his relationship with Joseph E. Johnston. Davis simply chose not to renew the feud. About the Atlanta campaign, for example, he wrote: "Whether we might have obtained more advantageous results by a vigorous and determined effort to attack are questions upon which it would be now neither useful nor pleasant to enter." By contrast, Johnston's *Narrative of Military Operations*, first published in 1874 and also available in a modern paperback edition (New York: Da Capo Press, 1959), is much more confrontational. Like some of the articles Johnston wrote for *Century* magazine in the 1880s and subsequently printed in the *Battles & Leaders* series (also still in print), Johnston often wrote as if he were engaged in a debate. In a style that produces far more heat than light, it is still possible to sense his anger over perceived mistreatment nearly a quarter century after the event. A collective reading of his postwar writings could easily suggest the conclusion that he did protest too much.

Others became involved in this "battle of the books," too. E. A. Pollard's bitterly anti-Davis screed, *The Lost Cause* (also available in a modern edition [Avenal, N.J.: Gramercy Press, 1994]) appeared in 1866 and was the first general history of the war by a Southerner. Pollard pulls no punches; he blames the loss of the war directly on Davis and calls Johnston "the military genius of the Confederacy" (p. 440). A contemporary pro-Davis argument can be found in Frank H. Alfriend, *The Life of Jefferson Davis*, published two years later in 1868 and no longer in print. More recently, moderate pro-Davis (and therefore anti-Johnston) sentiment can be found in Richard McMurry, *John Bell Hood and the War for Southern Independence* (Lexington: University Press of Kentucky, 1982) and Steven Woodworth's two books on Davis's relationships with his generals: *Davis and His Generals* (Lawrence: University Press of Kansas, 1991) and *Davis and Lee at War* (Lawrence: University Press of Kansas, 1994). Pro-Johnston arguments are evident in Gilbert Govan and James Livinggood's 1956 biography of the general entitled, *A Different Valor: The Story of General Joseph E. Johnston* (Indianapolis: Bobbs-Merrill, 1956) and Steven Newton's *Joseph E. Johnston and the Defense of Richmond* (Lawrence: University Press of Kansas, 1998).

The most recent biographies of Davis and Johnston are by William C. Davis (who is no relation), *Jefferson Davis, The Man and His Hour* (New York: HarperCollins, 1991) and Craig L. Symonds, *Joseph E. Johnston: A Civil War Biography* (New York: W. W. Norton, 1992). It is a biographer's job to see the world through the eyes of his subject without becoming an uncritical advocate, and each of these volumes is moderately sympathetic toward its subject, and generally (though not universally) critical of his counterpart. William C. Davis addresses the Davis–Johnston relationship itself in "Davis, Johnston, and Beauregard: The Triple

Play That Crippled the Confederacy," one of the essays in his *The Cause Lost: Myths and Realities of the Confederacy* (Lawrence: University Press of Kansas, 1996), 15–34. In it, Davis likens Johnston to the cowardly lion from *The Wizard of Oz*. Another thoughtful essay is Joseph Glatthaar's "Davis, Johnston, and Confederate Failure in the West," from his book *Partners in Command: The Relationships Between Leaders in the Civil War* (New York: Free Press, 1994), 95–133. Glatthaar concludes that "Joseph E. Johnston possessed a hodgepodge of strengths and weaknesses. . . . Yet a temperamental nature and limited vision inhibited him from elevating his talents to satisfy the demands of large-scale warfare" (p. 133).

There is a wealth of material available about the various campaigns in which Johnston participated, particularly the Peninsular campaign in 1862 and the Atlanta campaign in 1864. A particularly pertinent and valuable source on the former is Steven Newton's *Johnston and the Defense of Richmond*. And by far the most detailed account of the Atlanta campaign, one full of trenchant (and largely critical) assessments of both Johnston and Sherman, is Albert Castel, *Decision in the West: The Atlanta Campaign of 1864* (Lawrence: University Press of Kansas, 1992).

TWO: *Ambivalent Visions of Victory: Davis, Lee, and Confederate Grand Strategy*
EMORY M. THOMAS

Lee's most detailed military biography is by Douglas Southall Freeman, *R. E. Lee: A Biography* (New York: Scribner, 1934–35). Also important are Thomas L. Connelly, *The Marble Man: Robert E. Lee and His Image in American Society* (New York: Knopf, 1977) and Emory M. Thomas, *Robert E. Lee: A Biography* (New York: Norton, 1995). Richard M. McMurry, *Two Great Rebel Armies: An Essay in Confederate Military History* (Chapel Hill: University of North Carolina Press, 1989) is a good answer to Connelly. Significant, too, is Thomas Lawrence Connelly and Archer Jones, *The Politics of Command: Factions and Ideas in Confederate Strategy* (Baton Rouge: Louisiana State University Press, 1973). Russell F. Weigley in *The American Way of War A History of United States*

Military Strategy and Policy (New York: Macmillan, 1973) recognizes Lee's commitment to a battle of annihilation and the cost to the Confederacy of Lee's offensive campaigns. A strong summary statement is Charles P. Roland, *Reflections on Lee: A Historian's Assessment* (Mechanicsburg, Penn.: Stackpole Books, 1995).

Jefferson Davis is the primary focus of Steven E. Woodworth's *Jefferson Davis and His Generals: The Failure of Confederate Command in the West* (Lawrence: University Press of Kansas, 1990), which is the companion volume to Steven E. Woodworth's *Davis and Lee at War* (Lawrence: University Press of Kansas, 1995). Together these books offer an insightful critique of the Confederate president as war leader. The best available biography of Davis is William C. Davis, *Jefferson Davis: The Man and His Hour* (New York: HarperCollins, 1991), and author Davis is especially attentive to the military. Emphasis on the offensive–defense came originally from Frank E. Vandiver, *Their Tattered Flags: The Epic of the Confederacy* (New York: Harper's Magazine Press, 1970). Confederate strategy is the topic of Frank E. Vandiver, *Rebel Brass: The Confederate Command System* (Baton Rouge: Louisiana State University Press, 1956); Raimondo Luraghi, *The Rise and Fall of the Plantation South* (New York: New Viewpoints, 1978); Herman Hattaway and Archer Jones, *How the North Won: A Military History of the Civil War* (Urbana: University of Illinois Press, 1983); Richard E. Berringer, Herman Hattaway, Archer Jones, and William N. Still, Jr., *Why the South Lost the Civil War* (Athens: University of Georgia Press, 1986); and Gabor S. Boritt, ed., *Why the Confederacy Lost* (New York: Oxford University Press, 1992).

The Maryland Campaign of 1862 has a rich literature. Some important works include James V. Murfin, *The Gleam of Bayonets: The Battle of Antietam and the Maryland Campaign of 1862* (New York: Yoseloff, 1965); Stephen W. Sears, *Landscape Turned Red: The Battle of Antietam* (New York: Ticknor & Fields, 1983); and Gary W. Gallagher, ed., *Antietam: Essays on the 1862 Maryland Campaign* (Kent, Ohio: Kent State University Press, 1989).

On Gettysburg the standard work is still Edwin B. Coddington, *The Gettysburg Campaign: A Study in Command* (New York: Scribner, 1988). Other works of import include Gabor S. Boritt,

The Gettysburg Nobody Knows (New York: Oxford University Press, 1997); Gary W. Gallagher, ed., *The First Day of Gettysburg: Essays on Confederate and Union Leadership* (Kent, Ohio: Kent State University Press, 1992); Gary W. Gallagher, ed., *The Second Day of Gettysburg: Essays on Confederate and Union Leadership* (Kent, Ohio: Kent State University Press, 1993); Gary W. Gallagher, ed., *The Third Day at Gettysburg and Beyond* (Chapel Hill: University of North Carolina Press, 1994); Harry Pfanz, *Gettysburg: The Second Day* (Chapel Hill: University of North Carolina Press, 1987); and Harry Pfanz, *Gettysburg: Culp's Hill and Cemetery Hill* (Chapel Hill: University of North Carolina Press, 1993).

On the personalities at work in this war, see Joseph T. Glatthaar, *Partners in Command: The Relationships Between Leaders in the Civil War* (New York: Free Press, 1994).

THREE: *Jeff Davis Rules: General Beauregard and the Sanctity of Civilian Authority in the Confederacy*
T. Michael Parrish

The only scholarly biography of Pierre Gustave Toutant Beauregard is T. Harry Williams, *P. G. T. Beauregard: Napoleon in Gray* (Baton Rouge: Louisiana State University Press, 1955), a revealing study that is mostly negative toward Beauregard as a military commander. An outdated but sometimes interesting and sympathetic portrait is Hamilton Basso, *Beauregard: The Great Creole* (New York: Scribner, 1933). Beauregard provided the bulk of source materials and personally edited Alfred Roman's massive study, *The Military Operations of General Beauregard in the War Between the States, 1861–1865*, 2 vols. (New York: Harper and Brothers, 1884; reprint, New York: Da Capo Press, 1994), making the book, in effect, Beauregard's personal memoir and, in large measure, an extended denunciation of President Jefferson Davis.

The assertion that Jefferson Davis's personal hatred for Beauregard crippled the Confederacy's military fortunes is most clearly evident in William C. Davis, *The Cause Lost: Myths and Realities of the Confederacy* (Lawrence: University Press of Kansas, 1996), chapter 2. It also gives scant credit to Beauregard and argues that ultimately Jefferson Davis needed more generals like Robert E. Lee. See also Bell Irvin Wiley, *The Road to Appomattox* (New York: Atheneum, 1977), 33–35, 77–121; James R. Arnold, *Presidents Under Fire: Commanders in Chief in Victory and Defeat* (New York: Orion Books, 1994), chapters 6 and 7; Grady McWhiney, "Jefferson Davis and the Art of War," *Civil War History* 21 (June 1975), 101–12.

A mostly positive portrait of Beauregard emerges in Gamaliel Bradford's classic essay in his *Confederate Portraits* (Boston: Houghton Mifflin, 1914), chapter 4. See also Ellsworth Eliot, Jr., *West Point in the Confederacy* (New York: Baker, 1941), chapter 10.

A fairly balanced treatment of the strained relationship between Davis and Beauregard is available in two books by Steven E. Woodworth, *Davis and Lee at War* (Lawrence: University Press of Kansas, 1995), and *Jefferson Davis and His Generals: The Failure of Confederate Command in the West* (Lawrence: University Press of Kansas, 1990). See also William C. Davis, *Jefferson Davis: The Man and His Hour* (New York: HarperCollins, 1991). Woodworth describes Beauregard's consistently weak performance as a field commander most convincingly in "On Smaller Fields: General P. G. T. Beauregard and the Bermuda Hundred Campaign," in Woodworth, ed., *Leadership and Command in the American Civil War* (Campbell, Cal.: Savas Woodbury Publishers, 1995), 197–230. See also William Glenn Robertson, *Backdoor to Richmond: The Bermuda Hundred Campaign, April–June 1864* (Newark: University of Delaware Press, 1987).

Beauregard's setback at Shiloh and his pivotal abandonment of Corinth are also evaluated in Thomas L. Connelly, *Army of the Heartland: The Army of Tennessee, 1861–1862* (Baton Rouge: Louisiana State University Press, 1967), and Archer Jones, *Civil War Command and Strategy: The Process of Victory and Defeat* (New York: Free Press, 1992).

Much of the important correspondence between Davis and Beauregard is in Dunbar Rowland, ed., *Jefferson Davis, Constitutionalist: His Letters, Papers, and Speeches*, 10 vols. (Jackson: Mississippi Department of Archives and History, 1923). More definitive coverage is available in Lynda Lasswell Crist, Mary Seaton Dix, and Kenneth H. Williams, eds., *The Papers of Jefferson Davis*, 9 vols. thus far (Baton Rouge: Louisiana State University Press, 1971–97). See also U. S. War Department, *War of the Rebellion: A Compilation of the Official Records of the Union and Confederate Armies*, 127 vols. and index (Washington, D.C.: Government Printing Office, 1880–1901).

The problematic notion of Beauregard's genius, displayed as a prominent member of the so-called "Western Concentration Bloc" of military and civilian leaders, influencing Davis's strategic decisions is put forth in Thomas L. Connelly and Archer Jones, *The Politics of Command: Factions and Ideas in Confederate Strategy* (Baton Rouge: Louisiana State University Press, 1973), and Herman Hattaway and Archer Jones, *How the North Won: A Military History of the Civil War* (Urbana: University of Illinois Press, 1983).

Beauregard's brilliant defense of Charleston is described in E. Milby Burton, *The Siege of Charleston, 1861–1865* (Columbia: University of South Carolina Press, 1970), and Stephen R. Wise, *Gate of Hell: Campaign for Charleston Harbor, 1863* (Columbia: University of South Carolina Press, 1994). The last wartime meeting in North Carolina involving Davis and Beauregard is recreated in Michael B. Ballard, *A Long Shadow: Jefferson Davis and the Final Days of the Confederacy* (Jackson: University Press of Mississippi, 1986), chapter 4.

The solidification of civilian authority over military power in the United States prior to and during the Civil War is described cogently in Russell F. Weigley, "The American Military and the Principle of Civilian Control from McClellan to Powell," *Journal of Military History* 57 (October 1993): 27–58.

FOUR: *Davis, Bragg, and Confederate Command in the West*
STEVEN E. WOODWORTH

Negative treatments of Bragg are abundant, more positive ones extremely rare. The standard biography of Bragg, a two-volume set, *Braxton Bragg and Confederate Defeat* (Tuscaloosa: University of Alabama Press, 1991) falls into the smaller second category. The first volume was written by Grady McWhiney in 1969, the second by Judith Lee Hallock in 1991. Their combined product is moderately critical of Bragg, unblinking in its view of his faults but usually willing to try to understand his actions as well as condemn his mistakes. It also takes an honest view of the shortcomings of other Southern generals who contributed to Confederate defeat in the West. McWhiney's volume includes excellent campaign and battle accounts, while Hallock is at her best in describing the conflict of personalities that characterized the latter part of Bragg's Confederate service.

Stanley Horn's 1941 *The Army of Tennessee: A Military History* (Indianapolis: Bobbs-Merrill) set the tone and the agenda for much modern writing about the Confederate war effort west of the Appalachians. In this work Bragg appears as a snarling, half-demented villain. Although Horn's work is now badly outdated, many of his harsh criticisms of Bragg are echoed in current books.

Thomas L. Connelly's two-volume set, *Army of the Heartland: The Army of Tennessee, 1861–1862* and *Autumn of Glory: The Army of Tennessee, 1862–1865* (Baton Rouge: Louisiana State University Press, 1968 and 1971, respectively), superseded Horn and became the standard work on the army that Bragg commanded longer than any other general. In this analytical study, Connelly is highly critical of Bragg, but then he is highly critical of everyone else, bar none, so perhaps this can be counted as a fair treatment. In Connelly's pages, Bragg's every action and inaction get picked apart under a microscope, but his enemies within the army's officer corps receive the same treatment.

Modern battle studies that follow the extreme anti-Bragg vein of interpretation include Wiley Sword's *Mountains Touched with Fire: Chattanooga Besieged, 1863* (New York: St. Martin's Press, 1995) and Peter Cozzens's *This Terrible Sound: The Battle of Chickamauga* and *The Shipwreck of Their Hopes: The Battles for Chattanooga* (Urbana: University of Illinois Press, 1992 and 1994, respectively).

The author's own *Jefferson Davis and His Generals: The Failure of Confederate Command in the West* (Lawrence: University Press of Kansas, 1990) takes a different approach to Bragg, endeavoring to understand more than condemn his actions and assessing his potential value to the Confederacy. Looking at Bragg from the perspective of the Confederate president—and in light of what the president could or should have done with regard to him—puts his Confederate career in a different light.

Current scholarship continues to reexamine Bragg, and Edward Carr Franks' interesting recent article, "The Detachment of Longstreet Considered: Braxton Bragg, James Longstreet, and the Chattanooga Campaign" (in *Leadership and Command in the American Civil War*, Steven E. Woodworth, ed., Campbell, Cal.: Savas Woodbury, 1995) takes a long-needed careful look at one aspect of Bragg's generalship and suggests conclusions far different from those often repeated in previous works.

FIVE: *The General Whom the President Elevated Too High: Davis and John Bell Hood*
HERMAN HATTAWAY

Albert Castel, *Decision in the West: The Atlanta Campaign of 1864* (Lawrence: University Press of Kansas, 1994) is the magnum opus of an accomplished master. It sheds useful new light on its subject. Richard M. McMurry, *John Bell Hood and the War for Southern Independence* (Lexington: University of Kentucky Press, 1982) remains the best study of the general. Hood's own *Advance and Retreat* (1880; Lincoln: University of Nebraska Press, 1996) is revealing. C. Vann Woodward, *Mary Chesnut's Civil War* (New Haven: Yale University Press, 1981) is unsurpassed for insightful observations by an erudite contemporary. Thomas Lawrence Connelly and Archer Jones, *The Politics of Command: Factions and Ideas in Confederate Strategy* (Baton Rouge: Louisiana State University Press, 1973) is stimulating and very important, but somewhat difficult to read.

Lynda Lasswell Crist, Mary Seaton Dix, and Kenneth H. Williams, eds., *The Papers of Jefferson Davis*, 9 vols. thus far (Baton Rouge: Louisiana State University Press, 1971–97) is essential and sets a high standard for editorial execution.

William C. Davis, *Jefferson Davis: The Man and His Hour* (New York: HarperCollins, 1991) is the best biography today; but see

Felicity Allen, *Unconquerable Heart: The Life of Jefferson Davis* (Columbia: University of Missouri Press, forthcoming).

Charles Fair, *From the Jaws of Victory* (New York: Simon & Schuster, 1971) remains a favorite among military historians and deservedly so for its insights and pithy observations.

SIX: *"To Comfort, To Counsel, To Cure"*: *Davis, Wives, and Generals*
LESLEY J. GORDON

Pioneering and still insightful general studies of women and war include Francis Butler Simkins and James Welch Patton, *The Women of the Confederacy* (Richmond and New York: Garrett and Massie, 1936); Mary Elizabeth Massey, *Bonnet Brigades* (New York: Knopf, 1966); and Bell Irvin Wiley, *Confederate Women* (Westport, Conn.: Greenwood Press, 1975). A fascinating discussion of female roles and images in wars through Western history is Jean Bethke Elshtain, *Women and War* (New York: Basic Books, 1987).

Books that address white elite women and marriage in the antebellum and bellum South include, Anne Firor Scott, *The Southern Lady: From Pedestal to Politics, 1830–1930* (Chicago: University of Chicago Press, 1970); Victoria Bynum, *Unruly Woman: The Politics of Social and Sexual Control in the Old South* (Chapel Hill: University of North Carolina Press, 1992); Christie Anne Farnham, *The Education of the Southern Belle: Higher Education and Student Socialization in the Antebellum South* (New York: New York University Press, 1994); Bertram Wyatt-Brown, *Southern Honor: Ethics and Behavior in the Old South* (New York: Oxford University Press, 1982); Suzanne Lebsock, *Free Women of Petersburg: Status and Culture in a Southern Town, 1784–1860* (New York: W. W. Norton, 1984); Catherine Clinton, *The Plantation Mistress: Woman's World in the Old South* (New York: Pantheon Books, 1982); Elizabeth Fox-Genovese, *Within the Plantation Household: Black and White Women of the Old South* (Chapel Hill: University of North Carolina Press, 1988); Jean E. Friedman, *The Enclosed Garden: Women and Community in the Evangelical South, 1830–1900* (Chapel Hill: University of North Carolina Press,

1985); and Carol K. Bleser, ed., *In Joy and In Sorrow: Women, Family and Marriage in the Victorian South, 1830–1900* (New York: Oxford University Press, 1991). Karen Lystra, *Searching the Heart: Women, Men, and Romantic Love in Nineteenth-Century America* (New York: Oxford University Press, 1989), and Phyllis Rose, *Parallel Lives: Five Victorian Marriages* (New York: Knopf, 1984), deal broadly with Victorian love and marriage.

Studies that tie Confederate women and the homefront to the battlefront include George Rable, *Civil Wars: Women and the Crisis of Southern Nationalism* (Urbana: University of Illinois Press, 1989); Leann Whites, *The Civil War as a Crisis in Gender: Augusta, Georgia, 1860–1890* (Athens: University of Georgia Press, 1995); Drew Gilpin Faust, *Mothers of Invention: Women of the Slaveholding South in the American Civil War* (Chapel Hill: University of North Carolina Press, 1996); Edward D. C. Campbell, Jr., and Kym S. Rice, eds., *A Woman's War: Southern Women, Civil War, and the Confederate Legacy* (Charlottesville: University Press of Virginia, 1996); and Donna Rebecca Krug, "Women in the Confederacy," in *The Road to Total War*, edited by Detlef Junker (Cambridge: Cambridge University Press, 1997). *Divided Houses: Gender and the Civil War*, edited by Catherine Clinton and Nina Silber (New York: Oxford University Press, 1992), explores a variety of ways the conflict tried and tested both Northern and Southern gender roles.

There is not yet a consensus among historians regarding the short- and long-term effects of the Civil War on Southern marriage. Two of the best studies include Carol K. Bleser and Frederick M. Heath, "The Impact of the Civil War on a Southern Marriage," in Bleser, ed., *In Joy and In Sorrow*, 135–53; and Joan Cashin, "'Since the War Broke Out: The Marriage of Kate and William McClure," in Clinton and Silber, eds., *Divided Houses*, 200–212.

Female descriptions of wartime Richmond lend insight into the Davis marriage and Jefferson Davis's overall interaction with women. Besides the classic C. Vann Woodward, ed., *Mary Chesnut's Civil War* (New Haven: Yale University Press, 1981), see Virginia Clay-Clopton, *A Belle of the Fifties: Memoirs of Mrs. Clay of Alabama* (1905; rpt. New York: Da Capo Press, 1969); Mrs. (Constance Cary) Burton Harrison, *Recollections Grave and Gray* (New

York: Scribner, 1911); Sally B. Putnam, *Richmond During the War* (New York: G. W. Carleton and Co., 1867). A surprising treasure trove of various firsthand female accounts is Katherine M. Jones, *Ladies of Richmond: Confederate Capital* (Indianapolis: Bobbs Merrill, 1962).

Confederate generals' wives have rarely merited attention from scholars in their own right. Some biographers of Civil War generals, however, have recognized the importance of wives to their husbands's lives and careers and included these women in their studies. Three consulted for this essay include Grady McWhiney, *Braxton Bragg and Confederate Defeat*, vol. 1 (New York: Columbia University Press, 1969), Craig Symonds, *Joseph E. Johnston: A Civil War Biography* (New York: W. W. Norton, 1992), and Emory M. Thomas, *Robert E. Lee: A Biography* (New York: W. W. Norton, 1995).

Most Davis scholars acknowledge Varina's significance in her husband's life, although they do not collectively view her sympathetically or positively. Clement Eaton devotes an entire chapter to "The Women in Davis's Life," that includes a discussion of Varina in his *Jefferson Davis* (New York: The Free Press, 1977); and Hudson Strode, ed., *Jefferson Davis Private Letters* (New York: Harcourt, Brace, 1966), highlights correspondence between Jefferson and Varina Davis. Joan Cashin is presently at work writing a biography of Varina Howell Davis. She has published the beginnings of her findings in G. J. Barker-Benfield and Catherine Clinton, eds., *Portraits of American Women*, vol. 1 (New York: St. Martin's Press, 1991): 259–77.

An anthology examining the wives and marriages of several Civil War generals will soon appear, entitled *Intimate Strategies: Military Marriages of the Civil War*, edited by Lesley J. Gordon and Carol K. Bleser, to be published by Oxford University Press.

SEVEN: *The Image of Jefferson Davis as Commander in Chief*
HAROLD HOLZER

When this writer, together with Mark E. Neely, Jr., and Gabor S. Boritt, published *The Confederate Image: Prints of the Lost Cause* (Chapel Hill: University of North Carolina Press, 1987), we expressed the belief that "the subject needs more careful evaluation to help us better understand the historical impact of the icons that played so central a role in the emotional movement known as the Lost Cause."

That need persists, although important new literature abounds. The essential starting point on Confederate iconography is now Michael T. Parrish and Robert M. Willingham, Jr., *Confederate Imprints: A Bibliography of Southern Publications from Secession to Surrender* (Austin, Tex.: Jenkins, n.d.). This prodigious volume lists 9,497 examples of official and unofficial publishing in the Confederacy, including prints and sheet music. Its introduction convincingly links "the art of printing and the Confederate cause."

Understanding Jefferson Davis's image of himself is impossible without consulting his own memoir, *The Rise and Fall of the Confederate Government*, 2 vols. (New York: Da Capo, 1990), and Varina Howell Davis, *Jefferson Davis, Ex-President of the Confederate States of America: A Memoir* (orig. ed., New York: Belford, 1890), the latter now available in a paperback edition with an insightful introduction by Craig L. Symonds that explores, among other topics, the Davises' joint quest for "historical reputation" (Baltimore: The Nautical and Aviation Publishing Co. of America, 1990).

Other early biographies help the reader comprehend the Confederate president's status in the popular mind. Principally, one must consult Frank Alfriend's sympathetic *The Life of Jefferson Davis* (Cincinnati and Chicago, 1868), and Edward A. Pollard's hostile *Life of Jefferson Davis, With a Secret History of the Southern Confederacy* (Atlanta: National Publishing Company, 1869). A book that helped establish Davis's supposed wartime role as "president-general" is John B. Jones, *A Rebel War Clerk's Diary at the Confederate States Capital* (Philadelphia: Lippincott, 1866). John J. Craven's *Prison Life of Jefferson Davis* (New York: Carleton, 1866) helped cement Davis's image as a Lost Cause martyr. More recently, profound commentary on the feminized image of the captured Davis appeared in Nina Silber, *The Romance of Reunion: Northerners and the South, 1865–1900* (Chapel Hill: University of North Carolina Press, 1993).

Among recent biographies, the essential title is William C. Davis,

Jefferson Davis: The Man and His Hour (New York: Harper-Collins, 1991). Valuable material on Davis's aspirations as a military man can also be found in Steven E. Woodworth, *Jefferson Davis and His Generals: The Failure of Confederate Command in the West* (Lawrence: University Press of Kansas, 1990).

Much fine work has been done on the culture of the South during and after the Civil War. A groundbreaking study is Charles Reagan Wilson, *Baptized in Blood: The Religion of the Lost Cause, 1865–1920* (Athens: University of Georgia Press, 1980), and a major contribution is Gaines M. Foster, *Ghosts of the Confederacy: Defeat, the Lost Cause, and the Emergence of the New South* (New York: Oxford University Press, 1987), particularly the chapters on "Ceremonial Bereavement" and "Confederate Celebration." There is useful information, too, in Edward D. C. Campbell, Jr.'s entry on "Popular Culture" in Richard N. Current, ed., *Encyclopedia of the Confederacy*, 4 vols. (New York: Simon & Schuster, 1993). The apogee of generic study in this field was achieved by Michael Kammen in *Mystic Chords of Memory: The Transformation of Tradition in American Culture* (New York: Knopf, 1991).

In the debate over the part played in the outcome of the war by collective Confederate will, iconography has as yet achieved a minor role. That oversight needs correcting. Required reading on the topic is Richard E. Beringer, Herman Hattaway, Archer Jones, and William N. Still, Jr., *Why the South Lost the Civil War* (Athens: University of Georgia Press, 1986). An intriguing set of essays is presented in Gabor S. Boritt, ed., *Why the Confederacy Lost* (New York: Oxford University Press, 1992). And a fresh study that argues anew for older theories about Confederate defeat is Gary Gallagher, *The Confederate War* (Cambridge: Harvard University Press, 1997). Drew Gilpin Faust discussed Confederate literature, publishing, and music in *The Creation of Confederate Nationalism: Ideology and Identity in the Civil War South* (Baton Rouge: Louisiana State University Press, 1988), but touched only lightly on the visual arts.

Finally, insights about the Davis image can also be found in Roger A. Fischer, *Them Damned Pictures: Explorations in American Political Cartoon Art* (North Haven, Conn.: Archon Books,

1996), and the valuable monograph by Tucker Hill, *Victory in Defeat: Jefferson Davis and the Lost Cause* (Richmond, 1986). Davis illustrations also abound in many of the books published over the years for the general audience, including the multivolume Time-Life Civil War series, as well as that quaint but irresistible old scrapbook, Lamont Buchanan, *A Pictorial History of the Confederacy* (New York: Crown Publishers, 1951).

EIGHT: *Was the Best Defense a Good Offense?* *Jefferson Davis and Confederate Strategies* JAMES M. MCPHERSON

A good starting point for understanding the larger context of Confederate strategy is Russell F. Weigley, *The American Way of War: A History of United States Military Strategy and Policy* (Bloomington: Indiana University Press, 1977). Confederate and Union strategies are analyzed in relationship with each other in Archer Jones, *Civil War Command and Strategy: The Process of Victory and Defeat* (New York: Free Press, 1992). Incisive comparisons of several command relationships in both the Union and Confederacy can be found in Joseph T. Glatthaar, *Partners in Command: The Relationships between Leaders in the Civil War* (New York: Free Press, 1994).

For an introduction to the specific problems of Confederate strategy, a good place to begin is Frank E. Vandiver, "Jefferson Davis and Confederate Strategy," in Avery O. Craven and Frank E. Vandiver, eds., *The American Tragedy: The Civil War in Retrospect* (Hampden-Sydney, Va.,: Hampden-Sydney College, 1959), 19–32. See also Vandiver, *Rebel Brass: The Confederate Command System* (New York: Greenwood Press, 1956), and Grady McWhiney, "Jefferson Davis and the Art of War," *Civil War History* 21 (June 1975): 101–12.

Four essential books containing the latest research and insights on the issues treated in this essay are William C. Davis, *Jefferson Davis: The Man and His Hour* (New York: HarperCollins, 1991); Steven E. Woodworth, *Jefferson Davis and His Generals: The Failure of Confederate Command in the West* (Lawrence: University

Press of Kansas, 1990); Woodworth, *Davis and Lee at War* (Lawrence: University Press of Kansas, 1995); and Gary W. Gallagher, *The Confederate War* (Cambridge, Mass.: Harvard University Press, 1997). For Davis's leadership role during a crucial late-war period, see William J. Cooper, Jr., "A Reassessment of Jefferson Davis as War Leader: the Case from Atlanta to Nashville," *Journal of Southern History* 36 (May 1970): 189–204.

There are valuable observations about strategy as well as tactics in Grady McWhiney and Perry D. Jamieson, *Attack and Die: Civil War Military Tactics and the Southern Heritage* (Tuscaloosa: University of Alabama Press, 1982) and Paddy Griffith, *Battle Tactics of the Civil War* (New Haven: Yale University Press, 1989). The limitations that logistics imposed on strategy are analyzed in Edward Hagerman, *The American Civil War and the Origins of Modern Warfare* (Bloomington: Indiana University Press, 1988).

For the East versus West theme in Confederate strategy and allocation of resources, consult Archer Jones, *Confederate Strategy from Shiloh to Vicksburg* (Baton Rouge: Louisiana State University Press, 1961); Thomas Lawrence Connelly and Archer Jones, *The Politics of Command: Factions and Ideas in Confederate Strategy* (Baton Rouge: Louisiana State University Press, 1973); and Richard M. McMurry, *Two Great Rebel Armies: An Essay in Confederate Military History* (Chapel Hill: University of North Carolina Press, 1989).

Trenchant essays that analyze both Union and Confederate military strategy and leadership include T. Harry Williams, "The Military Leadership of North and South" and David M. Potter, "Jefferson Davis and the Political Factors in Confederate Defeat," both in David Donald, ed., *Why the North Won the Civil War* (Baton Rouge: Louisiana State University Press, 1960), 23–48, 91–114; and Archer Jones, "Military Means, Political Ends: Strategy" and Gary W. Gallagher, "'Upon Their Success Hang Momentous Interests': Generals," both in Gabor S. Boritt, ed., *Why the Confederacy Lost* (New York: Oxford University Press, 1992), 43–108.

Although strategy and military leadership are not the principal focus of Richard E. Beringer, Herman Hattaway, Archer Jones, and

William N. Still, Jr., *Why the South Lost the Civil War* (Athens: University of Georgia Press, 1986), the analysis touches on these matters at several points. Books by British as well as American authors that concentrate mainly on Union strategy and leadership should, nevertheless, be consulted for their comparative insights: J. F. C. Fuller, *The Generalship of Ulysses S. Grant* (London, 1929; reprint Bloomington: Indiana University Press, 1958) and *Grant and Lee: A Study in Personality and Generalship* (Bloomington: Indiana University Press, 1957); John Keegan, "Grant and Unheroic Leadership," in Keegan, *The Mask of Command* (New York: Viking, 1987); Basil H. Liddell Hart, *Sherman: Soldier, Realist, American* (New York, 1929; reprint New York: Praeger, 1958); Colin R. Ballard, *The Military Genius of Abraham Lincoln* (London, 1926; reprint Cleveland: World Publishing, 1952); T. Harry Williams, *Lincoln and His Generals* (New York: Knopf, 1952); Kenneth P. Williams, *Lincoln Finds a General: A Military Study of the Civil War*, 5 vols. (New York: Macmillan, 1949–59); and Herman Hattaway and Archer Jones, *How the North Won: A Military History of the Civil War* (Urbana: University of Illinois Press, 1983).

Contributors

LESLEY J. GORDON is Assistant Professor of History at the University of Akron. She has contributed several articles and encyclopedia entries to a variety of publications, including the *Encyclopedia of the Confederacy* (New York: Simon & Schuster, 1993). She is author of *General George E. Pickett in Life and Legend* (University of North Carolina Press, 1998) and co-editor of *Intimate Strategies: Military Marriages of the Civil War* (Oxford University Press, forthcoming).

HERMAN HATTAWAY is Professor of History and Religion Studies at the University of Missouri—Kansas City. He has authored and co-edited six books. His most recent work, *Shades of Blue and Gray: An Introductory Military History of the Civil War* (University of Missouri Press, 1997), was an alternate selection of the History Book Club.

HAROLD HOLZER serves as Vice Chairman of the Lincoln Forum. He is Vice President for Communications at The Metropolitan Museum of Art and has authored or co-authored twelve books on Abraham Lincoln and the Civil War, including *The Confederate Image: Prints of the Lost Cause* (University of North Carolina Press, 1987), with Mark E. Neely, Jr. and Gabor S. Boritt. His most recent book is *The Lincoln Mailbag, 1860–1865* (Southern Illinois University Press, 1998).

JAMES M. MCPHERSON serves as the George Henry Davis '86 Professor of American History at Princeton University. He has written a dozen books and edited another half dozen, including *Battle Cry of Freedom: The Civil War Era* (Oxford University Press, 1988), which won the Pulitzer Prize for History. His most recent book, *For Cause and Comrades: Why Men Fought in the Civil War* (Oxford University Press, 1997), won the 1998 Lincoln Prize.

T. MICHAEL PARRISH is Archivist at the Lyndon Baines Johnson Library, University of Texas at Austin. His publications include *Brothers in Gray: the Civil War Letters of the Pierson Family* (Louisiana State University Press, 1997), and *Richard Taylor: Soldier Prince of Dixie* (University of North Carolina Press, 1992).

CRAIG L. SYMONDS is Professor of History at the U.S. Naval Academy, where he has served as department chair and been awarded the Naval Academy's Teaching Excellence Award and the Research Excellence Award. He is the author or editor of fourteen books, including Lincoln Prize finalist *Joseph E. Johnston: A Civil War Biography* (Norton, 1992) and his most recent, *Stonewall of the West: Patrick Cleburne and the Civil War* (University of Kansas Press, 1997).

EMORY M. THOMAS serves as Regents Professor of History at the University of Georgia. His seven books include *Robert E. Lee: A Biography* (Norton, 1995). He has an essay in *The Gettysburg Nobody Knows* (Oxford University Press, 1997)and is working on *Robert E. Lee. An Album.* (Norton, forthcoming).

STEVEN E. WOODWORTH serves as Assistant Professor of History at Texas Christian University in Fort Worth, Texas. His major works include *Jefferson Davis and His Generals: The Failure of Confederate Command in the West* and *Davis and Lee at War* (University Press of Kansas, 1990 and 1995, respectively), each of which was a selection of the History Book Club as well as a winner of the Fletcher Pratt Award. His most recent book is *Six Armies in Ten-*

nessee: The Chickamauga and Chattanooga Campaigns (University of Nebraska Press, 1998).

GABOR S. BORITT serves as Director of the Civil War Institute and Robert C. Fluhrer Professor of Civil War Studies at Gettysburg College. He has authored, co-authored, and edited fourteen books, including *Lincoln and the Economics of the American Dream* (1978; University of Illinois, 1994) and, most recently, *The Gettysburg Nobody Knows* (Oxford University Press, 1997), a main selection of the History Book Club.